T0329976

PERSPECTIVES ON THE
HISTORY OF ECONOMIC THOUGHT
VOLUME VII

PERSPECTIVES ON THE
ADMINISTRATIVE TRADITION:
FROM ANTIQUITY TO THE
TWENTIETH CENTURY

Perspectives on the History of Economic Thought Volume VII

Perspectives on the Administrative Tradition: From Antiquity to the Twentieth Century

Selected Papers from the
History of Economics Conference 1990

Edited by
S. Todd Lowry

Professor
Department of Administration and Economics
Washington and Lee University
Lexington, Virginia, US

Published for the History of Economics Society
by Edward Elgar

Published by
Edward Elgar Publishing Limited
Gower House
Croft Road
Aldershot
Hants GU11 3HR
England

Edward Elgar Publishing Company
Old Post Road
Brookfield
Vermont 05036
USA

A CIP catalogue record for this book
is available from the British Library

A CIP catalogue record for this book
is available from the US Library of Congress

ISBN 978 1 85278 447 8

Printed and bound by CPI Group (UK) Ltd, Croydon, CR0 4YY

Contents

Acknowledgements

I wish to express my appreciation to the participants in the 1990 History of Economics Society conference held at Washington and Lee University in Lexington, Virginia, for their scholarly efforts and patience in the process of negotiation and selection of papers reproduced in Volumes VII and VIII of this series. The authors of the selected papers have been most patient and helpful, responding to suggested revisions and adapting their papers to the Elgar style.

I have also found the general editor of the series, Mark Blaug, pleasant to deal with, and the staff of Edward Elgar Publishing Limited very efficient and helpful.

Last, but not least, I wish to express my gratitude to Carolyn West Hammett for her initiative and services in organizing and hosting the meetings that gave rise to these papers and to Mary Hall Bobenia who worked up the printed programme and the abstracts of the papers for the meetings, and devoted many long and tedious hours to editing the selected papers for publication.

S. Todd Lowry
Washington and Lee University

Acknowledgements

Introduction
S. Todd Lowry

Our earliest record of human explanations of natural and social processes is in terms of anthropomorphized gods controlling natural events and setting in motion physical, zoological and civic patterns. These were, in fact, administrative explanations of how mythic individuals in authority got things done and how predictable patterns in nature and society were established. Under such an administrative umbrella, self-perpetuating patterns were assumed to continue. Human decision-making has, of necessity, exhibited an ongoing tension between the premiss that some things can best be done by *affirmative human action*, and that others can best be accomplished by *accommodating to natural propensities*. Farmers, for example, plant seed, cultivate it and harvest the produce – an administered programme, but they must adapt their activities to the implicit natural growth characteristics of the grain being raised. Artificers tend to make items that grow out of their own skill and artistic interests, but they soon find themselves applying these skills to the implicit pressures of mutually beneficial exchange. It is this ongoing tension between layers of rational decision-making or planning on the one hand and perceived social or economic necessities or processes on the other, that we wish to explore historically.

The papers collected in this volume were selected for the insight they give to the antiquity and continued influence of the administrative tradition. These contributions range from ancient Chinese economic policies to relatively contemporary ideas that bring out the countercurrent of administrative purpose and its theoretical premisses. The authors have not necessarily characterized their contributions in these terms, but the historical relevance and continuity of administrative purposes and their implicit and explicit theoretical foundations speak for themselves.

There are two primary facets in social thought, including politics and economics. The first is the determination of *ends* or objectives to be achieved. These may be highly individualized purposes, family sustenance, or religious or military dictates with admixtures of custom and habit. The second facet is the determination of *means* by which these ends may be achieved and the evaluation of their effectiveness. A corollary to this facet gives rise to the twin functions of affirmative manipulation of people and phenomena and even structured purposeful promotion and management of human behaviour patterns and natural tendencies. From the earliest times, the head of a family, tribal chieftain or village leader was compelled to 'do something about' problems that we would define today as involving production or distribution. This aspect of human activity evolved in more complex political economies and involves appropriation (taxation), adjudication (redress and punishment), and affirmative administrative implementation of programmes and policies. Throughout recorded history, people have legitimately recognized that their level of living was dependent upon agricultural production and political organization to promote subsistence, civic order, military defence and security. These were issues that could best be handled by efficiently structured positive action by individual farmers and charismatic leaders. As a result, a dual genre of protoeconomic theory in our premodern historical tradition has been made up of agrarian instructional tracts and what has often been called 'Wisdom Literature'. This latter is better known under the rubric, 'Mirror for Princes' literature. These documents have a surprisingly standardized form from the earliest beginnings of writing up to the eighteenth century. They are usually couched in terms of a letter of instructions to a newly crowned ruler or young prince preparing to assume his inherited responsibilities. These treatises feature advice on effective leadership, personnel management, efficient administration of public services, military affairs, tax policy, treasury matters and ultimately, care of the personal health of the sovereign himself.

Both of these traditions which emphasize agricultural and political effectiveness and efficiency in implementing purposeful programmes necessarily concern themselves with the positive description and analysis of many of the processes that we now study as modern economics. However, as our modern discipline has grown out of the upwelling of eighteenth century naturalism, the industrial revolution and the apparent extra-political character of the commercial and industrial process, it is all too easy to forget that the principles of efficient administration were an ongoing part of this transition and continued to be of primary importance.

Beginning with ancient China in the seventh century BC, James L.Y. Chang, in the first paper in this collection, brings out the sophisticated level at which Chinese intellectuals advised their authoritarian rulers on the efficient use of the principle of manipulating tensions between opposing forces, expressed in terms of the principle of 'the light-heavy'. What is even more remarkable is the clarity with which they could abstract nascent market forces in these terms and define the forces of supply and demand as capable of self-equilibration within prescribed zones of control, consistent with imperial purpose and interests. The ubiquity and continuity of this intellectual tradition in equilibrium theory makes much of our western speculation about the emergence of supply–demand analysis appear somewhat Eurocentric and ahistorical.

S. Ambirajan's paper on ancient Tamil thought in southern India, 300 BC–200 AD, presents the more traditional form in which early economic policy was framed. The ethical literature of early political entities had a deeper significance for political economy, however, when the ethical traditions were the guidelines for individual kings or emperors who had absolute administrative authority over a broad spectrum of the lives of their subjects.

Gloria Vivenza's paper on the evolution of Roman taxation identifies an extremely significant transition in administrative policy and, implicitly, economic perception. Her research deals with a change in the administrative basis for the raising of revenues. Under constant pressure to support the army, in the last days of the Republic and the beginning of the Empire, imposts ceased to be perceived as personal calls for service and financial support, but were administered as *ad valorem* levies on the land held by individuals. This policy shift from an emphasis on 'personal duty' to the state to one of institutionalized claims by the state on the 'physical productivity' of the country marks a transition in political-economic perspective whose continuity we can recognize in French Physiocracy in the eighteenth century.

Yassine Essid's essay documents the importance of ancient Greek thought in medieval Muslim economic writings. He calls our attention to a Greek tract, in the tradition of Xenophon's *Oikonomicus* that survives in several Muslim commentaries. This work by Bryson has been completely ignored by classical scholars, who have traditionally shown little interest in both economic literature and Muslim scholarship. A full compilation and translation of Bryson's treatise should be made available to European scholars.

S.M. Ghazanfar and A. Azim Islahi survey the thought of one of the prominent Muslim economic writers whom western historians of thought have tended to ignore despite evidence that their ideas were known by the leading Scholastics in Europe. These writers dealt with an active commercial economy with clearly defined administrative policies regulating the market while defining acceptable areas for the free play of market forces.

William D. Grampp's reappraisal of Cantillon puts in question the modernity of his analyses and, coincidentally, leaves one with the impression that Cantillon belongs in the earlier tradition of analysts whose observations were heavily overshadowed by an agrarian commercial system with a strong administrative tradition.

Philippe Fontaine's paper on Turgot reminds us that, while Turgot was crossing the threshold into modern economic thought, his emphasis on capital accumulation was still in the context of individual agricultural administration where landowners generate and plough back their own surpluses into the enhancement of production.

S. Zin Bae, a Korean banker from Paris, eruditely demonstrates that Quesnay and his Physiocrats drew on Platonist principles of authoritarian administrative efficiency. The conventional picture put before us of recognizing Quesnay as the source of the concept of *laissez-faire* is inconsistent with our knowledge that he was a partisan of one of the most absolute monarchies in Europe. The Physiocratic commitment to the Platonic premiss of a perfectible administrative efficiency to serve the national interest is a dominant theme here that is carried forward in the two papers that follow.

Françoise Duboeuf's contribution deals with the broader question of measurement in Adam Smith's political economy. She distinguishes Smith's acceptance of social differentiation from the naturalistic theory of differentiated social and economic roles put forward by Plato and echoed in Quesnay. As she interprets Smith, he accepted natural equality, but justified functional differentiation as a source of enhanced use value to the productivity and growth of the economy. Smith is seen, from this viewpoint, as following an emphasis upon the efficiency of the total society in the Physiocratic tradition with social effectiveness measured by the differentiated contributions of individuals and materials whose usefulness is subject to a social criterion. A similar interpretation is approached from another direction by the following paper.

John C. Winfrey's paper focuses on Adam Smith's value theory. He contends that Smith's concept of use value is tied to his emphasis on economic growth and carries a connotation of social purpose. This interpretation continues the Physiocratic emphasis on general social well-being and perpetuates use value as an administrative criterion rather than as a naturalistic reference for exchange value.

J.G. Backhaus's reinterpretation of Friedrich List's contributions to political economy emphasizes List's application of public administration using a broad range of techniques in pursuit of economic development. Within this framework, List develops and draws his analysis of economic forces and tendencies that are to be manipulated and nurtured.

W.D. Sockwell offers an interesting paper on the popularization of classical economic ideas during the nineteenth century. This paper is partially derived from Professor Sockwell's doctoral dissertation which received the History of Economic Society's prize for the most outstanding dissertation offered in the history of economic thought in 1989. Our interest in this investigation is in the role of affirmative feedback when theoretical analyses are reintroduced into the culture at a popular explanatory and instructional level, thus influencing the presumptive behaviour that gives rise to the analysis in the first place. This phase of social reinforcement of theory has an administrative aspect that is augmented by the enhancement of the intensity of formal education in our society.

Zoltan Kenessey resurrects the nearly forgotten 1923–4 national accounts of the Soviet Union, which represented pioneering efforts in national statistical analysis and inter-industry relations that most western European nations did not develop until after World War II. Such efforts, in the Physiocratic tradition, are, of course, most obviously appropriate to the needs of a command economy, but any economy that requires either private entrepreneurial or public administrative planning is now seen to be dependent upon formal systematic accumulations and analysis of information.

M.H.I. Dore's study of the theoretical and political background to the Gorbachev reforms in the Soviet Union investigates the theoretical approaches to administrative supervision of the economy. The varying appraisals of the appropriate amount of intervention and the renewed commitment to a wider zone of independent market adjustment under perestroika offer a case study of the theoretical and policy interactions of administration and volitional forces since the 1920s in the Soviet Union.

Finally, Mary Ann and Robert W. Dimand's paper on Benjamin Graham and theories of storage of materials or commodites takes us full circle, reminding us of relatively modern concerns for managing the materials balances in the economy in the interest of a more direct administrative control over actual supplies rather than control over prices. Throughout antiquity and into medieval times, in both the Muslim and Christian worlds, 'provisions policies' for the poor and 'staples policies' provided administrative control of essential commodities to protect the subsistence of the poor and commercial interests. Beyond these regulations, the open market was free to function in its prescribed arena. The Dimands review aspects of this tradition in its relatively recent expression in the 1920s and 1930s when macroeconomic materials policies were receiving attention.

All of the papers in this volume could be discussed in terms of their treatment of market forces and policy, but our interest here has been in drawing out the continuity and clarity of the administrative tradition in which individual and social sovereignty have been brought to bear on the economic problem, promoting rationality and efficiency consistent with administrative purposes with various delineations of the appropriate scope of market forces.

Contributors

S. Ambirajan, Department of Humanities and Social Sciences, Indian Institute of Technology, Madras, India

J.G. Backhaus, Rijksuniversiteit Limburg, Faculteit der Economische Wetenschappen, Maastricht, The Netherlands

S. Zin Bae, Puteaux, France

James L.Y. Chang, Virginia Military Institute, Lexington, Virginia

Mary Ann Dimand and Robert W. Dimand, Department of Economics, Brock University, St Catharines, Ontario, Canada

M.H.I. Dore, Department of Economics, Brock University, St Catherines, Ontario, Canada

Françoise Duboeuf, Université de Paris I, Panthéon – Sorbonne, Paris, France

Yassine Essid, Salammbo, Tunisia

Philippe Fontaine, Department of Economics, Harvard University, Cambridge, Massachusetts

S.M. Ghazanfar, University of Idaho, Moscow, Idaho

William D. Grampp, University of Chicago, Illinois

A. Azim Islahi, Aligarh Muslim University, India

Zoltan Kenessey, International Statistical Institute, Voorburg, The Netherlands

W.D. Sockwell, Berry College, Mount Berry Station, Rome, GA

Gloria Vivenza, Istituto Di Storia Economica E Sociale, Universita Di Verona, Italy

John C. Winfrey, Department of Economics, Washington & Lee University, Lexington, Virginia

1 The doctrine of 'light-heavy' and Kuan-Chong's economic policies

James L. Y. Chang

Kuan-Chong (*c.*730–645 BC), the renowned premier of the state of Chi in ancient China, introduced a series of economic programmes aimed at promoting the prosperity and power of the state under a controlled economy and feudalistic monarchy. During his 40-year premiership (685–645 BC), the state attained unprecedented economic and military supremacy and political hegemony.[1]

We know that after the death of the premier and probably during the period 400 to 300 BC, a number of anonymous scholars jointly published a book titled *Kuan-Tzu*, which means, literally, master Kuan.[2] Recapitulating the political, economic and other policies, the thought and teachings of Kuan-Chong, the work marked a milestone in the history of Chinese economic thought. It endeavoured to treat the people's well-being and the state's productive and distributive problems from an economic rather than a philosophical or ethical viewpoint. However, we don't know how large a portion of the book was written by the premier, and, to the extent that it was written by others after his death, how much and how far the contents deviated from the words and deeds of Kuan-Chong.[3] Nevertheless, despite these controversies, the significance of the work stands. The book comprises 86 essays, of which 76 remain. Section VIII, consisting of the last 16 essays subtitled 'Light-Heavy', reiterates Kuan-Chong's views on monetary and fiscal policies, governmental exploitation of monopoly rights, measures for promoting foreign trade and immigration, manipulation of commodity markets, and redistribution programmes. Most of these policies and their underlying concepts are narrated in the form of a dialogue between the premier and Duke Hun, the ruler of Chi, in no clear order.[4] Yet, as a whole, the 16 essays turned out to be the most original and sophisticated economic work of ancient China and it has generated a profound impact upon Chinese economic thinking not only throughout the ages but even today.

A central theme of the premier's economic policies is his plan of substituting taxes – the traditional source of government revenue – with income generated from state monopolies of key industries, and from controls and manipulation of the money supply and the prices of grain and other staples and necessities. Government activities of such a scale clearly indicated a grand design which, in turn, reflects at least an understanding or notion of the way the price system

1

and the ancient economy functioned. This notion, emphasized repeatedly in *Kuan-Tzu*, is the doctrine of 'light-heavy'. In the following pages I will attempt to elucidate the doctrine and to examine its application to policies of government finance, price control and monetary measures.[5]

I The doctrine

The term 'light-heavy' existed in Chinese literature long before Kuan-Chong's time, but the way it was used was so broad and general as to defy definition. Even in *Kuan-Tzu* the term is used in different contexts, some relating to military strategy, others to law, education, farming and politics, in addition to economic issues. 'Light-heavy' is, in effect, a homograph. Nevertheless, although no definition is given in section VIII of the book, we find a fairly consistent use of the term. In this article, I suggest that 'light-heavy' be defined as relatively low/relatively high prices or values.[6]

Let us take a closer look at the doctrine. Essentially, it indicates that if two products, say product A and product B, are compared with each other, and, if A is made relatively lighter, B would be relatively heavier in comparison with A. Clearly, all we have here is a truism. To establish a causal relation, let us now add: (1) other things being equal, and (2) that some of the products can be made lighter or heavier artificially. Now, applying this notion to a case often cited in the text: if the price of grain is compared to the price of other necessities such as textiles for whatever reason, when the price of grain is lowered (made lighter), other things being equal, the price of textiles would be higher (heavier). Put differently, the textile price of grain would be higher; a unit of grain would now command fewer textiles. This leads to the question: why is the price of a product increased or decreased in the first place? *Kuan-Tzu's* answer is: 'when people experience surplus [of a commodity] they would tend to value it cheaply' and 'when people experience a shortage [of a commodity] they would tend to value it dearly'. In addition, 'abundance lowers the value [of a product]; shortage raises it'.[7]

As to the factors and forces causing a product to be more abundant or scarce, the text offers the following:

1. Annual harvest: other things being equal, bumper crops bring abundance; crop failures bring shortages.
2. Seasonal variations: abundance in harvest seasons, shortage in spring and early summer.
3. Hoarding of a commodity by merchants or government: again, other things being equal, this leads to shortages of the product in marketplaces; dumping leads to abundance.
4. Centralization of a commodity gives rise to its shortage; decentralization creates its abundance. (Items 3 and 4 apparently overlap considerably.)

5. Tax collection – in kind – with short notice creates a shortage; the shorter the notice, the steeper the price climb of the taxable product. When tax was collected in the form of money, peasants in ancient China were forced to sell farm crops for money. Taxpayers' selling of farm crops would thus create an abundance of the crops in the market.
6. Obstacles hindering the movement of a commodity create its shortage. Actions easing its movement create its abundance.[8]

The effects of the six factors listed above, according to the text, on balance control people's predispositions to the abundance of shortage of grain and thus its price. The effects of the last four factors, on the whole, control people's predispositions toward their feelings and the prices or values of all items in marketplaces including two other stocks-in-trade: first, 'ten thousand goods', that is, a catch-all, for all other goods except grain; second, money or the circulating medium. Here, in one stroke, the authors of *Kuan-Tzu* aggregated all items in marketplaces into three categories: grain, all other goods, and money. The 'light-heavy' relationships between them are as follows:

When grain is light, *ceteris paribus*, all other goods would be heavy; when grain is heavy, all other goods are light.
When grain is light, *ceteris paribus*, money would be heavy; when grain is heavy, money is light.
When money is light, *ceteris paribus*, grain (and/or all other goods) would be heavy; when money is heavy, grain (and/or all other goods) are light.

Interrelationships of the three aggregates are stated only in one-to-one terms. At the same time, the authors also expressed their disbelief that the price relations of the three aggregates would ever reach a fixed proportion. Instead, they saw endless changes and movements in price ratios.

The authors also assumed grain to be the only product whose price could go up and down independently. Irregularities in the annual harvest or seasonal variations, for example, were some of the reasons for grain's abundance or shortage and price changes. This assumption is apparently self-contradictory since, as will be noted later, the authors also recommended manipulation of the money stock in order to influence commodity prices. Such a recommendation clearly admitted the autonomy of the value of money.

II Application of the doctrine
In *Kuan-Tzu*, the doctrine of 'light-heavy' was put to practical use in many areas of governmental administration, including economic planning. In the following, we shall focus on the application of the doctrine to three types of government economic policies.

Government finance

The type of society the authors of *Kuan-Tzu* had in mind was primarily a monarchical-feudalistic market society populated by four classes of people: gentry-scholars, peasants (the mass majority), artisans and merchants. In this society, which actually prevailed at the time of *Kuan-Tzu*'s publication, the productive and commercial activities were simple: producers, consumers and traders were working mainly for their own interests and well-being; the economy was partly but increasingly monetarized; the price of grain and other basic products fluctuated seasonally and often violently.[9] Looking at the society from the standpoint of the monarch, the writers of *Kuan-Tzu* saw the profits from price variations grabbed by the merchants and barons, who accumulated wealth and power at the expense of the peasants and grassroots population. If government pursued a non-interference policy, distributive inequality would be increasingly intensified and the state's political and economic stability endangered. The text considered profits from these sources a legitimate revenue of the sovereign.[10]

Another theme that dominates the thinking of *Kuan-Tzu* is its distaste for taxation. In the book many types of taxes were discussed but all were dismissed because of either their negative impact on production or their burden to the populace.[11] Since citizens always 'resent being bereaved but rejoice at receiving', the ruler would be well advised to keep himself 'in full sight when handing out gifts but out of sight when plotting larcenies'.[12] This simply says that wise kings would have much to gain if they broadcast their almsgiving but conceal their plans to impose taxes and levies. The honesty displayed by the writers of *Kuan-Tzu* here was unprecedented. But what is more important is 'their attitude toward government finance, which helps us to understand their attempt to minimize taxes – to about 5–10 per cent on land output and comparably light levies on other objects – and to maximize 'invisible' revenues.[13] The text affirms that revenues so obtained are under the control of the state 'without begging the citizens'.[14]

What 'invisible' revenues are available to the government? The authors of *Kuan-Tzu* identified two major sources. First there is government income from the monopoly on the supply of salt, iron and a few other natural resources such as timber, leather and hide, together with hunting and fishing rights. Since all land in ancient China was the property of the sovereign, any output extracted from land, river or sea was subject to a rental payment to the state. The state of Chi, located in present Shangdong province in eastern China, was well endowed with fertile land, a long coastline and salt and mineral resources. Since both salt and iron products were necessities, the Chi government was in a good position to control their marketing and prices.[15] As noted earlier, hoarding and concentration of a commodity tend to create a shortage of the item and to affect its price in the marketplace. The authors of the book noted that a moderate upward adjustment of the salt price would generate more revenue than a poll tax. Moreover, since the distillation of salt is non-technical, 'by boiling sea water, [the state of Chi] would be well-situated to tax other states'. The text also pointed out that even for a poorly endowed state it is expedient to consider price control of necessities as a source of government revenue.

Another type of 'invisible' revenue, *Kuan-Tzu* suggested, derived from government operations in buying and selling grains and other necessities. *Kuan-Tzu* affirmed that the ruler ought to watch closely the price movements of basic commodities and throw his weight around by purchasing them in harvest times or bumper crop years and selling them when they are in short supply. Profits thus obtained would otherwise be seized upon by speculating merchants. Thus, according to the text, government trade in the staples market not only generates substantial revenue but also prevents the rise of powerful merchants, and alleviates the inequality between the rich and the poor.

How adequate were these 'invisible' revenues in the government budget? Unfortunately, no empirical data are available. The authors of *Kuan-Tzu*, however, were quite confident that they would be more than sufficient to keep taxes at low levels.

With regard to government spending policies, *Kuan-Tzu*, like most other ancient works in China, emphasized economy and restraint and condemned luxury and lavishness. An important exception is its recommendation of government spending to maintain employment in hard times.[16] The essay 'Chen Ma Soo' asserted:

> at times of drought or flood, when people's annual output is ruined, palace and pavilion projects ought to be undertaken to employ the destitute who possess neither dog nor pig. Projects as such are designed not to add pleasure and beauty but rather to sustain the state economy.

The emphasis lies in the phrase, 'in hard times', since, in normal times, the text noted, 'mobilization of massive numbers of workers in mansion and castle constructions' would force 'people to ignore their fundamentals'. Simple and crude as they are, these remarks conceivably constitute one of the earliest countercyclical fiscal policy statements.

Closely related to the countercyclical programmes named above is the authors' suggestion of spending by the well-to-do to prevent secular stagnation.

> Lengthen the mourning period so as to occupy people's time, and elaborate the funeral so as to spend their money. Relatives visit each other [during such occasions] – this is to strengthen kinship .... To have large caves for burial is to provide work for poor people, to have magnificent tombs is to provide work for artisans. To have large inner and outer coffins is to encourage carpenters, and to have many pieces for enshrouding is to encourage seamstresses.[17]

Kuan-Tzu was not the only ancient document recommending public and private spending for maintaining economic stabilization and adequate employment, although it offered the most systematic plan.

Price control

Two types of price policies are recommended in the text: one deals with domestic, the other with international prices. The authors of *Kuan-Tzu* realized that domestic commodity prices tended to swing widely and to destabilize the political and economic system if the government maintained a hands-off stance. If the price of grain, for example, were too low, consumers would benefit but peasants would be hurt. Low-priced grain also tended to flow out of the state and undermine the state's power and wealth.[18] Restless peasants would tend to emigrate to other states, resulting in depopulation, a situation every state in East Chou times endeavoured to avoid in view of the general underpopulation in China during that period. If the domestic grain price stayed high, the authors noted, agricultural production would be encouraged and foreign grain would flow in but consumers would be unhappy, creating a different kind of discontent. Furthermore, wild price fluctuations, *Kuan-Tzu* asserted, would breed merchant speculation and annexation, creating concentration of land and intensifying social unrest. *Kuan-Tzu* thus argues for the maintenance of a reasonably stable price.

But what is meant by a reasonably stable price? In *Kuan-Tzu* it is certainly not a fixed price, nor an adjustable peg, but more akin to a system of a managed float, with government authorities keeping an eye on market trends and stepping in every now and then to curtail strong fluctuations, such as in the price of grain, in order to keep markets functioning in a more orderly way. The following conversation between Duke Hun and Kuan-Chong describes the authors' notion of a 'reasonably stable price'.

> Duke Hung asked: 'Is it feasible to keep the leveling price (of a commodity) fixed?' Kuan-Chong replied 'No, the leveling price guides and moves with the market (buying and selling) by shifting itself up and down; it can never be fixed at a given numeral.' Duke Hung: 'What if the leveling price is fixed and adjusted periodically?' Kuan-Chong responded: 'It is not advisable to maintain an adjustable fixed price system, since the arrangement would harden price movement, freeze production, and stiffen economic activities.'[19]

In connection with domestic price stabilization policies, two more points are worth noting. First, state activities in grain trade enabled the government to acquire a large volume of the food staple as well as a strong influence in the grain market. Since grain assumes a special position in agrarian societies, government, now with money and a large supply of grain on hand, also gained control over other prices.[20] Second, government price stabilization policies at home involving the buying and selling and redistribution of grain and other staples applied not simply intertemporally, but also interregionally, especially when regional famine occurred.

Kuan-Tzu's international price policies are dominated chiefly by the authors' giving priority to commodities over money and their preference for open trade. The text noted repeatedly that 'the five grains and rice are the basis of people's livelihood', but 'pearls, jade are high-grade moneys; gold, medium grade; coins, lower grade. All three neither provide warmth, nor fill the stomach.'[21] The next question is how to encourage an inflow of grain and other desirable products? The authors suggest a high price policy through the storing of grain and these products by state agencies so as to keep them scarce and dear in domestic markets. Higher prices would naturally attract imports.[22] Since the authors' notion of wealth is goods and products, more imports would mean greater wealth for the state. Thus, if the government will 'keep price high [internally] when it is low externally, keep our wares heavy when they are light abroad, make things scarce [at home] when they are abundant outside; our leading position would be assured'.[23]

Kuan-Tzu's policy of promoting international exchange is revealed by its favourable treatment of foreign merchants and the establishment of hostels for visiting businessmen. 'Guests coming in a carriage should be provided with free meals; those in two carriages, free meals and horse feed; those in three carriages, meals for servants too.'[24]

Monetary policies

The text assumes that the value of money is chiefly determined by the quantity in circulation. A well-known passage states, 'If 90 per cent of the money stock is summoned by the government, leaving 10 per cent in circulation, money tends to be heavy, all goods light.'[25] What it says is that if the lion's share of the circulating medium is withheld by the government, leaving only a small portion in circulation, the value of money would tend to be high, and the price of goods low. In addition, 'when money is heavy all goods would be light', and 'when money is light all goods would be heavy',[26] meaning that the value of money is inversely related to the price of all goods, including grain.[27]

The statements quoted above call for a few remarks:

1 The 90 per cent/10 per cent division of the circulating medium between the holdings of the state treasury and the marketplace, presumably a change from an earlier division say, 50 per cent/50 per cent (but this 50/50 ratio is not given), certainly appears out of proportion, even by ancient China's standards. However, exaggeration, especially in quantities and figures, is a matter of *Kuan-Tzu*'s style, and these figures should not be taken literally.

2 During the period 500–300 BC, paper and credit money were nonexistent in China. So 'money' or 'the circulating medium' refers mainly

to hand-to-hand copper coins. But two other forms of money, – gold bars and pearl and jade, as noted earlier, known as 'middle' and 'high' grade moneys – were also available.

3   When the government proceeded to decrease the quantity of money in circulation in ancient China, the only expedient and practical way was to sell its stockpile of commodities; on the contrary, easy money calls for government purchase of commodities in marketplaces.

However, if government holding of the circulating medium is increased by a sale of its commodity stockpiles, more goods and less money would be available in marketplaces. Both changes would thus create a downward pressure on prices. Yet, crude as it was, *Kuan-Tzu*'s assumption of the inverse relation between the quantity and the value of money is noteworthy. The work deserves credit as one of the earliest publications introducing a crude quantity theory of money.

In *Kuan-Tzu*'s terminology, when grain is 'light', money would be 'heavy'. The situation would call for 'shooting down a "light" with a "heavy"', so as to reverse or slow the fall in the price of grain. The policy, as noted earlier, is aimed at evening out excessive price fluctuations. The same principle holds when the grain price is too high. In this case, the grain is 'heavy' but money 'light'; the government could then dump its grain holding (a 'heavy') in exchange for money (a 'light') so as to prevent continued price rises.[28]

Let us now take a look at *Kuan-Tzu*'s monetary policies, price control and government finance measures in their entirety. The authors of the text knew well that the production, output and price variations of grain and other goods were determined primarily in the private sector, in which government influence is, at best, indirect and limited. But they also realized that mintage is a divine right of the sovereign, and state control over the money stock is direct and powerful. By turning the money stock in the private sector up and down, the state is able to manipulate market prices and reap substantial profits.[29] In the authors' thinking, the profit would be large enough to replace most, if not all, taxes. This being the case, a policy of minimum taxes could be maintained by the state's commercial activities, or, more specifically, by the government's 'out-of-sight' or 'invisible' revenues. With adequate government revenues, the state would be well positioned to carry out its plans to promote wealth, prosperity and economic and military might. In addition, the state's buying and selling of commodities also contribute to price stability and more equal distribution of income.

Kuan-Tzu's monetary policies are not simply a matter of abstract thinking; they are, in effect, highly empirical. In the essay 'Chi-Fa' ('The Seven Standards'), the text affirms that 'disregarding statistical records and computations while planning national projects is like crossing a rapid without a watercraft.' In the essay 'State Guidelines' (actually 'State Guidelines Based on Socioeconomic Statistics'), the text points out that 'It is essential to maintain a tally on the state's land, population, consumption, expenditures, money stock of each village, county, and the entire state; administration of state plans without comprehension of statistical data is unthinkable.' Again, in the essay, 'Inquiry', the whole discussion is devoted to nearly a hundred questions which each village and county administration is instructed to investigate, collect and record. A few of these questions are: How much land is there in each village and county? How much of these lands are of high, medium and low grades? How much is the per family and total annual yield? What are the types of produce? How large is the population in each village and county? Then, comparing each locality's annual yield with its population and consumption, the next question is: how much is the surplus or deficit, in terms of food products, textiles and other basic necessities? Records so compiled would then offer a basis for the management of state purchase and redistribution operations. More importantly, these data, which were kept only for official use, enabled the administration to monitor the necessary amount of 'loan funds' and the quantity of the circulating medium in each locality and in the state as a whole.

Notes

1. Kuan-Chong's time was characterized by the diminishing power of the Eastern Chou dynasty (771–249 BC) when the feudal lords, preoccupied by interstate conflicts, were overlooking their homage responsibilities. It was also a time when the northern and western nomads invaded China frequently; yet neither the Chou king nor any state was strong enough to offer nationwide resistance or to unite all vassal states. Thus the prime minister of Chi (one of a half-dozen mightier states) proposed to his lord, Duke Hun of Chi, and the Chou king, a series of measures to restore peace, order and the dignity of the king. His proposal included policies to halt the interstate warfare, to compel vassal states to observe their liege duties, and to guard against the tribal invaders collectively. These proposals, in effect, called for the establishment of a hegemonic state, one which would be widely respected by all, and economically, morally, and militarily capable of the task. Under Kuan-Chong's leadership, the state of Chi became the first to achieve hegemony ('Pa' in Chinese). In 667 BC, the Chou king established Duke Hun of Chi as the 'First Noble'. Following Chi, four other states acquired the same status. They were Sung, Tsin, Ch'in and Chu, which ended its hegemony in 591 BC.

2. The time of publication suggested in the text is based on the following: first, some events which occurred after Kuan-Chong's lifetime are noted in the book; second, Ssu Ma Chien, the grand historian (145–87 BC), Han Fei Tzu, the legalist theoretician (c.280–233 BC), and Chia Yi (201–169 BC), the author of *Hsin Shu* (New History), all made references to the wide circulation of the book; and, third, the style of writing and the topics discussed seemed to fit well with the period, 400–300 BC. Nevertheless, a few questions are not yet settled: whether the book was published over a period of time, and, if so, over how long a period; also, because of the variations of style and the repetitions of some topics, I believe that more than one author was involved in the writing, but we have no way of knowing how many.

3. Although the book attempted to record Kuan-Chong's thought, and the prime minister himself might have contributed a part of it (for example, the essay 'Kuo Shoc', see Ma (1979: 212)), we must distinguish Kuan-Chong from the authors of *Kuan-Tzu*. Hereafter the former will be referred to as Kuan-Chong or the premier, the latter as the authors of *Kuan-Tzu*, or interchangeably as the text or the book.

4. Throughout the last 2 000 years, numerous researchers have endeavoured to collate, edit, authenticate, rectify and, in some cases, reconstruct the text. Liu Hsiang (79–8 BC), a

scholar appointed by Emperor Cheng of the Early Han Dynasty, was the first of many men of letters to collate and edit the text. Since the original *Kuan-Tzu* has been partly lost and partly corrupted, works on *Kuan-Tzu* became a highly specialized endeavour. In addition, largely because of its breadth, *Kuan-Tzu* has attracted the attention of philosophers, historians, sociologists and political scientists. In the area of Chinese economic thought, its main thread was clarified about 70 years ago: see Liang (1930, 1936a, 1936b), Holi (1935), Hu (1962–81, 1988), Fu (1983), Ma (1979). An English translation, by Maverick (1954) is also available. Hu translated one of his works into English in 1988; a chapter of this work is devoted to the economic thought of *Kuan-Tzu*.

5. Other economic policies of *Kuan-Tzu*, such as redistribution of income, population and land, and agricultural programmes, though integral parts of the *Kuan-Tzu* system, are not considered in this paper.

6. In *Kuan-Tzu*, price and values are used interchangeably, so we have no choice but to stick to this usage.

7. Ancient Chinese economists had attempted to develop a theory of price determination. Here, according to the authors of *Kuan-Tzu*, market prices are determined essentially by people's feelings of the abundance/shortage of the product in question. See the essay 'Kuo Shoo', one of the most important essays in Section VIII of *Kuan-Tzu*.

8. Relative scarcity obviously holds a pivotal position in the text; words like 'demand' and 'supply' are implied, but never occur in the text.

9. *Kuan-Tzu* is perhaps the earliest publication in China which explicitly assumes a human nature based on self-interest. Both Han Fei, the Legalist theoretician (c.280–233 BC) and Ssu Ma Chien, the grand historian (145–87 BC), as noted earlier, also assumed the acquisitive nature of human beings.

10. Ancient Chinese writers, like their contemporaries in other cultures, treated the words 'sovereign' and 'government' synonymously.

11. People's criticism of heavy taxes in Eastern Chou times were widespread, as is evident in all documents published by the Confucianists, the Moaists and the Taoists.

12. 'Kuo-shoo'. However, the government financial policies sound less wicked if one also considers governmental aid to the old, the weak and the poor.

13. In a few passages the authors seem to argue for zero taxes rather than minimum taxes. Interpretation of these passages is still controversial, perhaps indicating the existence of some inconsistencies in the text.

14. Similar expressions also appear in 'Chen Ma Su', an essay in Section VIII of *Kuan-Tzu* and in at least seven other essays.

15. Recognizing the inefficiency and potential corruption of government commercial operations, the authors of *Kuan-Tzu* recommended the production of salt and iron by private concerns under government contracts. Profits of the operation would be shared so as to preserve adequate private incentives. However, control of marketing and supply remained completely in the hands of the government.

16. For a review of the work-relief policies in ancient China, see Yang (1957). Yang's re-examination continued into medieval China when Fan Wen-cheng, Governor of Western Chekiang Province, launched a similar programme with remarkable success.

17. Ibid.

18. *Kuan-Tzu* held a different concept of wealth from that of the European mercantilists. For *Kuan-Tzu*, wealth is represented mainly by the output of grain, silk, domestic animals, houses and natural resources, not money.

19. In the essay, 'Light-Heavy B', an essay in Section VIII, *Kuan-Tzu*, the 'Leveling price', or 'hung' in Chinese, is one of ancient Chinese economists' vague notions of 'equilibrium price'.

20. In ancient China, when *Kuan-Tzu* was published, money, mainly in the form of copper coins and gold bars, prevailed side by side with a barter system. In effect, grain and silk were also accepted as media of exchange. A good example of this interchangeability was government agricultural loans, which were carried out partly in terms of money and partly in grain and other staples. Typically, the government loaned money to peasants in planting seasons but received grain as repayment in harvest times.

21. 'Kuo Shoo'.
22. Clearly this is self-defeating, since higher domestic prices and continued inflow of imports of the goods in question cannot be sustained permanently.
23. 'Light-Heavy B'.
24. Ibid.
25. 'Shan Kuo Gew', an essay in Section VIII, *Kuan-Tzu*.
26. 'Shan Chuan Shoo', an essay in Section VIII, *Kuan-Tzu*.
27. The great majority of economic historians in the People's Republic of China incline to look down upon the quantity theory, including the one introduced by *Kuan-Tzu*. Their attack on *Kuan-Tzu* in this regard is however exceptionally and partly reasonable, since the money these earlier authors had in mind was commodity money with an intrinsic value.
28. In the text, dumping grain in the marketplaces to curb its price hike is also referred to as 'draining a "dear" with a "cheap"'. In this case the grain is dear but that excess can be 'drained' away by something 'cheap'. Put differently, the government unloads its grain hoard at a cheaper price in order to lessen the price climb of grain in the market.
29. *Kuan-Tzu*'s plan to replace tax revenues with government commercial profits reflects, to a large extent, the experience of Kuan-Chong, who was a successful businessman. His insight into market dynamics and price movements undoubtedly found its way into *Kuan-Tzu*. The applicability of personal experience to a state programme is certainly controversial, but the impact of *Kuan-Tzu*'s strategy on later Chinese economic thinkers, including San Hung Yang (152–80 BC), a prime minister of the Western Han dynasty, is deep rooted.

References

Chang, Bing-Lin (1919), *Kuan-Tzu Yu-yui* (Further ideas of *Kuan-Tzu*), Shiwen-she.

Chang, James L.Y. (1987), 'History of Chinese Economic Thought: Overview and Recent Works', *History of Political Economy*, **19** (3) (Fall), 481–502.

Fu, Bao-san (1983), 'Lun Kuan-Tzu Ching-chon Kuo-pien de Ching-chi Ssu-hsiang Tee-she Wen-tea' ('*Kuan-Tzu*'s Light-Heavy Essays: Comparison with other *Kuan-Tzu* Essays'), *Ching chi Ko-shueh*, **2**, 62–9; **3**, 54–8.

Fung, Yu-lan (1952), *A History of Chinese Philosophy*, trans. Derk Bodde, Princeton: Princeton University Press.

Ho, Ting Gwang (1935), 'Kwantze, Seventh Century BC: A Study of His Economic Ideas, with Reference to Recent Economic Thought', PhD dissertation, American University, Washington, DC.

Hsiao, Kung-chuan (1979), *A History of Chinese Political Thought*, trans. F.W. Mote, Princeton: Princeton University Press.

Hu, Jichuang (1962, 1963, 1981), *Chung-Kuo ching-chi ssu-hsiang shih* (History of Chinese Economic Thought), 3 vols, Shanghai.

Hu, Jichuang (1988), *A Concise History of Chinese Economic Thought*, Beijing: Foreign Language Press.

Hu Shih (1930), *Chung-kuo che hsueh shih ta kan* (An outline of Chinese History of Philosophy), 15th edn, Shanghai: Chuan Shang.

Huan Kuan (1973), *Yan Tie Lun* (Discourses on Salt and Iron) (81–73 BC), Part trans. Esson M. Gale, Taipei: Ch'eng Wen Publishing.

Huang, Han (1936), *Kuan Tzu Ching-chi Ssu hsiang* (Economic Thought of *Kuan-Tzu*), Shanghai: Shanghai Commercial Press. English trans. in Maverick (1954).

Kuo Mo-ruo (1954), 'Chimi Pien Yan-jiu' ('A Study of the Essay on Chimi', *Kuan-Tzu* XII), *Lishih Yan-jiu*, **3**, 27–62.

Kuo Mo-ruo, Yiduo Wen and Wei-yu Hsu (1956), *Kuan-Tzu Ji-jiao* (Collected Authentication of *Kuan-Tzu*), Beijing: Ko-shu Chu-ban she.

Liang, Ch'i-ch'ao (1930), *History of Chinese Political Thought*, New York: Harcourt Brace.

Liang, Ch'i-ch'ao (1936a), *Yin-ping-shih ho-chi* (Collected Works of the Icedrinkers' Studio). Shanghai: Chunghua Shu-chu.

Liang, Ch'i-ch'ao (1936b), *Kuan-Tzu Chuan* (A History of *Kuan-Tzu*) Chungking: Chong-hua Shu-chu.

Ma, Fei-bai (1979), *Kuan-Tzu Ching-chon Pien Sing Chuan* (New Interpretation of the Ching-chon Essays of *Kuan-Tzu*), Beijing: Chong-hua Shu-ju.

Maverick, Lewis (ed.) (1954), *Economic Dialogues in Ancient China: Selections from Kuan-Tzu*, New Haven, Conn: Yale University Press.

Rickett, W.A. (1985), *Guanziz: Political, Economic, and Philosophical Essays from Early China*, Princeton, NJ: Princeton University Press.

Ssu-ma Chien the grand historian, 145–87 BC, *Shi Chi* (Records of the Historian).

Tang, Ching-gao (1957), *Kuan-Tzu*, Taipei: Commercial Press.

T'ang Ch'ing-tseng (1964), *Chung-kuo Shang Koo Ching-chi ssu hsiang shih* (History of Chinese Ancient Economic Thought), Taipei: Koo-tin Shu-wu.

Yang, Lien-sheng (1952), *Money and Credit in China: A Short History*, Cambridge, Mass: Harvard University Press.

Yang, Lien-sheng (1957), 'Economic Justification for Spending – An Uncommon Idea in Traditional China', *Harvard Journal of Asiatic Studies*, **20**, 36–52.

2 Economic wisdom in ancient Tamil society: the acquisition and use of wealth in ancient Tamil literature
S. Ambirajan

It is not easy to come to any definite conclusion about the precise time and place of the origin of modern economic thinking. You can locate it as recently as you like – for instance in 1881, when Leon Walras's classic was published – or take it back to the times of Moses and his Ten Commandments. The choice of origin depends upon what is meant by 'economics', and it is clear that there can be no universally accepted definition. What is, however, clear is that the nature of economics has undergone changes depending on how 'economists' have practised their profession. Crudely speaking, we can see three stages:

- The stage of 'Protoeconomics', as J.J. Spengler calls it. This is the notion of economic ideas before it became a formal body of theory (Spengler, 1980, pp. 3–8).
- When political economy became a separate discipline, but with no community of specialist professional economists.
- The stage when there is a body of accepted economic theory practised by professionals.

By the very nature of their training and inclination, and the environment in which they operate, the objectives for which the ideas are formulated and applied, and their worldview, economists in each of the three stages are very different creatures. Expecting to see a linear progress of economic theory through these three stages, as, say, Schumpeter or Blaug do, is to ask for the impossible. One needs different sets of ground rules to evaluate the writings of 'economists' belonging to each of these three stages of the evolution of the discipline. There are no doubt some concepts and ideas that seem common to all three, but the similarity is more apparent than real. The origin of the concept, the usage, meaning and significance attached to the stages, can all be fundamentally different. So even such a notion as 'scarcity' or 'money' may mean very different things to the 'economist' of the second century BC in India and an economist in present-day Australia.

The purpose of this paper is to make a preliminary examination of the economic ideas that were prevalent in the Tamil country, i.e. south India comprising the present-day states of Tamilnadu and Kerala. While some attention has been given to the economic ideas of ancient India – mainly the north Indian tradition – hardly anything has been written on the economic ideas of ancient south India.[1] In his *Indian Economic Thought: A Preface to its History*, Joseph Spengler treats India almost as a homogeneous entity without looking at the varieties of regional experience. A particularly glaring omission is his non-recognition of the uniqueness of the Dravidian experience. Because he concentrates all his attention on Kautalya's *Arthashastra* and the *Dharmashastra* texts, Spengler has not been able to shed light on the contributions of the south Indian variant of ancient Indian economic thought.

The sociocultural differences between the Sanskritic north and the Dravidian south were considerable in the pre-Christian era. The respected ideals of a largely homogeneous Tamil society were romantic love, heroism in war and spontaneous generosity. It was a much less complicated society than that of the Aryan north with its sacredotalism, metaphysical disquisitions, myths, philosophies and social differentiation. Roughly from the second century AD onwards, a composite culture began to evolve with the cultural fusion of north and south. Even before the second century AD the cultures did not remain totally isolated but it was still possible to speak of the uniqueness of the southern Dravidian/Tamil civilization. Despite its simple structure, the society had its own institutions, it had a worldview, and it had its law-givers.

Much of our knowledge about this period (*c*.300 BC to AD 200) comes from the corpus of literary sources known as Sangam literature. Sangam is a Tamilized word of Sanskrit origin, which originally referred to the Buddhist Sangha, meaning an association. In the early period of south Indian history there had been three such associations, one succeeding another: the First Sangam, Second Sangam and the Last Sangam, all patronized by the Pandyan Kings ruling from Madurai. Despite its fragmentary character, there is enough material to make a preliminary study of the economic opinion that prevailed during this early period of Tamil history. The following are the basic texts:

Tolkappiam (verse)	Grammatical work but contains accounts of social arrangements

Ettutokai (verse)
   Purananooru
   Ahananooru
   Paditrupattu
   Kalitokai
	Anthologies of poems not all of them available now. In all, eight such anthologies are extant, providing a lot of information about the life and times

Kuruntokai
Ainkurunooru
Natrinai
Paripadal

Pattupattu (verse)	Known as 'Ten Idylls'. Written by individuals,
Pattinappalai	these contain detailed descriptions of life in
Maduraikkanchi	towns and villages
Malaipadugadam	
Porunaratrupadai	
Tirumurugatrupadai	
Perumpanatrupadai	
Sirupanatrupadai	
Kurinjipattu	
Nedunalvadai	
Mullaipattu	
Epics	Epics with strong storylines and themes
Silappadhikaram	
Manimekhalai	
Padinenkilkanakku (verse)	Eighteen didactic texts. This group includes
	the *Tirukkural, Naladiar* and *Palamoli*, all
	extremely important for the study of the moral
	ideas of the period. Of these *Tirukkural* is the
	most important.

The broad theme of literary composition was *porul*, which was dealt with under two aspects, namely *aham* and *puram*. These words are translated usually as 'interior' ('subjective') and 'exterior' ('objective'), meaning that some poems deal with feelings, and others deal with social interactions outside the family such as heroism during wars and generosity at other times. While, strictly speaking, *ettutokai* and *pattupattu* dealt with these subjects, they are rich in suggestion and enable us to attempt a reconstruction of the socioeconomic life of the period. But more importantly – and especially in the *puram* works – there is considerable normative content.

The economic environment in which this literature flourished was as simple as it was poor. There were a few wealthy people – mostly kings and merchant princes living in big cities – and they seem to have led quite opulent lives. There was considerable external commerce, as evidenced not only by Tamil literary sources but also by contemporary foreign sources such as the Greek text *Periplus of the Erythraen Sea* (AD 80) and the Alexandrian mapmaker Ptolomey's *Map of the World*. The trade was bilateral and goods were exchanged for goods (or precious metals) at the important trading cities.

From the available numismatic evidence, it appears that the ancient Tamils did not have a system of mints issuing currency and coins, but used the Roman silver and gold coins that were imported into India in exchange for goods.

By this period, the south Indian economy had long since passed from a kind of pastoralism to settled agriculture. Ancient Tamils divided the landscape into five types: *mullai* (pastoral), *kurinji* (hilly), *marudam* (arable), *neidal* (coastal) and *palai* (wasteland). The nature of the south Indian geography was such that it was almost wholly agricultural except in the south-western parts. A Sangam poet in *Natrinai* conjures up the following vision of a prosperous and hardworking agricultural labouring class (P.T. Srinivasa Iyengar, 1929, p. 179):

> You, ploughmen who have yoked the buffalo and are ploughing the field, you have built up many stacks of paddy, which look like artificial hills. You open your eyes when the cool dawn breaks. Your hands hanker for balls of rice mixed with soup in which bits of the meat of the black-eyed varal fish float. You eat to the full and go along with your wives to plant the seedlings in the wet clay. (60)

There are copious references to other craftsmen, such as the blacksmith, potter, carpenter, weaver, spinner, goldsmith and others. However it is the farmer who predominates. The economy was dominated by small settlements of agriculture with minor craft professions attached to it. While foreign trade is much noticed because it is essentially a large urban seaport city phenomenon, there are only stray references to internal trade. But the frequency of references to the salt trade gives the impression that salt was produced in the coastal regions, and people living in other regions necessarily had to buy from the itinerant traders.

The system of government that presided over this economy was monarchical. The state at this stage was still rudimentary but was in the process of becoming more and more stable. The king was obviously the holder of all secular power. While he presided over the capital cities, protecting the welfare of the good and punishing the wicked, the actual administration of the country was in the hands of the elders of the villages, who met under a banyan tree to look after the village's communal affairs. Decisions were based on what everyone agreed as right, reasonable and proper rather than on some obscure codified written Law. And yet there was enough complexity for thinkers to be concerned about the correct functioning of the society. This concern shows itself in the ancient Tamil literature under two heads:

1. in fragments of literary texts with an economic content from both the Sangam poetry and the Epics;

2. in didactic texts that give advice to people in general – including kings – on matters of economic interest.

An overall picture emerges which has the following broad features:

●   There was an economic worldview that was life-affirming rather than extolling the ascetic life.
●   There was a body of prescriptions suited to achieve a steady-state economy in the context of the existing social arrangements and economic compulsions created by nature.
●   Economic opinion was encompassed within a moral universe.

It is not surprising to see the Tamils of two millenia ago, like all ancient peoples, not treating their economic life as something divorced from other aspects of their existence. Life for them was an integrated whole comprising a variety of aspects and stages. This whole was also something that is extremely complex and not amenable to easy understanding through formulae.

The Indian view of life had four component parts: *Dharma* meaning a system of eternal values which give guidance to an individual *vis-à-vis* his relationships with other individuals, society and nature; *Artha* dealing with what we would call politics and political economy; *Kama* meaning the emotional aspects of the family relationships; and *Moksha*, which was concerned with the preparation for the afterlife. In early Indian tradition virtuous life and righteousness were supreme. It was Kautalya who placed politics and economics above even *Dharma*. In other words, according to him, *Dharma* could be freely violated for political and economic objectives. However, this primacy of position given to *Artha* was refused by the Dharmasastras and, in combination with the spread of Buddhism and Upanishadic teaching, this enabled the dethronement of the ideology that treated polity and economy as autonomous and above all else. In this sense, early Tamils followed the post-Kautalyan ideology as exemplified in the Dharmasastras. (Subramanian, 1977, pp. 33–5).

Early Tamil thinkers not only saw human life as a whole, but were also convinced that it could be meaningful only in terms of a set of universal values. This is seen clearly in *Tirukkural*, which has often been called 'The Book of Universal Wisdom'. It is divided into three sections: Virtue, Wealth and Love, which roughly correspond to the three aspects of human existence that have been part of the Indian tradition – *Dharma*, *Artha* and *Kama*. Critics have pointed out that the Tamil word *Aram* is not quite the *Dharma* that the early Indian thinkers of the Sanskritic tradition wrote about (Kamaliah, 1973, ch. 5). However such subtleties apart, the fact remains that not only virtue gets the primacy of position; the work also emphasizes how virtue is what leads human beings to the fullfilment of the other facets of human life:[2]

> Virtue wins glory and wealth: what better
> key to excellence in life? (31)

> Pleasure emanates from virtue alone:
> all else is stale and weary. (39)

While early Sangam poetry extols acts like killing in war, stolen love, etc. as permissible behaviour, the virtue of the later Sangam age, mellowed by the non-violent doctrines of Jainism, is one of universal love, compassion and truthfulness which would totally abhor such moral aberrations. Take for example the following couplet from *Tirukkural*:

> Wisdom's way is sharing food with others
> and sustaining all that lives. (322)

Early Tamil writers had a clear notion about the ultimate objectives of human existence and this has a great bearing on their views on economic matters. This notion of the ultimate aim of human life was underpinned by two basic beliefs: the impermanence of things and the power of Fate or Destiny. Sangam thinking again and again draws our attention to this aspect of human life. For example, *Naladiyar* begins with three chapters, each of ten quatrains, with self-explanatory titles such as Impermanence of Wealth, Impermanence of Youth and the Impermanent Body. In their words:[3]

> There is no passing the fixed day (of death). No one
> On earth has escaped death, and fled, and gone free.
> You who hoard up wealth, give it away! Tomorrow
> The funeral drum will beat. (6)

Tiruvalluvar says the same thing in a beautiful couplet:

> Wealth grows, like a crowd in a dancing hall:
> and scatters too, like the crowd. (332)

Tiruvalluvar has ten couplets on destiny, and he too talks about the power of fate:

> Of what use amassing millions? Except
> as ordained, you don't enjoy? (377)

One would have expected that these two beliefs – the notions of impermanence and Destiny – would have given economic thought a life-denying or ascetic twist. But notwithstanding the praise of renunciation under certain circumstances, the thought that emerges is extremely life affirming.

The impact of these two beliefs led law-givers to give importance to the way wealth was earned rather than question the necessity of wealth as such. To start with, early Tamil economics had a clear idea of what poverty can do to the human psyche. Again and again, the thinkers stress that poverty is not something to be welcomed by everyone and that it degrades human beings. *Naladiyar* makes the point trenchantly:

> A person of noble birth, suffering in want
> Is despised as being even lower than a corpse. (281)

Tirukkural is equally emphatic:

> Out of the affliction named Poverty
> A thousand others ensue. (1045)

> Easier to sleep amidst flames than have
> a wink amidst poverty. (1049)

There was no doubt that wealth was needed, not only for guarding against poverty, but also for a variety of other reasons. An early Sangam anthology, *Kalitokai*, says

> To give to the poor
> To conquer the enemy
> To enjoy sensual pleasures
>   you need wealth. (11, 1–3)

Tiruvalluvar affirms:

> A Prince should gather wealth, for no sharper
>   weapon can humble his foes. (759)

> That man who has justly amassed wealth can
>   win also Virtue and Love. (760)

The most frequent reason given for acquiring wealth is to relieve poverty. There are literally hundreds of poems both in the earlier heroic and in the later didactic works on the theme of the necessity to earn so that the needy poor can be helped. An *Ahananooru* poem claims:

> In order to lead the Life of Dharma
> In order to prevent the misery of begging
>   Wealth is essential. (155, 1–3)

Naladiyar says:

This is the duty of a true man –
   To shelter all, as a tree from the fierce Sun
And to labour that many may enjoy
   What he earns
As the fruit of a fertile tree. (202)

Tiruvalluvar of course goes straight to the point:

Wherefore the accumulation of wealth,
   unless it leads to sharing? (212)

Another didactic work, *Tirikadugam*, is equally terse:

Acquire wealth in order to give. (90)

Not only is wealth to be acquired for giving, Tiruvalluvar goes further and argues that, if wealth is neither enjoyed by oneself nor given to the deserving poor, the possessor is a disease to society.

The wealth of the unloved is like the fruit
   of a village poison-tree. (1008).

This does not mean that the prevailing ideology encouraged affluent living. Thus a *Purananooru* poet:

What you eat is a measure of food
You need no more than a pair of dresses
All the rest of your wealth is superfluous
The advantage of wealth is that it could be given
To imagine you will enjoy all your wealth is a self-deception. (189)

While there has been no bar to acquiring wealth, both the poets and the law-givers were emphatic that wealth should be acquired only by virtuous means. Ends do not, for them, justify the means. Thus *Paditrupattu* talks about *Palar Pugazh Selvam*, which means that the public praise only that wealth which has been acquired by fair and right means. *Tirukkural* has many couplets praising the acquisition of wealth by righteous methods:

Give up gains, though useful, if ill acquired;
   ends don't justify the means. (113)

Make indigence no excuse for evil;
   it will but make thee poorer. (205)

Where wealth has been won by unblemished means
   there is both virtue and joy. (754)

Not only the right means are to be followed; one *Purananooru* author goes to the extent of saying that, unless a person has a detached attitude towards riches, he cannot become wealthy.

But, then, what is the right method of acquiring wealth? There is a great deal of unanimity as to how wealth should be earned. Industriousness, ceaseless effort and love of work are absolutely vital, according to *Tirukkural*:

> Resolved effort leads to prosperity;
> Sloth brings about poverty. (616)

These qualities are specific to the gathering of wealth, but whether in the process of acquiring wealth or not, it was expected that individuals would be always truthful, not cause harm to others, guard themselves against idleness, forgetfulness and negligence, exercise self-control, and so on. In order to emphasize a work ethic, all the writers pass severe strictures on beggary and idleness. Tiruvalluvar is explicit:

> What though fate denies labour's due return?
> Effort is its own reward. (619)

> Not to beg is a million times better than
> begging even for one's food. (1061)

> It's cheeky assumption that begging
> can wipe out one's poverty. (1063)

The extolling of 'giving' and condemnation of 'receiving' may seem contradictory. But if seen in the economic-environmental context of the times in which the ideas emerged, this makes perfect sense. It was a time when natural forces determined economic conditions. The very fact that writers of the period anxiously spoke of the need to have timely rains indicates how a quirk of nature at any time could reduce the most industrious to a position of absolute poverty. In the absence of organized state charity to deal with crises, what is needed is the acceptance of social responsibility by individuals to help their fellow human beings when they are in temporary distress.

While the general thrust of the argument in ancient Tamil writings is that an individual's economic well-being depends partly upon his past actions and partly upon his present industriousness, this does not amount to giving sanction to a form of open freedom for all economic behaviour. What they want to emphasize is that humankind is a family, and that those fortunate to have wealth should help the indigent. There is a famous *Puranaanooru* poem which brings out this sentiment beautifully:[4]

> Any town our home-town, every man a kinsman
> Evil and good are not things brought

by others; neither pain, nor relief of pain
Death is nothing new. We do not rejoice
that living is sweet, nor resent it
for not being so. (192)

Tiruvalluvar too has expressed similar ideas:

He who practises sharing truly lives;
the rest are as good as dead. (214)

Indeed they would argue that the extreme poverty created by man's inhumanity
is not to be tolerated because there is nothing divinely ordained about poverty.
Tiruvalluvar again:

If the Ordainer wished that some should beg,
let Him too roam and perish! (1062)

So far we have talked of wealth in the abstract. Wealth for the ancient Tamil
thinkers (as for most ancient civilizations) was agricultural prosperity. The
literature again and again refers to the importance of agriculture for both
individual prosperity and for state power. Thus when Tiruvalluvar talks of
agriculture, he almost sounds Physiocratic:

Varied are the employments, but to wield
the plough is basic, though hard. (1031)

The linchpin of society, the farmers
support all others as well. (1032)

They live best who live by the plough; others
eat out of the farmers' hands. (1033)

The farmers' rich harvests make their King strong;
other Princes bow to him. (1034)

Labour input is of course vital,

With energy men achieve wealth; without,
What's it that they can attain? (591)

as are correct agricultural practices:

Ploughing, manuring, weeding, watering,
guarding – all five are needful. (1038)

But it was to water as the life-sustaining element that early Tamil economics
attached so much importance, in a way emphasizing the role environment plays

in the economic life of any country or society. Tiruvalluvar, for example, devotes one of the four invocatory chapters to the praise of rains (the other three being 'In Praise of God', 'In Praise of the Renunciants' and 'In Praise of Virtue'). According to Tiruvalluvar, the abundance of rain is a source of much happiness and its absence is the cause of much misery:

> Unfailing rain ensures the earth's largesse:
> it's the elixir of life. (11)

> With water scarcity, disorder reigns
> and duties come to a stop. (20)

Similarly the epic *Silappadhikaram* starts with a song of Benediction in which rainbearing clouds are given prime place.

And the supply of water is the function of good government. This leads us to the views of the ancient Tamil thinkers on the state. The king was very important in their view of society. A *Purananooru* poem puts this in no uncertain terms:

> Foodstuff is not the life nor water;
> The King is the Life of the World. (186)

But no king can be above *Dharma* or righteousness, and he has to be careful in performing his duty to provide a just administration. If he faltered in his duties, he would lose his kingship. Again Tiruvalluvar:

> The king who wantonly perverts justice
> will lose both his wealth and realm. (554)

There was unanimity of opinion that if the king swerved from justice and righteousness, even the heavens would refrain from giving rains; according to Tiruvalluvar:

> Were the King himself to swerve from justice,
> the seasonal rains would fail. (559)

The author of the epic *Manimekhalai* puts this in the mouth of the tutelary goddess:[5]

> ....Oh son of the King!
> If the King swerve from right,
> the prosperity of the land will fail
> If equity fail, rain will cease to fall
> If rain cease to fall, human life will fail,
> Human life is to the king as his own life
> So all things fail when the King fails in virtue.

The earlier *Purananooru* poem said the same thing without making a causal connection between misrule and the failure of rains:

> Kings get the blame, whether
> Rains fail or output decline
> And unnatural things occur in men's ordinary lives
> Such is the usage of this wide world. (35)

Not only were the kings enjoined to be fair-minded, they were also expected to play an active part in the economic affairs of the country. The king should develop the resources of his kingdom, enrich the treasury, preserve what had been acquired and spend well to increase the welfare of the people. As Tiruvalluvar says:

> A wise Prince augments and conserves his wealth,
>   and spends it worthily too. (385)

Of all the Sangam works, *Tirukkural* comes nearest to being what was called *Speculum principis* or 'Mirror of Princes', the name given since the early days of monarchy to the large body of writing incorporating systematic and pointed advice intended for the benefit of reigning kings or princes training to become monarchs.[6]

On expenditure, the early Tamil economists firmly believed in a state which provided law, order, defence and public works. Although Sangam poets almost as a rule emphasized the value of knowledge and education, there is no mention of the king formally sustaining educational institutions. But from the repeated reference to the vital importance of making gifts to learned men, we might conclude that providing education was considered a proper avenue for state expenditure. This is because the method of disseminating knowledge was by learned men presenting their ideas through public discourse.

Ideal society to the Sangam poets seems to have been an economy with a large population of sturdy, industrious, educated peasant proprietors. The duty of the king was to preserve such a society. A *Purananooru* poem says:

> Don't listen to the calumnies of the fickle minded
> But look after the welfare of the Farmers
> And by that look after the rest
> Even your enemies will respect you then. (35)

What do the farmers need most? Water, of course. The king is exhorted to preserve water. Thus a *Purananooru* poem (Sesha Iyengar, 1933, p. 256):

Therefore, Oh Cheliyan, great in war,
   despise this not;
Increase the reservoirs for water made
Who binds the water, and supply to fields
Their measured flow, these bind
The earth to them. The fame of others
   passes swift away. (18)

The writings of the period thus specify only broadly on what areas the king should expend the state's resources. On the whole, the king is given great freedom to do as he likes subject to the moral obligation of not hurting his subjects and being fair to all. But they warned that the king should not indulge in expenditure indiscriminately. As Tiruvalluvar says:

One who lives grand beyond his means will crash,
   and leave not a rack behind. (479)

In every action there are benefits and costs:

Think of these three: investment, return, gain –
   and then embark on action. (461)

There are enterprises that tempt with great profits but which may lead to the loss of everything:

The Wise will not rashly speculate, and
   lose the capital itself. (463)

Hence the Prince is exhorted to take decisions only after careful deliberation:

Thinking should precede action; it's folly
   to act first and think later. (467)

Discussion preludes decision, to lead
   on to prompt execution. (671)

The king should take into account every aspect of the project:

What decide an action are its nature,
   time, place, assets and the means. (675)

The king's right to tax was well recognized by the economists of the time. Tiruvalluvar says that a prosperous nation is one which is quite capable of paying any amount of taxes to the king in times of need. The authors thought that land taxes, escheats, customs duties and reparations were legitimate sources of income for the state. But whatever the source of income – even if it was as a result of a successful war – it should be collected without unduly hurting the taxpayers. Indeed, the incomparable Tiruvalluvar in order to emphasize his distaste of cruel exactions says clearly that wealth that is secured by discarding compassion on the part of the king and without love on the part of citizens is to be avoided:

> An extortionist King is a robber
> who cries 'Stand and Deliver'! (552)

Actually it is counterproductive:

> As well grow rich by evil means as store
> water in an unbaked pot. (660)

This idea is expressed by the *Purananooru* poet, Pisir Aandhaiyar, in his advice to the Pandyan King Nambi (Sesha Iyengar, 1933, p. 257):

> If an elephant take mouthfuls of ripe
>   grain on it, the twentieth part of an
> acre will yield it food for many days.
> But if it enter a hundred fertile fields
>   with no keeper
> Its foot will trample down much
>   more than its mouth receives.
> So if a wise King who knows the path
>   of right take just his due
> His land will prosper yielding myriad
>   fold.... (184)

The texts have ample advice for the king as to how he should go about collecting his dues. The poet Moondrurainar in his *Palamolinanooru*, postulates three canons of taxation:

1. Taxes should be collected from citizens when they are prosperous and not when they are in dire straits due to natural calamities like the bee collecting honey only from fully honey laden flowers. (244)
2. Taxes should be collected regularly without leaving it late to collect in one go just as you milk your cow daily instead of trying to do it at the end of the week. (245)
3. Do not use cruel methods to collect taxes even if your intention is to use the proceeds only for their benefit. (246)

It can be seen that the ancient Tamils had developed a fairly comprehensive idea of the nature of state finance. In some respects this way of looking at the king's income and expenditure as a separate category and emphasizing the great care kings should take in managing their fiscal affairs continued to constitute – though in very different forms depending upon the systems of government – the basis of public finance until a few decades ago.

A striking thing about ancient economic opinion is the near-total absence of matters connected with a money market, i.e. credit, interest rates and usury regulation, which constitute an important feature of the economic writings of all other ancient civilizations. The economic literature of northern India (both *Arthasastra* and *Dharmasastras*), some of which have heavily influenced south Indian thinkers, are very vocal about the role of interest rates and what should be the individual's attitude and state's policy towards it. This is all the more surprising because of the copious references to trading communities,[7] merchant princes, vast internal trade and flourishing international trade throughout this period. There is also enough evidence to suggest that there was a market for landed property and there are descriptions of documents used in property transfer.

All we find in the Sangam literature are stray references to the actual act of borrowing and lending. There is a poem in *Purananooru* (316, 5–7) which describes how a warrior pawns his sword to borrow food for distributing to the needy poor. In the same anthology (163) there is a reference to *Kuriethirppu* which means borrowing a certain quantity and returning the same later. The didactic text *Palamoli* uses the word *Tanisu*, which means lending. It exhorts people not to lend within their family and also enjoins creditors (211) not to give loans without security. There are two *Purananooru* poems (327, 3; 156, 4–6) which give instances of creditors waiting outside the palaces to retrieve what they had lent from indebted poets who were about to receive presents from kings. In the didactic text, *Innanarpadu* (the 40 quatrains that mention items that bring unhappiness and should therefore be avoided) there is a sentence which says that to be indebted is to be miserable (11). But, again, there is no objection to the activity of lending or to high rates of interest.

There can be no doubt that people borrowed money from others who were prepared to lend. But did the creditors get anything in return? The anthologies, the epics and the didactic works are all silent on this issue. One cannot completely dismiss the possibility that surviving literature is unrepresentative of the total literary output of those times. However, even Tiruvalluvar, the great synthesizer and certainly the most eloquent and terse mouthpiece of ancient Tamil wisdom concerning the norms of human behaviour, is silent on this issue of interest rates.

One can only hazard the opinion that in the sort of worldview that was projected in the Sangam period there was no question of any type of human action that would take advantage of another individual's adversity being condoned. As we have seen, the prevailing ideology seems to have been: 'if somebody is in need, don't lend but share what you have'.

More than charity, we must remember that this was a heroic society where the noblest pursuit was considered heroism in war. The object of war was not only to show one's heroism, but also to accumulate riches by honest plunder. As the late K. Kailasapathy said: 'Heroic society is notoriously competitive. This overriding spirit of the age .... [is] seen in the accumulation of wealth'. But the aim is not further accumulation of wealth, as it would be in a modern capitalist society. In a commercial society the wealth would be used to invest and make profits. Wealth becomes an object in itself. But in a heroic society it is very different. Kailasapathy continues:

> The purpose of amassing riches, not merely as an end in itself but as a means to entertain friends, kinsfolk, and suppliants, and thereby acquire name and fame, although expressed in a domestic context, comes very close to the warrior's idea of the spoils of war – trophies and prizes – as prestige items to be given and exchanged. (Kailasapathy, 1968, p. 253)

Another aspect to be considered is that, during this period, apart from the heroic theme there was also the theme of distribution. Although the economy was slowly transforming itself, even in the second century after Christ when most of the didactic works were written, some of the old socioeconomic formations had remained intact. One aspect of the society is the distribution of resources by a consensus, however achieved. The *Tolkappiam*, the ancient grammatical work, in its 58th sutra talks about *Paal varai Deyvam*, which literally means 'the deity that allots the shares'. This deity is often invoked when distribution matters come into the picture. Early Sangam society was composed of communities that believed in sharing and did not have a rigid conception of private property. In this context this deity is nothing more than, as S. Ramakrishnan has said, 'divine validation of the egalitarian sharing that was the mode of distribution in the tribes of food gatherers and hunters living in conditions of what may be called primitive communism' (Ramakrishnan, 1980, pp. 62–3). In the course of the hunters acquiring spoils many may have helped. Hence there were two modes of distribution. One was *Paatheedu*, which refers to sharing by the actual hunters; the other was *Kodai*, which refers to giving to ironsmiths, drummers, etc. who had also contributed to the hunting expedition. Each actually participates in the physical act of earning, in which case he is entitled to a share of the wealth produced, or one who is unable to participate in the process of earning wealth due to natural causes is entitled to help from his fellow human beings. There can be no unearned income, to use a modern legal phrase for indicating the income of a rentier. In short everyone had an entitlement to the total output of the community.

Given this ambience, a money market could not develop and thrive. It was only after the end of the heroic age, followed by the dark ages consequent on the Kalabhara invasion, that a climate ripe for trading in money was created.

By the time the Kalabhara interregnum was over and the Pallava and Chola empires were stabilized from the ninth century onwards, there is ample evidence for the existence of interest rates and rules for regulating usury based on the *Dharmasastras* (Nilakanta Sastri, 1975, pp. 599–600).

Early Tamil economic opinion is essentially a code of conduct for individuals and their rulers in so far as economic life is concerned. The problem of scarcity was very much the economic problem of the ancient Tamils as it is of modern economics. But unlike modern economic thinking, which sees its origin in man's insatiable desires and its solution in better management and increased productivity, ancient Tamil economists saw the origin of scarcity in past actions and its solution in living a virtuous and contented life as well as universal brotherhood. Early Tamil economic ideas are part and parcel of an integrated humanistic worldview which emphasized that the problems encountered by man have to be solved by him alone. The Sangam authors were no theorists who derived a set of policy prescriptions for rulers or explained the behaviour of individuals from first principles. On the contrary they were empirical, practical and pragmatic but with a strong belief in a moral order. This moral order would shun a view that extolled the virtues of individual selfishness because it could maximize the welfare of the society. Early Tamil economics emphasized communal life marked by contentment, compassion, propriety and honest effort – a moral economy in fact. Their aim was to populate the country with good people living in harmony with their fellow human beings and with nature around them. The sort of noble or virtuous men they had in mind is best expressed in a *Purananooru* poem:[8]

> This World lives because
> some men do not eat alone, even
>   the sweetest things,
> not even the food of the gods
> earned by grace and penance.
> They have no anger in them;
> they do not fear evils that other men fear
> nor sleep over them
> they give their lives for glory
> but will not touch the gifts of the whole worlds
> if it should be tainted
> they have no faintness in their hearts
> and strive not for themselves
> but for others
> this world is
> because such men are. (182)

Notes

Professor Barry Gordon, Professor Todd Lowry and Sri T.N. Ramachandran provided many valuable comments and suggestions. Any remaining errors of fact or interpretation are my own.

Numbers in brackets after the verses quoted in the text refer to the works concerned.

1. See Rangaswami Aiyangar (1965), Shah (1954) and Pusalkar (1962). An exception is B. Natarajan's Sornambal Endowment Lectures for 1960–61 delivered at the University of Madras. See Natarajan (1975). Mention may be made of Mu. Vaithilingham (1989) in which there are papers that discuss the presence of socialist ideas in early Tamil literary works.
2. All translations of *Tirukkural* verses are from K.R. Srinivasa Iyengar (1988).
3. *Naladiar* translations are from Wm. Theodore de Bary (1958), pp. 67–9.
4. A.K. Ramanujan's translations are from Zvelebil (1973), pp. 16–18.
5. Translation by Prema Nandakumar in a private communication.
6. B. Natarajan has claimed that Tiruvalluvar's views come nearest to those of Adam Smith because for both political economy 'is a collection of recipes for the statesman aiming at enriching of both the people and the sovereign' (Natarajan, 1975, p. 52). Despite being aware of the danger of reading too much into the ancient literary texts, Natarajan nevertheless does not shy away from drawing parallels between the views of Tiruvalluvar and modern writers like Galbraith. At one stage he goes to the extent of declaring: 'Valluvar's ideas on poverty are an elaborate poetical anticipation of Marshall's ideas' (ibid., p. 21).
7. *Pattinappalai* (verses 194–212) indicates the respect traders of the port city of Kaverippoompattinam enjoyed. We are informed that they (a) treated others' property like their own and looked after them; (b) never shortchanged others; (c) always spoke the truth; and (d) did not indulge in profiteering.
8. A.K. Ramanujan's translation in Zvelebil (1973), pp. 17–18. See also *Nattrinai* (233, 7–9; 72, 1–2), *Kuruntokai* (252, 6–8), *Maduraikkanji* (192–4), *Kurinjippattu* (13–18).

References

De Bary, Theodore (1958), *Sources of Indian Tradition*, Vol. I, New York: Columbia University Press.

Kailasapathy, K. (1968), *Tamil Heroic Tradition*, Oxford: Oxford University Press.

Kamaliah, K.C. (1973), *Preface in Kural*, Madras: M. Seshachalam.

Natarajan, B. (1975), *Economic Ideas of Tiruvalluvar*, Madras: University of Madras.

Nilakanta Sastri, K.A. (1975), *The Colas*, Madras: University of Madras.

Pusalkar, A.D. (1962), 'Economic Ideas of the Hindus', in *The Cultural Heritage of India*', Vol. II, Calcutta: Ramakrishna Mission Institute of Culture.

Ramakrishnan, S. (1980), *Tirukkural Oru Samudayapparvai*, Madurai: Meenatchi Puthaka Nilayam.

Rangaswami Aiyangar, K.V. (1965), *Aspects of Ancient Indian Economic Thought*, Varanasi: Banaras Hindu University.

Sesha Iyengar, T.R. (1933), *Dravidian India*, Vol. I, Madras: C. Coomarasawmy Naidu & Sons.

Shah, K.T. (1954), *Ancient Foundations of Economics in India*, Bombay: Vora & Co.

Spengler, J.J. (1980), *Origins of Economic Thought and Justice*, Carbondale: Southern Illinois University Press.

Spengler, Joseph (1971), *Indian Economic Thought: A Preface to its History*, Durham: Duke University Press.

Srinivasa Iyengar, K.R. (1988), *Tiruvalluvar Tirukkural Lights of the Righteous Life*, Calcutta: Classics of the East Series, M.P. Birla Foundation.

Srinivasa Iyengar, P.T. (1929), *History of the Tamils from the Earliest Times to 600 A.D.*, Madras: C. Coomarasawmy Naidu & Sons.

Subramanian, V. (1977), *Cultural Integration in India*, Delhi: Ashish.

Vaithilingham, Mu (ed.) (1989), *Tamil Ilakkiyangalil Poduvudamai*, Salem: Then Thamizh Pathippakam.

Zvelebil, Kamil (1973), *The Smile of Murugan On Tamil Literature of South India*, Leiden: E.J. Brill.

3 Economic theory and policy implicit in the land tax in ancient Rome: republican and early imperial period

Gloria Vivenza

The theoretical discussions of the Romans on land taxation have not survived and probably were never formulated in a complete manner. But from the facts and from juridical evidence (together with other sources, for example the land surveyors' writings) something may be reconstructed.

The historical background, in simple outline, is the following: the land was the main basis of wealth throughout all of ancient history (despite the extraordinary growth of many renowned commercial cities and the development of a monetary economy in certain periods); and the main public expense was the army. The juridical background was equally simple: land was the political basis of Roman citizenship and every Roman paterfamilias in old times owned a plot in which nobody else could have any rights. So the private property of the Roman citizen (*dominium ex iure Quiritium*) was exempt from taxes because it had the character of an independent sovereign estate. Throughout the history of the Roman Republic there is evidence of the ongoing effort to conciliate the citizen's right to a *dominium* (which is marked with *immunitas*, i.e., exemption) and the necessity of the state to cover the expense of the army by drawing ultimately on the primary resource, the land. In the first periods of Roman history, defeated enemies frequently had to pay heavy war indemnities, which enriched the treasury; the other gain of war, booty, had the dual benefit of supplying the state with money and reinforcing ties between the commander and the soldiers (Gabba, 1977, pp. 20–22). It is interesting to note that the taxation upon the provinces, imposed later, may be interpreted as a rationalization of the booty and war indemnities (Lo Cascio, 1986, p. 30); while the tie between commander and soldiers was still alive in late republican times, when the great military leaders distributed to the troops the properties of their opponents. The survival of traditional elements shows the original relationship between war and finance. The land of the vanquished enemies was conquered, confiscated, distributed among Roman citizens or left undivided to the state, but never charged with a tax. The idea of a predial tribute was alien to the Roman mind before the conquest of the provinces.

The theoretical background is ultimately based on Greek and oriental ideas, which the Romans applied according to circumstances. For instance in early republican times, when the army needed support only occasionally, since it was composed of landowners who could supply themselves, the Senate had recourse to the *tributum civium*, which was a direct tax, not on the land, but on the person and proportioned to the *census*. So the wealthiest men paid the highest *tributum*: this is a reflex influence of the Greek ideology based on the difference between arithmetical and geometrical equality (Nicolet, 1976b, pp. 111–37). Another example relevant to the Roman conquest of the provinces is the oriental-Hellenistic principle that in the monarchies the king was the owner of all the land, and the right of property was his grant, for which a tax was paid. The Romans found this principle applied with the *lex Hieronica* in their first province, Sicily, and they kept it in place, substituting themselves for the previous sovereign. In this way they began to exploit the provinces (to export the taxation, it has been said) (Gabba, 1977, p. 27). No theory about this has survived, but Cicero calls the provincial land *vestra praedia, vestrae possessiones* (your fields, your possessions), addressing the Roman citizens, and the provincial tribute *quasi victoriae praemium ac poena belli* (the prize of victory and the penalty of war) (Cicero, *de lege agr*. III, 15; 2 *Verr.*, 3, 12–13). The Roman state behaved like the lawful owner of the provincial land, while in Italy normally it had no rights in the property of citizens, except in cases of public utility. On the Italic soil, the only land of which the state was proprietor was the *ager publicus*, the land conquered but not yet divided and distributed among Roman citizens. Here the state owned the land, and when single citizens were allowed to use it the state required the payment of a tax that was not to be reckoned as land tax (it was rather an usufruct or location). It is considered here for two main reasons: first, it was the only land in Italy of which the state could be declared the owner and to which it had some right. Second, it had a very important role in Gracchan politics because a fiscal burden on *private* property was then applied for the first time in Italy. The history of the pre-Gracchan period shows the decline of small proprietorship and the consequent impoverishment of the lowest classes of the *census*. When the authorities failed to send out colonies to peripheral countries (e.g., Cisalpine Gaul), Tiberius Gracchus proposed to set up the *proletarii* on the large concessions of *ager publicus* occupied by the Roman aristocracy in central and southern Italy. The land was given to the new proprietors as private, but they had to pay a tax to the state. This was a new type of property in Italy and was a contradiction in terms for the Roman mind. This tax had a short life (the fact that the attempt was repealed by the Roman ruling class means, to my mind, that the conception of property/sovereignty was still very strong in Italy).

But the Gracchan attempt had another important consequence: it opened the way to the confiscations carried out during the civil wars to reward the armies of the conflicting generals (Tibiletti, 1955, pp. 281–2).[1] With one important difference: the land used was not public (or exclusively public), but mainly private. From Sulla onwards, the political enemies of the victorious general were declared *hostes reipublicae*, their land confiscated and declared *ager publicus* and then distributed to the soldiers of the general. In short, what survived of the Gracchan enterprise was the rationale of conquest, not that of taxation: to put a burden on a private property (in Italy) was considered unacceptable, but to seize the land and distribute it to the citizen-soldiers was an old tradition in Roman politics, with the difference that, in early times, the land was that of enemies. Now it was land of Roman citizens – declared enemies, it is true.

The real problem was to find the land for an enlarged army. From 106 BC the army was opened to *proletarii*; moreover, the civil wars led to the emergence of charismatic personalities (chiefs of the army) who built their power on the personal loyalty of troops, and the commitment to reward them. Moreover, the troops had to be maintained after their discharge, that is to say, settled on a plot of land (the only 'pension' conceivable for a Roman citizen in republican times). It was difficult to find land to distribute in Italy, as the soldiers preferred to stay near home, instead of moving to remote provinces, so the practice of confiscation of estates and their distribution became widespread. The land was given to the soldiers as *dominium* (no land tax), but, as Cicero rightly understood (Cic., *de officiis* I, 27), the right of property was no longer sacred as before. Citizens of the opposite faction received the treatment that in the past had been reserved for defeated enemies. Until the end of the Republic, each of the conflicting parties was following the tradition that conquering people used to settle their citizen-soldiers on a *dominium*. Yet the growing scarcity of land (i.e. Italian land sufficient for all), together with the widening of the army corps, rendered it impossible to solve the problem without violent political struggle and frequent upsets of rights to landed property. Economic conflict did not erupt between *immunitas* and public finance because for a long time the political domain of Rome could continue to pass this burden on to the provinces. So the battle raged over Italian soil, in spite of the Gracchan legislation which shows (with its two new points: taxes on the private land, and the settlement of a colony out of Italy, at Carthage) an awareness of the necessity to abandon traditional patterns. It was the strong opposition of the ruling class that did not allow these Gracchan policies to be implemented.

With Augustus there began a change that continued under his successors. The character of Roman government, which had predominantly political features during the Republic, took on a more and more administrative and bureaucratic structure in the imperial age. The first emperor wanted to appear conservative, and tried to resolve his financial problems without dramatic changes, at least in appearance. He did not touch the 'taboo' of Italian *immunitas* (although he threatened it) (Cass. Dio LVI, 28), but he made some major innovations: he instituted a special reserve for the troops, the *aerarium militare* (AD 6), which was regularly supplied by the income from a tax that was levied for the first time on Roman citizens. It was not yet a land tax, but one on inheritances. (Indirect taxation is not considered in this study, so we do not dwell upon the other source of supply for the *aerarium militare*, a tax on sales.) Previously, in 13 BC, Augustus had made another decision of the greatest importance: soldiers were no longer rewarded with land, but with sums of money (Nicolet, 1984, pp. 109 and 126, n.74). Moreover, Augustus could get a thorough description of the resources, both economic and human, of the empire, thanks to the development of the census, which he also applied to the provinces. He had an administrative compendium of the military forces and of the public income/expense (*breviarium totius imperii*); and this gave impetus to the progress of geographical knowledge for political and economic purposes (Nicolet, 1989, chs VI, VII, VIII). Was Augustus aware of the difference between the former practice and the present necessity of drawing resources from the economy of the whole empire? We can only say that the shift towards domestic taxation seems to proceed at the same rate with the gradual disappearance of the Roman consciousness of being the 'ruling people' and with the supremacy of the unique sovereign who knew very well that there was now little new land to conquer, that the army was now a standing army, and the bureaucracy always growing (the tetrarchy quadrupled the courts and increased the number of legions) (Jones, 1964, Vol. I, pp. 51–60). After the first turning point under Augustus, the main points were the edict of Caracalla in AD 212, which gave Roman citizenship to all provincial peoples,[2] and the reform of Diocletian, which is no part of our subject at the moment.

From here onward, it appears that troops were maintained with supplies derived from landed property, but by a more direct system. The landowner had to furnish the food, clothing and weapons for the troops, in proportion to how much (and how productive) land he owned. To obtain this support it was indispensable to value the estates, the products, revenues and so on, so an improvement in the detail and accuracy of the cadastre and in the classification of land took place in the imperial age. Of the valuing technique involved by these developments we know very little: the *forma censualis* of Ulpianus (*Dig.*, 50, 15, 4) does not say how the proprietor makes his *aestimatio*; the fiscal classifications of land in Pannonia and Syria give only a relationship between the kind of cultivation and the surface. From many indications, however, it appears that the value of land is always linked to the rent (De Neeve, 1985).

The new 'bureaucratic' administration reveals an important difference from republican times. While the *tributum civium* was decided mainly by the same persons who had to pay it (the ruling class formed by the wealthiest men, who consented to pay provided that the decision of when, if and how much to pay was of their own making), the imperial taxation was of course independent from the will of the individuals being taxed. When Diocletian, at the end of the third century AD, introduced a conventional fiscal unit, the tax became almost mathematical. This emperor also removed the privilege enjoyed by Italian soil to be exempt from land taxes: now land throughout the empire was all on the same footing. This development is confirmed, too, from the land surveyors: the original measurement of the assigned holdings, which had juridical but not fiscal purposes, was later used to characterize the land for fiscal purposes (Hygin. Grom., pp. 167–8 Thulin). But notwithstanding the acknowledged importance of land, that is of agricultural productivity for the central administration of tribute, very few emperors tried to improve this side of the economy.[3] The usual practice, at least in the later empire, was to 'impose', after a thorough calculation of the needs of the state, the total production that each fiscal unit had to furnish in view of the tax (Jones, 1964, Vol. I, p. 65). We could say that the Romans learned financial administration from the need to maintain their army, and from the different requirements the army had at different times. The land always maintained the troops, but it was, for a long time, the land of the provinces. For their own land in Italy, the Romans did not conceive the possibility of taxation, because this would have detracted from their personal sovereignty and authority. When they came in contact with oriental-Hellenistic economies, they applied the idea of state property in the land in the provinces, which was subject to taxation. There is some controversy over the question of whether the provincial tax, usually a tenth of the product, but not everywhere, is to be considered a tax or a rent. According to T. Frank (1927, p. 144) it was too low for a rent; but F. de Martino (1979a, p. 374) says that juridically a tenth is the share of the crop which belongs to the owner of the land.

On the Romans' Italian properties, something similar, but not identical, was possible only on the *ager publicus*, to which the community (the collectivity of citizens) had a right. In the development of Roman history, we can note that during the Republic the ruling class crushed all attempts to tax private land (in Italy). In the imperial period, however, in which a direct taxation on landed property is recognizable from the early principate at least in the imperial provinces (Luzzatto, 1953, Vol. IV, p. 82), a complex evolution (and improvement) of administrative techniques led to a general taxation of provincial land and then to an 'impersonal' land tax calculated on objective (cadastral) information. This was extended to Italian soil as well. The idea of the right of the sovereign had emerged and become absolute, while the independence of the Roman citizen based on free land had disappeared.

In short, we can say that in republican times the state could define its authority only in relation to the public land (*ager publicus*), and the provincial land: the first as common land, the other by right of conquest. In this period the declaration for *census* was made personally by the landowner. Control over the measure of the estate for fiscal reasons, as well as on the productivity of land (and its classification), though not wholly unknown in republican times, began systematically only when authority over all territory of the state belonged to the emperor. This led to the idea that the tax was due from the property, not from the person. This may be, I believe, a constant pattern in history, at least in Italy. In the nineteenth century A. Messedaglia noticed, in his famous parliamentary report on the cadastre, that the proprietor's declarations are typical of early estimates in medieval Italy, and are always the first form of ascertainment, as long as the tax retains a personal (not a real) character (Messedaglia, 1936, p. 207).

In this paper we have taken into consideration mainly tributes which were not properly land taxes, but these were analysed to explain the origin of the land tax of the imperial period, which was a real tax. Work is not completed on this subject, but with more research I hope that the economic thought behind this economic behaviour will be clearer. It is already possible to see in this case of Roman economics the cross-influence of Greek political thought and Roman jurisprudence. For instance direct taxes of every kind (on the person as well as on property) were considered, in ancient Greek sources, as marks of slavery and distinctive features of a tyrannical government (Pseudo Aristot., *Oecon.* II, 1, 4; Xenoph., *Cyr.* IV, 5, 15). The obstinate Roman refusal to charge with duty the *dominium ex iure Quiritium*, on the other hand, originated as we know in Roman law. But every attempt to offend the *dominium* was considered tyrannical policy, whether it was a land tax, a confiscation, or an expropriation; and Cicero (in *de officiis* I, 43; *vide* Gabba, 1979, p. 128) describes Caesar and Sulla as having 'tyrannical' characteristics for this reason. In the late second century AD Tertullian still defines the tax as *nota captivitatis* (Tertull., *Apol.*, 13, 6).

Other instances have been cited briefly in the previous pages: the political and philosophical significance of the *tributum* proportioned to the *census* for the elites of the Roman ruling class and the impact of oriental ideas and practices on Roman provincial politics. It is, perhaps, appropriate to observe that the land tax was completely and thoroughly applied in the Roman Empire when the emperor was close to being a despot similar to the best oriental examples – and this would prove once again that the Greeks were right!

Notes

1. The difference between the Gracchan procedure (recovery of land from the *ager publicus*) and the following (recovery of land from private estates) was a legal one; but the Roman ruling class, which made use of its possessions on the *ager publicus* and could transmit them to its heirs, considered them real ownership and felt the Gracchan politics like true expropriation.

2. According to Cassius Dio, citizenship was given to the provincials with the aim of obliging them also to pay the taxes of Roman citizens (Cass. Dio LXXVII [LXXVIII], 9, 3-5).
3. One of these was Trajan; E. Lo Cascio (1978).

References

This paper is a shortened version of work in progress on Roman land taxation with particular reference to its cadastral aspects. It is a very broad and simple outline, which cannot take into consideration the complex discussions and the rich bibliography existing on the main subjects I refer to. Here I include only the essential references for an initial survey of the subject.

Brugi, B. (1897), *Le Dottrine Giuridiche degli Agrimensori Romani Comparate a quelle del Digesto*, Padua: Drucker.

Cardascia, G. *et al.* (1977), *Armées et fiscalité dans le monde antique*, Paris: Centre National de la Recherche Scientifique.

Ciccotti, E. (1960), 'Lineamenti dell'Evoluzione Tributaria nel Mondo Antico', in G. Stefani (ed.), *I Tributi e l'Amministrazione Finanziaria nel Mondo Antico*, Padua: Cedam.

Clerici, L. (1943), *Economia e Finanza dei Romani*, Bolgona: Zanichelli.

D'Amati, N. (1962), 'Natura e Fondamento del "Tributum" Romano', in *Annali della Facoltà di Giurisprudenza dell'Università di Bari*, 16, pp. 145–69.

De Martino, F. (1958–72), *Storia della Costituzione Romana*, Naples: Jovene.

De Martino, F. (1979a), '*Ager Privatus Vectigalisque*', in *Diritto e Società nell'Antica Rome*, Rome: Editori Riuniti.

De Martino F. (1979b), *Storia Economica di Roma Antica*, Florence: La Nuova Italia.

De Neeve, P.W. (1985), 'The Price of Agricultural Land in Roman Italy and the Problem of Economic Rationalism', *Opus*, 4, pp. 77–109.

Frank, T. (1927), '*Dominium in Solo Provinciali* and *Ager Publicus*', *Journal of Roman Studies*, 17, pp. 141–61.

Frank, T. (ed.) (1933), *An Economic Survey of Ancient Rome*, Baltimore, Md: Johns Hopkins University Press.

Gabba, E. (1973), *Esercito e Società nella Tarda Repubblica Romana*, Florence: La Nuova Italia.

Gabba, E. (1977), 'Esercito e Fiscalità a Roma in Età Repubblicana', in Cardascia *et al.* (1977).

Gabba, E. (1979), 'Per un'Interpretazione Politica del *De Officiis* di Cicerone', in *Rendiconti dell'Accademia Nazionale dei Lincei*, 34, pp. 117–41.

Grelle, F. (1963), *Stipendium vel Tributum. L'Imposizione Fondiaria nelle Dottrine Giuridiche del II e III Secolo*, Naples: Jovene.

Jones, A.H.M. (1964), *The Later Roman Empire 284–602. A Social, Economic and Administrative Survey*, Vol. 1, Oxford: Blackwell.

Lo Cascio, E. (1978), 'Gli *Alimenta*, l'Agricoltura Italica e l'Approvvigionamento di Roma', in *Rendiconti dell'Accademia Nazionale dei Lincei*, 33, pp. 311–52.

Lo Cascio, E. (1986), 'La Struttura Fiscale dell'Impero Romano', in M. Crawford (ed.), *L'impero Romano e le Strutture Economiche e Sociali delle Province*, Como: Edizioni New Press.

Luzzatto, G. (1953), 'La Riscossione Tributaria in Roma e l'Ipotesi della Proprietà-Sovranità', in G. Moschetti (ed.), *Atti del Congresso Internazionale di Diritto Romano e di Storia del Diritto*, Vol. IV, Milan: Giuffrè.

Marquardt, J. (1888), *De l'organisation financière chez les Romains*, trans. A. Vigié, Paris: Ernest Thorin.

Messedaglia, A. (1936), *Il Catasto e la Perequazione*, Bologna: Cappelli.

Neesen, L. (1980), *Untersuchungen zu den direkten Staatsabgaben der römischen Kaiserzeit*, Bonn: Rudolf Habelt.

Nicolet, C. (1976a), *Tributum. Recherches sur la fiscalité directe sous la république romaine*, Bonn: Rudolf Habelt.

Nicolet, C. (1976b), 'L'idéologie du système centuriate et l'influence de la philosophie politique grecque', in W. Seston, *et al.*, *La Filosofia Greca e il Diritto Romano*, Vol. I, Rome: Accademia Nazionale dei Lincei.

Nicolet, C. (1984), 'Augustus, Government, and the Propertied Classes', in F. Millar and

E. Segal (eds), *Caesar Augustus. Seven Aspects*, Oxford: Clarendon Press.

Nicolet, C. (1989), *L'Inventario del Mondo. Geografia e Politica alle Origini dell'Impero Romano*, Bari: Laterza.

Tibiletti, G. (1955), 'Lo Sviluppo del Latifondo in Italia dall'Epoca Graccana al Principio dell'Impero', in AA.VV., *Storia dell'Antichità, Relazioni del X Congresso Internazionale di Scienze Storiche*, Vol. II, Florence: Sansoni.

Weber, M. (1967), *Storia Agraria Romana*, Milan: Il Saggiatore.

4 Greek economic thought in the Islamic milieu: Bryson and Dimashqî

Yassine Essid

The new interest taken in the history of Islamic economic thought and the diversity of the massive literature produced in this field that has come to be known as Islamic Economics, bring to the attention of the historian of economic thought the importance of circumspection in choosing the objectives of one's research.

Today caution imposes itself on any historian as the territory of research in our field becomes more densely inhabited with would-be historians of economic thought whose intentions are not always commendable and whose efforts in this field often serve ideological purposes.

My objective in this paper is, to begin with, to do justice to the contributions that have been neglected by historians of economic doctrines or, when mentioned at all, have been reduced to footnotes. A closer look at the work of J.A. Schumpeter shows the great importance placed on Greek authors. On the other hand, Arab-Muslim thinkers have been ostracized. Still, when we look closer at their contributions in this field, and especially at the bonds that link their thought to the Greeks, we discover that they are too important to be neglected. Further, studying Arab-Muslim writers permits us to fill the 'Great Gap' of five centuries Schumpeter has identified, an alleged gap that became endemic in the books and manuals dedicated to the history of economic thought (Ghazanfar, 1988). It is very curious that historians of economic thought, usually so concerned to draw filiations and so quick to find a deceased precursor for every theorist, have remained silent about the contributions of Arab-Muslim authors. Schumpeter has simply carried on a tradition that has been going on since 1800, and is relevant to Greeks as well as Arab-Muslim authors.

With regard to the history of economic thought, Muslim historians and professional economists reacted against this situation and since the 1960s we have witnessed a revival of Islamic economic thought. This revival, which has already a 'past', was undertaken by two trends of thought with different objectives.

As to the first trend, Arab-Muslim authors are here the source of information of the intellectual heritage. The purpose of the historian is to prove that the Arabs had a specific body of ideas and that their contributions in this field were as relevant as those of their western contemporaries in discussing economic exchange, value theory and price formation. In this confrontation, Arab historians usually start by counting ideas and/or anything that would suggest for them the presence of something of interest to the economic discipline put forward by this or by that Muslim author. They then estimate the consequences of these, put them to the test of modern theories and evaluate their originality. Such a method usually leads to false comparisons if not to some erroneous conclusions.

The second trend divided between moderates and extremists, was occasioned by the resurgence of Islamic fundamentalism and is an integral part of a social project. The concern here is not so much to valorize but rather to reconsider the economic conceptions from the perspective of an ideal future society that will be governed according to Islamic norms and values.

Despite these two trends I choose to stand on the broader historical footing: in other words, to stand outside the dispute over the significance of the later precursors of economic thought. Unlike the accepted opinions shared by the most professional economists of the institutes of Islamic Economics (see ICRIE publications), Arab-Muslim economic thought as well as some economic or commercial institutions considered and mentioned as typically Islamic do not start with Islam but are deeply rooted in preceding ancient civilizations.

In discussing certain ideas we consider nowadays as economic, Arab-Muslim thinkers have drawn ethical standards not only from Islamic but also and above all from foreign ethical sources, mainly Greek and Persian. My aim here is to treat Islamic economics from the viewpoint of the continuity of cultures. I am deeply persuaded that this method will link rather than divide, will reconcile rather than part our civilizations.

Greek economic thought in Islamic milieu: Bryson and Dimashqi

Oikonomia was known among Arab-Muslim philosophers, *falasifa*, as *Ilm tadbir al-Manzil* (domestic philosophy) or the science of household management. This science consisted according to al-Tûsi (1964), 'in supervising the state of this community in such a way as necessarily produces general attainment to the perfection which is sought in accordance with association'. The Arab-Muslim philosopher here refers to the second of the three sciencers belonging to the Aristotelian scheme of practical philosophy: father, mother, children, slaves and food supply. In order to function properly the household requires the cooperation of all these elements. This depends primarily upon the man of the house, who must look to the best interest of the family and to the maintenance of order. The economy of the house includes the totality of all its human relationships, the relationship of man to wife, parents to children, lords to servants, and the carrying out of their duties in the home. This, of course, is immediately recognizable as a paraphrasing of the description of the household found in Book I of Aristotle's *Politics*.

This Greek doctrine inspired not only Arab-Muslim philosophers but another category whose concern would look quite foreign to the *falasifa's*: the merchants. In the corpus of Arab literature there exists a practical manual of advice for merchants which reproduces large parts of a lost text of the neo-Pythagorean Bryson (Sheikho, 1921, pp. 161–79). This text, which survived only in Arabic translation, was copied and elaborated more or less in detail by a line of Arab-Muslim authors such as Ibn Sinâ (1906, 978–83, 1036–42, 1073–8), al-Tûsi, al-Frâbi (Al-Frâbi, n.d.), al-Ghazâli (1910), and al-Dawwâni (Al-Dawwâni and Jalal al-Din, 1839). We may consider the *Kitâb al-Ishâra ilâ Mahasin al-Tijârqa* (The Book of Knowledge of the Beauties of Commerce and Cognizance of Good and Bad Merchandise and the Falsifications of Tricksters) (Al-Dimashqî, 1917) of Abûl-Fadl Ja'far b. 'Ali al-Dimashqî, probably a merchant of Damascus who lived in the twelfth century AD, the golden age of oriental commerce. At first glance, this appearance of a neo-Pythagorean text seems surprising in the same way that it seems strange to find a merchant taking an interest in Hellenic culture. This wonder vanishes completely as we glance through the pages of the book.

The first chapter of this *Kitâb* or manual deals with the essence of wealth. There are four kinds of 'wealth':

mute wealth, mainly gold and silver;
consumption goods, merchandise, jewellery, copper, lead and raw material;
real estate;
livestock or living goods, animals, slaves.

The wealthy individual is here considered a respected person who deserves people's esteem because he is rich, not in need, and because he makes good use of his fortune.

The second chapter deals with the need for money. Paraphrasing the author, because of the necessity of transactions the carpenter who needs a pair of shoes finds a shoemaker who needs a door, similarly with the man who has wheat and needs oil, and because it is difficult to know what exact quantity of each good one has to give to match another quantity of another good we tried to find something which corresponds to all the goods for any specific value and in a material of solid substance. Then the need for money arose. In virtue of its existence and by equating a little of its kind with a great amount of other things, gold and silver were used to permit people to dispense with the inconvenience and trouble of transporting provisions to remote places. In this way Dimashqî tried historically to legitimize trade activity. This discussion parallels the exposition found in Book II of Plato's *Republic*, 317 b. It is to satisfy the multiplicity of needs that men came to be organized in society.

Thinking about the origin of gold and silver as money goes a step beyond the conditions that gave birth to the necessity of exchange that is, essentially, an explanation of social organization itself. The benefits of trade are optimized by the merchant's activity. This Muslim view, following Bryson, is a significant advance on the Aristotelian position in which trade for commodities for their use value was accepted. However, the Aristotelian analysis was hostile to mercantile activity for its own sake. The reason was, of course, that most merchants were metics (resident aliens) or foreigners, and not trusted members of the Greek community.

Then comes a chapter on the ways to test gold, various commodities and their prices, ways of distinguishing bad merchandise from good, craft and industries, and advice to merchants. On all these subjects Dimashqî remained very close to Bryson and the chapter on the excellence of trade is nothing more than a parallel to the chapter on the acquisition of wealth in this neo-Pythagorean text.

After praising trade activity Dimashqî states the duties of the different classes of merchants.

> The wholesaler (*Khazzân*) is a merchant who buys cheap and sells dear, in other words buys when the goods are abundant and the demand weak and sells in inverse ratio to that. The temptation to cheat and to make big and unjustified profits is hidden there, and that is the reason why it is necessary to state how risky and uncertain is the merchant's business. Because steady traffic and relative safety of the roads contribute to the growth of trade and fluctuations of prices, the wholesaler must investigate not only the state of the market, but also the distance and danger of the roads as well as the scarcity of wares.
>
> The travelling merchant (*Raqqâd*) is a merchant who moves with his merchandise from place to place. He has to establish a list of prices anywhere he goes. If he needs to buy something and calculate his profit he should refer to that list, compare the different rates with the different places and add to that the customs duties and the transportation costs.
>
> The exporting merchant's (*Mujahhiz*) prosperity rests on the good or bad choice of his agents. (Al-Dimashqî, 1977)

Finally comes a chapter on the administration of wealth.

Regarding the management of funds, expenditure should not exceed income. No expenditure is justified on anything that it is impossible to turn into a product account such as properties that cannot be cultivated or jewels desired only by a very few persons.

With regard to expenditure the merchant should guard against meanness, cheese-paring, extragavance and dissipation, affectation and vainglory, and bad management.

Dimashqî's pragmatic theory of prices

Discussions on prices among Arab-Muslim authors generally bear a common stamp owing to the fact that problems related to prices, their fluctuations and interference or non-interference in their formation, are faced according and by reference to the theological principle that it is only God who raises and lowers prices. This attitude, far from being prejudicial to the quality of their analyses, improved them but at the same time set a limit on the scope of their investigation.

Arab-Muslim thinkers, jurists or theologians, because of this very limit did not succeed in developing clear economic conceptions. Discussions on prices were usually integrated into discussions of retail trade, an activity engaged in by shopkeepers of the city market who were generally considered to be speculators who made profits by taking advantage of the fluctuations in supply and demand and were most frequent targets of the jurists' injunctions and the object of the manuals on market supervision. The wholesale merchant, the importer–exporter, was outside the market area and thus avoided the market inspector's jurisdiction.

With reference to what has been said, the treatise of al-Dimashqî seems doubly instructive: because it is written by a professional, a well-read merchant who had enough education to write down his ideas about prices and because it illustrates economic thinking free of any theological consideration.

Dimashqî does not worry about who is responsible for the movement of prices, God or man, or both, but rather he tries to determine how to take into account and take advantage of their fluctuations in order to anticipate the market value of goods. His objective was to buy or sell at a good price. Price fluctuations were no longer believed to follow an implacable law. On the contrary, they were the result of and subject to forces a merchant was expected to understand and manipulate if he wanted to prosper. That is the reason for the absence in Dimashqî's book of any reference to the traditional debate about the divine control of prices. This avoidance of theological explanations of price persists despite the author's religious background, which is expressed in other parts of the book.

For a merchant, price variations of goods are a crucial problem. We can even state without exaggeration that the greatest part of a merchant's activity, all his know-how, seems to be reduced to his ability to anticipate price fluctuations and keep them under control.

According to Dimashqî, all goods have their median price *Qîma Mutawasita, Si'r Mutawassit/Mu'tadil*) to which they tend as to an ideal state. When putting a price on a good, or appraising its value, one way would be to refer to its place of production, like Indian baskets or coral. Another way would be to ask trusted experts in the field, those who are familiar with its current and/or usual price after correction for the ordinary and extraordinary variations to which the commodity is subject. These variations have causes that we could qualify as *economic*: abundance or scarcity, proximity or remoteness of its market point and *institutional* factors that are intrinsic to mercantile activity such as its dependence on local conditions, customs duties, insecurity of the roads, disorganization, and the imposition of prices by the central government. These are circumstances which could disrupt the supply/demand mechanism and consequently the median price.

By coining this new concept of median price, Dimashqî has treated the problem on the ethical level. We are here far from the shopkeepers' mentality so discredited in the *hisba* books of market behaviour, those shopkeepers who are delighted when prices are high and people suffer and who look sorrowful when prices are low and people prosper. Dimashqî's concept matches perfectly his conception of what trade should be. The median price is the just price, a price which brings profit to the merchant without endangering the community interests and, in a larger sense, it is nothing more than the optimal state of the market – the equilibrium price (*al-Si'r al Mu'tadil*). This concept has surely an Aristotelian flavour and we have here a good example of the transposition of the notion of the golden mean into the merchant's activity.

On the whole, Dimashqî's book reflects a commercial ideal that is incarnated in the small enterprise and is oriented towards a limited market. It incorporates the ideal of a moderate business submitted to the exigencies of a just price and a moderate profit covering the needs of a family household. The word *merchant* is not synonymous with greed and display of wealth. By relying on Greek ethics Dimashqî succeeds not only in creating a model of good investment, but also in bringing the text of Bryson into line with both Islamic and mercantile realities.

References

Al-Dawwani, and Jalal al-Din (1839), *Akhlaqî al-Jalali*, trans. W.T. Thompson as *Practical Philosophy of Muhammedam People*, London.

Al-Dimashqî (1917), *Cairo: Matba'at al'Mu'ayyid*, trans. into German by H. Ritter as 'Ein Arabishes Handbuch der Handelswissenschaft,' *Der Islam* 7:1917, 1–97.

Al-Frabi (n.d.), *Risala fi l-Siyasa*, L. Sheikho. Imprimerie Catholique.

Al-Ghazali (1910), *The Alchemy of Happiness*, trans. Cl. Field, London.

Al-Tûsi, Nasiruddin (1964), *Akhlak al-Nasiri*, trans. G.M. Wickens as the *Nasirean Ethics*, London.

Ghazanfar, S.M. (1988), 'Scholastic Economics and Arab Scholars: The "Great Gap" Thesis Reconsidered', paper presented at the History of Economics Society National Meeting, Toronto, Canada, June.

Ibn Sina (1906), 'Athar Majhoul li Ibn Sina', *al-Mashriq*, 2.

ICRIE publications: International Centre for Research on Islamic Economics, King Abdul Aziz University, Jeddah, Saudi Arabia.

Sheikho, Louis (1921), 'Risalat Rufus fi Tadbir al-Menzil', *al-Mashriq*, 3.

5 Explorations in medieval Arab-Islamic economic thought: some aspects of Ibn Taimiyah's economics

S.M. Ghazanfar and A. Azim Islahi

Introduction

Our purpose in this paper is to explore and present some aspects of the economic thought of a medieval Arab-Islamic scholar, Taqi al-Din Ahmad bin 'Abd al-Halim, known as Ibn Taimiyah (661–728 AH/AD 1263–1328). In the intellectual history of Islam, he 'is classified as a reactionary'. Also; 'there was very little in the theological development of Islam up to his own day that escaped Ibn Taimiyah's highly developed historical sense' (Peters, 1968, pp. 200–1). His discussion of economic issues tends to be quite normative, with extensive positive analysis, quite like that of other Arab and Latin Scholastics (e.g., Abu Hamid Al-Ghazali, 1058–1111; Nasir al-Din Tusi, 1201–74; Ibn al-Ukhuwah, d.1329; St Thomas Aquinas, 1225–74, and others). While some of Ibn Taimiyah's works have been translated into English and other languages, the present paper relies primarily on the original Arabic-language sources.

With reference to medieval Arab-Islamic scholarship, Ibn Taimiyah stands out distinctively as one of at least 35–40 prominent scholars who wrote on a variety of specific economic issues – some even wrote separate treatises (see for example, Abu Yusuf, 731–98; Al-Farabi, 870–950; Tusi, 1201–74). Unfortunately, however, there is hardly any Arab-Islamic scholar whose economic thought is familiar in the profession or incorporated in the relevant literature. Such neglect is only tangentially rectified by some English-language literature on the economics of a late-medieval Arab-Islamic scholar, Ibn Khaldun (1332–1404). About 25 years ago, Joseph Spengler wrote an excellent paper on this scholar, and while referring to Arab-Islamic literature of the era, he observed that 'the knowledge of economic behavior in some circles was very great indeed, and one must turn to the writings of those with access to this knowledge and experience if one would know the actual state of Muslim economic knowledge' (Spengler, 1964, p. 304). Part of the stimulus for the present paper comes from Spengler's suggestion. Further, it might be noted that another scholar, also writing on Ibn Khaldun, referred to him as 'among the fathers of economic science', but, quite erroneously, that he was

45

'an accident of history...without predecessors and without successors' (Boulakia, 1971, p. 1118).

It is appropriate, in the present context, to briefly refer to the controversial 'great gap' thesis, propounded by Joseph Schumpeter in his classic, *History of Economic Analysis*. According to this thesis, the several centuries between the Greeks and the Latin Scholastics (particularly St Thomas Aquinas) were simply 'blank centuries', during which nothing of relevance to economics was written (Schumpeter, 1954, p. 74). Such a claim is untenable, though Schumpeter perhaps was not aware of Arab-Islamic literature on economics, especially given the cultural context in which he wrote (see Ghazanfar, 1988; also Ghazanfar and Islahi, 1990).[1]

In the same vein, it is interesting to note that much of the existing economic literature assumes that, as with numerous other concepts, the idea of classifying market forces into demand and supply is a relatively recent development in the history of economic thought. Again, there is Schumpeter's endorsement: 'As regards the theory of the mechanism of pricing, there is very little to report before the middle of the eighteenth century' (1954, p. 305). As with his 'great gap' thesis, this conclusion also completely disregards the contributions of Arab-Islamic scholars (and some European scholars) on this important topic. Certainly, as early as the thirteenth century, Ibn Taimiyah provided a rather sophisticated discussion of the behaviour of markets, as we shall see below.

Ibn Taimiyah's discourses extended to many diverse fields, not unlike most other Arab-Islamic and Latin-Christian scholars of the era. Similarly, his writings emphasized the 'holistic' intellectual approach. However, one finds considerable economic content – normative as well as positive – in his writings, similar to that found in the works of his Arab and Latin counterparts. Consistent with the intellectual tradition of the time, however, his scholarship was not dominated by economic aspects of life, nor does one discover the esoteric abstractions and theoretical constructs to which contemporary economics has become accustomed. His style was quite similar to that of other Arab and Latin scholars, though somewhat unlike the more refined and abstract approach followed by Ibn Khaldun (1332–1404).[2] Instead, one chiefly encounters in their texts theological-philosophical ratiocination. Treatises on a specific field would hardly have been compatible with the prevailing 'integrative' approach to learning. Further, like other scholars of the era, Ibn Taimiyah mixes philosophical, religious, ethical, sociological and economic considerations in his discourses.

We begin with a brief synopsis of the socioeconomic environment in which Ibn Taimiyah lived and wrote, as well as a few remarks about his life. This will be followed by a discussion of Ibn Taimiyah's economics. For purposes of this paper, we shall restrict ourselves chiefly to a discussion of his views on the operations of a free market economy – which, in order to ensure that public welfare is not threatened, is to be administered and supervised through the institution of *hisbah*. However, he had a great deal to say on other significant economic issues – for example the role of money, the right to private property, the role of the public sector (including price regulation), public finances, various types of business organizations, problems of income-wealth distribution, poverty, and so forth. Only brief comments will be offered on these aspects of Ibn Taimiyah's economics.

Ibn Taimiyah: the environment and his life

Born in Harran (then Syria, now Turkey) in 1263, Ibn Taimiyah spent most of his life in Damascus (Syria) but also partly in Cairo. Both Syria and Egypt were part of the first Mameluke Dynasty (1260–1382), and Ibn Taimiyah's greatest achievements belong in this period. Egypt and Syria represented the centres of learning during the Mameluke period. According to Hitti,

> Damascus and Cairo, especially after the fall of Baghdad (due to Mongol invasions) and the disintegration of Moslem Spain (after the crusades), remained the educational and intellectual centres of the Arab world. The schools founded and richly endowed in these two cities served to conserve and transmit Arab science and learning. (Hitti, 1951, p. 651)

The struggle between the rationalism of the Greek philosophy and the comprehensive, unitive and intuitive quality of Islamic thought, however, continued in the Mameluke period and is reflected in the writings of numerous Arab-Islamic scholars, including Ibn Taimiyah.

Mameluke society was stratified into four distinct classes. First there were the rulers (the Mamelukes) themselves, whose chief occupation was the conduct of the state. Second, there were the *ahl al-'amamah*, or 'turban men', employed in various professions, for example as public administrators, jurists, educators and religious scholars (*ulama*). This group represented the link between the rulers and the general public; and the Mamelukes often feared them because of their influence and their tendency to criticize the rulers for any breach of religious injunctions (Suyuti, 1968, pp. 97, 99). Third, given the intense commercial activity of the time, there was the rich class of traders and merchants. The fourth group was made up of the rest – farmers, labourers, craftsmen, small shopkeepers and the poor. The farmers were in the majority, and about the worst economically, mainly because of heavy taxation (Ibn Iyas, 1960, p. 30). A collective tax levied on a village, regardless of income level, was called by Ibn Taimiyah *al-mazalim al-mushtarakah*, i.e., a joint or common injustice (Ibn Taimiyah, AH 1381–7, Vol. 30, 338–9).

As for the nature of economic life during this period, some insights can be gained from several sources. According to Lane-Poole,

> It was an age of extraordinary brilliance in almost every aspect. In spite of the occasional records of scarcity and high prices, the wealth of the country, whether from its fertile soil or from the ever-increasing trade with Europe and the East, was immense, if the fortunes of the individuals are any test. (Lane-Poole, 1925, p. 313)

The Mamelukes were aware that their success depended on the strength of the economy, along with their army. They fully exploited the sources of wealth, and developed agriculture, trade and industry. Since the population's basic needs depended upon agriculture, this sector received first priority. Industry also flourished in the Mameluke era. Egypt was prominent in such industries as sugar, textiles, iron and steel, armaments, utensils and ornaments, shipbuilding and transportation. Indeed, Egypt and Syria were centres of trade and commerce long before the advent of Islam. According to Hitti,

> The concessions offered by al-Adil and Baybars (Mamluk rulers) to the Venetian and other European merchants stimulated an exchange of commodities and made Cairo a great 'entrepot' of trade between East and West.... Damascus, Tripoli, Antioch, and Tyre were among the leading centers of industry. (1951, p. 639)

Commenting on the economic conditions of this era, Heaton says,

> Muhammadanism regarded trade as a worthy occupation, ties of rule and religion facilitated long-distance trade and travel; and since the Asiatic end of the Moslem world possessed many industrial or agricultual skills and products which were superior to those of the European end, the West benefited by the lessons it learned from its new masters. (Heaton, 1948, pp. 51–2)

Ibn Taimiyah's life was one of commitment and struggle on three fronts. As a soldier, he fought against the Mongol invasion from the East, while the Mediterranean territories were still in ruins at the hands of the Crusaders (Ibn Kathir, 1966, Vol. 14, pp. 8–10). As a radical scholar, he fought against the stagnant Islamic teachings of the previous four centuries. And as a reformer he attacked the social and political ills that surrounded him, and even criticized the rulers and other jurists and scholars (Al-Mubarak, 1970, p. 847). As the iconoclastic radical-reformer that he was, he was imprisoned on several occasions. During his imprisonment he was not allowed to read, write or have any contacts with his students. He spent the last months of his life in a Damascus prison, where he died in 1328 at the age of 65.

Given the depth of his religious convictions and knowledge of Islamic scriptures, Ibn Taimiyah was thoroughly familiar with the writings of various other Islamic scholars (e.g., Al-Farabi, 870–950; Ibn Sina, 980–1036; Ibn Hazm, *d*.1086; Al-Ghazali, 1058–1111; Ibn Tufail, *d*.1186; Ibn Rushd, 1126–98, and others), as well as the inherited reservoir of Greek knowledge.

However, 'though poles apart from Al-Ghazali, he is nevertheless to some extent under his influence, but more under the influence of Ibn Hazm and his *Zahirism*' (Ali, 1967, p. 25, quoting Goldziher). While Al-Ghazali attempted 'to accommodate all movements and tendencies in contemporary Islam, such as mysticism, rationalism, dogmatism, etc. (as legitimate branches of one tree), Ibn Taimiyah sought to cleanse Islam from everything which was, to his mind, incompatible with Islamic shariyah' (ibid.). Thus, Goldziher characterizes Ibn Taimiyah as not belonging to a definite school of thought but being a 'Muslim on his own' ('Muhammadner auf eigene Faust') (Goldziher, 1884, p. 188). Nevertheless, Ibn Taimiyah is generally associated with the Hanbali school of Islamic jurisprudence, although he often differed with – as well as drew upon – each of the four schools mentioned earlier. He was critical of the excessive rationalism of Greek philosophy. 'Like Kant (*d*.1804), he did not believe that reason could lead us to the knowledge of the Ultimate Truth. And, as against the deductive method, Ibn Taimiyah emphasized the need and importance of the inductive and empirical method' (Umaruddin, 1963, pp. 725–6).

By the thirteenth century the Islamic way of life had become dominated by numerous un-Islamic customs and rites and false innovations (such as tomb worship), and by certain forms of Sufism (mysticism) which enervated the message of Islam. Ibn Taimiyah attempted reforms in both directions. Sufism preached a life of seclusion and strict 'otherworldliness' (Ibn Abd al-Hadi, 1938, p. 27). Ibn Taimiyah was vehemently opposed to such un-Islamic concepts and practices. Although his reformist views found little favour in his own time, almost all historians have recognized his deep impact on the most prominent reformer of the eighteenth century, Muhammad bin 'Abd al-Wahhab (*d*.1792), whose ideas have been influential in contemporary Saudi Arabia (Laoust, 1971, p. 950).

As a deeply religious man, he believed false concepts of his faith would lead to mass exploitation and social upheaval. Consistent with the prevailing ethos, he believed (as did his Arab and Latin counterparts), that religion and the state should be closely linked – the separation of one from the other had not yet happened. In his view, without the coercive power of the state, religion would be in jeopardy; and without the discipline of the revealed message, the state would become tyrannical (Ibn Taimiyah, 1971, p. 189).

Ibn Taimiyah's economic thought

Versatile scholar that Ibn Taimiyah was, it is natural that economic matters should receive considerable attention in his writings. He had seen – indeed, lived – the socioeconomic upheavals of the time (especially the Crusades and the Mongol invasion), as well as the plight of the poor and the exploitation by the ruling class. He found additional inspiration in the fact that Islam as a religion and a way of life focused specifically on the prevailing economic problems and prescribed guidelines for solutions.

Being a prolific writer, Ibn Taimiyah authored at least 18 books on various topics. However, much of his economics is to be found in two books: *Al-Hisbah fi'l-Islam* (*Public Duties in Islam: The Institution of the Hisbah*) and *al-Siyasah al-Shariyah fi Islah al-Rai wa'l-Raiyah* (*Public and Private Law in Islam*), both of which are available in the English language (see Holland, 1982, and Farrukh, 1966). While in the first book he discusses the operation of markets, and reasons for public sector intervention in economic affairs, in the latter volume as well as in his *Fatawa*, he deals with public sector economics (the role of the public sector generally, including matters of public spending, taxation, borrowing, the role and functions of money, usury, currency debasement, infrastructure, issues of income distribution and poverty, and so forth). Further, given his tendency to digress frequently, his economic views are also scattered throughout his other books – especially in his *Fatawa*, or legal rulings.

In the following pages we shall focus primarily on Ibn Taimiyah's views relating to the operations of a free market economy, paying some attention to public sector intervention in the markets directly and through an administrative institution called *hisbah*. Also, we shall briefly present Ibn Taimiyah's views on some other economic topics.

Operations of the free markets
At the outset it must be stated that while Ibn Taimiyah never uses the term 'competition' (a concept that emerged much later in the evolution of economic thought), or describes the conditions of perfect competition in contemporary jargon, it is clear that his awareness of the 'competitive market' assumptions is unambiguous. He writes that 'to force people to sell objects which it is not obligatory to sell, or restrict them from selling a permissible object, is injustice and therefore, unlawful'. In contemporary terms, this clearly refers to full freedom to enter or exit a market. Further, he is critical of collusion between buyers and sellers (Ibn Taimiyah, 1976, p. 25). He emphasizes knowledge of the markets on the part of participants (ibid., pp. 49–50). He had a clear perception of the well-behaved, orderly market, in which knowledge, honesty, fair play and freedom of choice were the essential ingredients. So it is with this contextual background that one must appreciate and evaluate Ibn Taimiyah's analysis of 'free market economics'.

Market demand and supply   Ibn Taimiyah understood well the functioning of the voluntary exchange, free market economies, and how prices tended to be determined through the forces of demand and supply. He states (AH 1381–7, Vol. 8, p. 583):

Rise and fall in prices is not always due to injustice [*zulm*] of some people. Sometimes its reason is deficiency in production or decline in import of the goods in demand. Thus if the desires for the good increase while its availability decreases, its price rises. On the other hand if availability of the good increases and the desires for it decrease, the price declines. This scarcity and abundance may not be caused by the action of any people; it may be due to a cause not involving injustice, or, sometimes, it may involve injustice.

This statement partly reflects a commonly held view at the time: that rising prices are the result of injustice, or transgression, on the part of sellers, or possibly the result of manipulation of the market. However, Ibn Taimiyah argues, there could be other factors. He states that rising or falling prices could be due to market pressures. Then he discusses some of the factors that influence demand and supply and his insights, while not quite as elegant as one finds in contemporary texts, are remarkably profound for the era he represented. He mentions two sources of supply: domestic production and imports of the goods demanded. A change in supply is described as an increase or decrease in the availability (supply) of the good. He describes 'demand for a good' (*raghbat fi'l shai*) in terms of 'desires for the good' – suggesting 'taste' in contemporary terms, a key determinant of demand (another being 'income', which he does not mention explicitly).

The above quotation from Ibn Taimiyah clearly suggests what we now call 'shifts' in demand and supply schedules, though he did not use this jargon. Thus, at a given price, demand increases and supply decreases, leading to a price rise. Or, conversely, at a given price, supply increases and demand decreases, leading to a price decline. Similarly, depending upon the extent of change in supply and/or demand, the change in price may be large or small, or none at all. Various such possibilities seem to be implied in the above quotation. Elsewhere, he is much more explicit (Ibn Taimiyah, 1976, p. 24):

If people are selling their goods according to commonly accepted manner without any injustice on their part and the price rises due to decrease of the commodity [*qillat al shai'*] or due to increase in population [*kathrat al khalq*], then this is due to God's doing.

Here Ibn Taimiyah suggests that the reasons for price increase may be either a decrease in supply or an increase in population (number of buyers) – that is, an increase in market demand. Thus, a price increase due to reduced supply (leftward shift) or increase in demand (rightward shift) is described as an 'act of God' – obviously referring to the impersonal nature of the markets.

From the foregoing, it is obvious that Ibn Taimiyah distinguishes between two factors that may cause shifts in demand–supply schedules and thus affect the market price: automatic market pressures and sellers' transgression (i.e. due to hoarding).

It might also be noted that while Ibn Taimiyah traces the effects of changes in demand and supply on market prices, he does not seem to identify the effect of higher or lower prices on quantity demanded or supplied (i.e. movements along the respective schedules). However, in his *Hisbah* he refers to an earlier jurist, in that 'administrative setting of too low a price that leaves no profit results in a corruption of prices, hiding of goods (by sellers) and destruction of people's wealth' (Ibn Taimiyah, 1976, p. 41). He seems to be aware of a direct relationship between price and quantity supplied. Further, he is also pointing to the disincentive effects from an 'administratively fixed' price which is 'too low' (obviously relative to some 'normal' price), and which could reduce profits and encourage hoarding.

Other factors affecting market demand and supply   Elsewhere, Ibn Taimiyah identifies some other determinants of demand (and supply) which can affect the market price – such as (1) intensity and magnitude of demand, (2) relative scarcity or abundance of a good, (3) credit conditions, and (4) discounts for cash payments. The following brief quotations are illustrative (Ibn Taimiyah, AH 1381–7, Vol. 29, pp. 523–5):

> People's desire [*al-raghbah*] is of different kinds and varies frequently. It varies according to the abundance or scarcity of the good demanded [*al matlub*]. A good is much more strongly desired when it is scarce than when it is available in abundance.
>
> It varies also depending on the number of demanders [*tullab*]. If the number of persons demanding a commodity is large, its price goes up as against when their number is small.
>
> It is also affected by the strength and weakness of the need for the good and by the extent of the need, how great or small is the need for it. If the need is great and strong, the price will increase to an extent greater than if the need is small and weak.
>
> [The price also varies] according to [the customer] with whom exchange is taking place [*al mu'awid*]. If he is well-off and trustworthy in paying debts, a smaller price from him is acceptable [to the seller] which [price] would not be acceptable from one known for his insolvency, delay in payment or refusal of payment due.
>
> In talking about the desirability of contracts, he says, 'This is because the purpose of contracts is [reciprocal] possession by the two parties [to the contract]. If the payer is capable of payment and is expected to fulfill his promise, the objective of the conract is realized with him, in contrast to the case if he is not fully capable or faithful regarding his promise. The degrees of capability and faithfulness differ. This applies to the seller and the buyer.... The price of what is available is lower than the price of what is not [physically] available. The same applies to the buyer who is sometimes able to pay at once as he has money, but sometimes he does not have [cash] and wants to borrow [in order to pay] or sell the commodity [to make payment]. The price is lower in the former case.'

An increase in the number of buyers thus causing an increase in price (other things constant) is indeed well recognized. However, the size of need as distinct from the intensity (both may be viewed as suggesting 'tastes') refers to the commodity's place in the basket of goods desired by the buyer. If this interpretation is correct, Ibn Taimiyah has associated high prices with intensity of need as well as the good's relative importance in the totality of a buyer's requirements. The converse then would also follow. Further, Ibn Taimiyah suggests the relevance of credit to sales. The above quotation implies that if credit transactions are common, sellers must face uncertainties as to future payments (say, between a more versus less creditworthy customer) when quoting prices. Further, he is also aware that a seller might offer 'discounts' for cash transactions. Clearly, Ibn Taimiyah's arguments not only demonstrate his awareness of demand–supply forces, but also his concern about the incentives–disincentives, uncertainties and risks involved in market transactions. Both represent significant contributions to economic analysis, especially when one bears in mind the era during which Ibn Taimiyah was writing.

Public sector intervention in the markets   While Ibn Taimiyah's vision of economic affairs is essentially free market oriented, he does not advocate unbridled functioning of the 'invisible hand'. He discusses certain circumstances which might warrant price regulation and controls – specifically when there are market imperfections (monopolistic practices) and/or when there are national emergencies (famine, war, etc.). As noted earlier, when talking of 'administratively fixed prices' he cautions against excessive regulation, for the incentives of the profit motive might be blunted.

With regard to market imperfections, Ibn Taimiyah recommends that if sellers abstain (through hoarding) from selling their goods except at a higher price than the customary or 'normal' price and people need these goods, then they will be required to sell them at the 'price of the equivalent' (Ibn Taimiyah, 1976, p. 25). Incidentally, this concept is synonymous with what is also described as a 'just price'. Further, if there are elements of monopoly (especially in the markets for food and other necessities), the state must intervene to ensure that monopoly power is restricted (ibid., pp. 25–6). Ibn Taimiyah proposes a basic principle for the removal of market-generated injustices: 'If abolition of injustice in its entirety is not possible, one is obliged to eliminate it to the extent possible' (ibid., p. 26).

While Ibn Taimiyah would oppose any price regulation or controls when price increases are the result of 'natural' market forces, he advocates price controls under certain conditions. He distinguishes 'two types of price-fixing – unjust and invalid and just and valid' (ibid., p. 24). Thus it would be unjust price-fixing, and therefore to be prohibited, if the price rise that was being 'fixed' was the result of free play of competitive markets – due to diminished supply or increased demand, or whatever the 'natural' circumstances.

However, in times of emergency, such as famine or war, Ibn Taimiyah recommends government price controls and forced sale of essential commodities, such as foodstuffs; such controls are classified as 'just and valid'.[3] He says, 'It is for the authority to compel a person to sell his goods at a fair price when people are in need of it. For example, when he has surplus food and people are faced with starvation, he will be forced to sell at a just price' (Ibn Taimiyah, 1976, p. 24). However, sellers could not be compelled to sell, except in cases of necessity (ibid., p. 26).

Administration of the markets through hisbah

Any discussion of Ibn Taimiyah's views on the functioning of markets will be incomplete without reference to the institution of *hisbah* – a term that is not found in the Qur'an, yet whose functions and goals are attributed to the Islamic scriptures.[4] It was an institution through which a number of economic activities, not otherwise conducted in the public interest through the free play of the markets, were supervised and administered. However, the scope of *hisbah* went beyond economic matters: it also encompassed the moral and spiritual well-being of the society as well as the supervision of social and civil activities. In broad terms, and given the context of Islamic society, Ibn Taimiyah defined the aim of *hisbah* to 'promote what is good and forbid what is evil' (*al-'amr bi'l ma'ruf wa-n-nahi 'an al-munkar*), particularly in those areas where the authority of other public officials could not reach (Ibn Taimiyah, 1976, p. 18). According to a contemporary Islamic scholar, *hisbah* represented an administrative control function of 'the government through persons acting especially in the field of morals, religion and economy, and generally in the areas of collective or public life, to achieve justice and righteousness according to the principles of Islam and commonly known good custom of the time and place' (Al-Mubarak, 1970, pp. 73–4).

The public official entrusted with *hisbah* was known as the *muhtasib*, with supervision of the markets being one of his main responsibilities. Thus he exercised comprehensive administrative control and surveillance over trade and economic activities. Some specific areas of such 'market' administration included the following (Ziadeh, 1963, pp. 34, 55): (1) supply and provision of necessities (foodstuffs, etc.); (2) supervision of industry (product standardization, arbitration, minimum wages, etc.); (3) supervision of services (including professions such as physicians, surgeons, pharmacologists, teachers, innkeepers, etc.); and (4) supervision of trading practices (weights and measures, product quality, enforcing laws against hoarding, usurious and other forbidden practices). It may be noted that the concept of *muhtasib* has its contemporary parallel in *ombudsman*, though the former is much broader in scope.

Apart from these activities, the *muhtasib* performed the municipal function of ensuring that, in the construction of buildings and structures, nothing prejudicial to public safety would happen (Ziadeh, 1963, pp. 48, 49, 93). Similarly, he would oversee the location of industries for reasons such as encouraging similar businesses to locate in the same area, and protecting industries from damage from others – for example 'pollutant' industries might not be allowed to locate near pharmacies and cloth merchants (ibid., p. 95).

Extending well beyond economic matters, the *muhtasib*'s obligations encompassed 'orders and prohibitions concerning God, God in relation to man, man's affairs, both public and private' (Foster, 1970, p. 140). The comprehensiveness of the *muhtasib*'s responsibilities is well described by Ibn Taimiyah himself (1976, pp. 19–20):

> The *muhtasib* shall enforce the Friday and other congregational prayers, ensure truthfulness of conduct and behavior, repayment of deposits; and he shall forbid such evil behavior as telling lies, dishonesty, improper weights and measures, fraud in industries, trades, and religious matters, etc.

While our purpose in this paper is mainly to present some aspects of Ibn Taimiyah's economics, of which *hisbah* is an important element, it is appropriate to briefly place this institution in an historical perspective, from the standpoint both of its significance and its origin.

Although Ibn Taimiyah advocated the free play of market forces, he was not a believer in invisible hand – an 'eighteenth-century discovery of the rational resource-allocating capacities of the self-regulating market system...' and 'a postulate which would have been unintelligible as late as medieval times' (Lowry, 1987, pp. 240, 249).[5] The state plays an active role in Ibn Taimiyah's economy, being the custodian of public interest, chiefly through the institution of *hisbah* – and, guided by the Islamic scriptures, the *muhtasib* was responsible for ensuring that all economic agents fulfilled their obligations toward one another and scrupulously adhered to appropriate norms of behaviour.

As an 'Islamized' institution, the *hisbah* remained in existence through the greater part of the Muslim world until the beginning of the twentieth century. However, similar state-sponsored administrative institutions, with varying nomenclature and primarily restricted to economic matters, also prevailed during the earlier Greek and Roman civilizations (from which – especially the Greek – medieval Islam inherited considerably, both in learning as well as in cultural-institutional adaptations).

In the Greek tradition, the activities of the marketplace (called *agora*) were administered ('with a whip in hand', according to Foster, 1970, p. 129) in the public interest, by the market inspector, or *agoranomos*, to 'ensure the proper functioning of the *oikonomia*', with 'emphasis on stability and self-sufficiency' (Lowry, 1987, pp. 238, 240). Subsequently, 'especially under the influence of Rome, the agoranomia evolved from a post of market inspector to that of a prominent public benefactor ... and the office of the Roman aedile was the source of this influence, and the Greek word agoranomous came to mean what the Latin word 'aedile' meant' (Foster, 1970, p. 130). The range of functions of the Roman *aedile*, however, fell somewhere between those of the Greek *agoranomos* and the Islamic *muhtasib*.[6]

To the extent that Ibn Taimiyah's *hisbah* relates to matters of the marketplace, this institution reflects administrative control and direction over economic activities similar to that found in the Graeco-Roman tradition, 'with an arena of open competition within the prescribed boundaries of public interest'. However, what is significant about Ibn Taimiyah's contribution is that it 'added an elaboration of the zone of market relationships that functioned without direct intervention when constrained within the broader oversight of officials committed to protecting the public interest' (communication from Lowry, 22 August 1990).

Is there any connection between the terms *hisbah* and *muhtasib* and the earlier traditions? According to Foster, the word 'agoranomos in the sense of aedile had dropped out of use by the end of the third century' and was replaced by 'prefect' (*eparch* in Greek) during the Byzantine age – though the term *agoranomos* also remained (Foster, 1970, p. 134). Nevertheless, any connection 'is dubious because the word "agoranomos" does not appear in inscriptions after the fourth century' (ibid., p. 135). After tracing the use of various terms in the early Islamic world, this historian concludes, 'The connection of any functionary called "agoranomos" and the Islamic "muhtasib" seems impossible' (ibid., p. 139). Further, 'The muhtasib had a whole set of other duties that appear uniquely Islamic and which were derived from the claim of Muslim law to regulate every aspect of an individual's public and private life' (ibid., p. 141).[7]

Additional corroborative evidence comes from the *Encyclopaedia of Islam*. Thus, while 'the origin, apparently very old, of the office of *hisba* is no clearer ... it is possible that both the office and the name were introduced in the Muslim period without there being any connection' with earlier traditions, since 'there exists no record of the *agoranomos* in the Greek inscriptions for three hundred years before the Arab conquest'. Further, there 'is no reason to insist that [the term *hisba*] could not have appeared without inspiration from outside' (*Encyclopaedia*, p. 487). However, the issue is not without controversy (see Glick, 1971).

Some other topics in Ibn Taimiyah's economic thought

While Ibn Taimiyah's discussion of competitive markets, given the *hisbah*-related limits, represents his most important contribution to economic thought, he also discussed several other topics – and each could well be the subject of separate studies. However, given the scope of the present paper, a mere glance at some of these may be presented (see Ibn Taimiyah, AH 1381–7, Vol. 29 primarily; also Ibn Taimiyah, 1976 and other sources):

(i) In the context of market price determination, Ibn Taimiyah discusses two concepts quite frequently in his writings: compensation of the equivalent (*'iwad al-mithl*) and price of the equivalent (*thaman al-mithl*). He elaborates, in that the 'equivalent' 'will be measured and assessed by its equivalent and this is the essence of justice [*nafs al-adl*]' (AH 1381–7, Vol. 29, p. 521). Elsewhere, he distinguishes between two kinds of prices: unjust and prohibited, and just and permissible; and he considers the 'price of the equivalent' as the just price (1976, pp. 24–5).

In defining the 'compensation of the equivalent', Ibn Taimiyah says that it 'is the equivalent amount of that particular object in the prevailing usage. It is also referred to as the rate and custom' (AH 1381–7, Vol. 29, p. 522). Further, 'the correct evaluation of the just compensation will be based on the analogy and assessment of a thing by its equivalent. And this is the real justice and real accepted usage' (ibid., p. 521). Such concepts initially represented guidelines for justice and for matters of litigation. Thus what began as defining justice in ethical-moral terms eventually evolved into economic terms.

In contrast to the 'compensation of the equivalent', the concept of the 'price of the equivalent' arises when there is actual sale, purchase and exchange of goods. Thus, 'The price of the equivalent is that rate at which people sell their goods and which is commonly accepted as equivalent for it and for similar goods at that particular time and place' (ibid., p. 345). Elsewhere he suggests the price of the equivalent to be one which is established by the free play of market forces (1976, pp. 25, 42). Further, Ibn Taimiyah also talks in terms of 'wage of the equivalent' and 'profit of the equivalent' (ibid., pp. 34, 37).

It might be mentioned that Al-Ghazali also talked in similar terms during the eleventh century, as did St Thomas Aquinas during the thirteenth century (see Ghazanfar and Islahi, 1990). So while the notion of a just or fair price was present in Islamic jurisprudence from the earliest times, Ibn Taimiyah is the first Arab-Islamic scholar who discussed such concepts in considerable detail. And through evolutionary metamorphosis, it seems, the word 'just', originally reflecting the religious-ethical spirit of the times, transformed into 'natural' with the Physiocrats, 'normal' with the Classicals, and eventually 'equilibrium' with Marshall and others. In each case what began as a chiefly normative concept increasingly became interpreted as a 'positive' consequence of free markets (see Dempsey, for example, for some controversial aspects of the issue).[8]

(ii) Ibn Taimiyah discusses economic issues relating to property rights in a manner analagous to the Roman and Greek viewpoints, as well as the

Latin-Christian perspectives. He discusses property rights at three levels: individual, social and state.

According to Ibn Taimiyah, the individual is indeed free to acquire property, subject to moral constraints. This right has been accorded so that he may meet certain obligations, but as soon as he transgresses the *shariyah* (laws of Islam, based on the Holy Scriptures and the Traditions and their interpretations) his rights will be subject to state intervention. However, there is no doubt that Ibn Taimiyah regards private property as a basic institution and it would be incorrect to think that the state is supreme in this regard, as the rights of the individual are inviolable while he acts within the 'scriptural bounds', for the sake of 'social good'. Further, consistent with his market orientation, he advocates private ownership and enterprise. Indeed, throughout his writing, the right to private property is simply assumed as given.

(iii) Ibn Taimiyah discusses in some detail the issues relating to barter economic systems, the evolution, nature and functions of money, currency debasement, as well as an early version of Gresham's Law (a concept also suggested by Al-Ghazali earlier, but one that is often associated with the fourteenth-century French scholar, Nicholas Oresme, 1328–82, and, in the contemporary literature, with the Englishman, Thomas Gresham, 1519–79) (Ibn Taimiyah, AD 1381–7, Vol. 29, p. 469).[9] Further, he discusses the Islamic position relating to usury in detail, concluding with similar injunctions to those found in the writings of Greek philosophers, St Thomas Aquinas and other medieval scholars. Aside from the scriptural prohibitions of usury, Ibn Taimiyah provides detailed economic arguments – something also pursued by Al-Ghazali earlier, though not as extensively.

(iv) Ibn Taimiyah discusses the socioeconomic role and functions of the state quite thoroughly. Promotion of socioeconomic justice being the supreme goal of Islamic society, the state must secure a balance between the rights of individuals and power of the state. But, he argues, the state must pursue such goals as the eradication of poverty, amelioration of gross income and wealth inequalities, regulation of markets to minimize the evils of market imperfections, economic planning to provide the necessary socioeconomic infrastructure, just and efficient enforcement of the laws (including taxation), and so forth. The essence of Ibn Taimiyah's economics, as well as his view of the state's responsibilities, is well expressed in a letter to the ruler of the time. He advised the ruler to combat starvation, to satisfy the basic needs of the people, to help the oppressed, to listen to those in distress, and to enjoin good and forbid evil, for he considered such actions to be the pillars of justice and goodness. He insists that it is the state's responsibility that every person is assured a minimum standard of living sufficient for him to fulfil his obligations to his faith, family and to his fellow citizens (Ibn Taimiyah, AH 1381–7 Vol. 24, p. 280).

Concluding remarks

Based on Ibn Taimiyah's original writings, we have explored and presented some aspects of the economic thought of an eminent thirteenth-century Arab-Islamic scholar. Writing several centuries before the well-known European classical economists, Ibn Taimiyah was the product of an era when man, not matter, was the measure of all things and economic concerns were secondary – the ultimate test of all human endeavours being one's salvation. Such were the underlying assumptions of medieval scholarship generally, whether Arab-Islamic or Latin-Christian.

Ibn Taimiyah demonstrates, among other things, rather detailed knowledge of the operations of a voluntary exchange, market economy that 'naturally' evolves among freely-acting individuals, motivated by self-interest and mutual necessity – though such environment is conditioned and guided by a divinely inspired code of ethics and moral values. He shows deep understanding of the forces of demand and supply. He talks of the 'intensity and size' of demand and various sources of supply, as well as incentives generated by the profit motive. He identifies several factors which affect demand and supply (shift the schedules, as one would say in contemporary terms). He even identifies several characteristics of what we today call 'perfectly competitive markets'. Further, he insists that it is no transgression on the part of market participants if prices of goods increase due to competitive market forces. And, therefore, there is no reason for public sector intervention – unless there are market imperfections or emergencies such as famine or war. Moreover, in the manner of his Arab and Latin contemporaries, as well as Greek and Roman predecessors, Ibn Taimiyah would have limited faith in the self-regulating market mechanism, though he advocated the free play of competitive markets. Thus he stressed the public institution of *hisbah*, to be entrusted to a 'grand ombudsman' called the *muhtasib*. The explicit purpose of this institution was, given the Islamic scriptures, the administration and supervision of economic activities in the public interest – 'to promote what is good and to forbid what is evil'. The *muhtasib* was the Islamic version of the earlier Greek *agoranomos* and Roman *aedile*, though the former's responsibilities were much broader.

Further, we earlier noted Schumpeter's remark on the pricing mechanism – 'there is very little to report before the middle of the eighteenth century'. He also observed that 'The contribution of even the brightest lights, such as Barbon, Petty, Locke, do not amount to much...' (Schumpeter, 1954, p. 305). However, it is clear that, contrary to Schumpeter's observations, 500 years earlier Ibn Taimiyah (and before him, Al-Ghazali in particular) had provided a rather lucid analysis of the demand and supply forces as they relate to price determination (although Ibn Taimiyah did not talk of price determination in terms of value theory, or in terms of the relative scarcity or abundance of goods and money supply). To the best of our knowledge, it was not until the eighteenth century that any European scholar discussed such topics with the kind of rigour evident in Ibn Taimiyah's writings centuries earlier.[10]

Ibn Taimiyah wrote in an age when economics as a science, or even as a separate discipline, had not yet emerged. One is impressed by his perceptions of the market mechanism and the forces of demand and supply, as well as the problems of market imperfections and distortions, and their effects upon consumers and producers. He is concerned with the questions of monopoly, hoarding, and price manipulations. He also explored several other topics relevant to the discipline of economics (e.g., barter transactions, the role of money, public finances, property rights, distribution of income and poverty, etc.).

At the societal level, however, Ibn Taimiyah's primary concern is the establishment of a just economic order. Further, his concern for socioeconomic justice is vividly expressed in his assertion that a regime committed to justice, even if it has certain moral failings, is superior to a regime of 'pious tyranny'. As for the pursuit of economic activities, he says, wealth is superior to poverty even in the moral sense, for while poverty gives rise to rights, wealth imposes obligations such as mutual help and sharing. And, according to Henri Laoust, Ibn Taimiyah's 'doctrines are favorable to the organization of an active economic society for the reason that, in the absence of such organization, wealth which is static will soon tend to diminish and finally disappear altogether' (Laoust, 1939, p. 441).

Clearly, Ibn Taimiyah deserves to be acknowledged as among the distinguished pioneers of modern economic thought.

Notes

The authors are, respectively, Professor of Economics, University of Idaho, Moscow, Idaho; and Reader in Economics, Aligarh Muslim University, Aligarh, India. The authors are indebted to Professor Todd Lowry of Washington and Lee University, Lexington, Virginia, for several useful suggestions. Any shortcomings, however, remain the authors' responsibility.

1. Schumpeter might well have reflected an institutionalized, cultural phenomenon concerning Arab-Islamic scholarship, aptly described by Normal Daniel as 'a cultural filter in acquiring knowledge from an alien source considered to be tainted' (Daniel, 1975, p. 87). In the same vein, with regard to western attitudes toward Arab-Islamic thought generally, Montgomery Watt says, 'the difficulty is that we are the heirs of a deep-seated religious prejudice which goes back to the "war propaganda" of medieval times'; Watt also stresses the influence of western scholars' own cultural and intellectual heritage by adding, 'yet we should not allow ourselves to forget that we are not wholly freed from the entail of the past . . . .' (Watt, 1979, p. iv).

2. The fact that Ibn Taimiyah and numerous other medieval Arab and Latin Scholastics, as well as their Greek and Roman predecessors, did not discuss economic issues in terms of the formal analysis evident with more recent scholars must not persuade one to diminish

or dismiss their contributions. Doing so would be, according to Polanyi, tantamount to compounding 'two meanings that have independent roots. We will call them the substantive and the formal meaning. . . . The latter derives from logic, the former from fact.' In making the distinction, Polanyi states, 'It is our proposition that only the substantive meaning of economic is capable of yielding concepts that are required by the social sciences for an investigation of all the empirical economies of the past and present' (Polanyi, 1968, pp. 139–40).

3. Commenting on the possibility of price controls under such circumstances, Samuelson, for example, writes, 'Patriotism is more effective in motivating people to brief acts of intense heroism than to putting up day after day with an uncomfortable situation.' He goes on, 'Such emergency measures work very well in emergencies but may create more and more distortions the longer they are in effect. Economists therefore tend to recommend that such direct fiats be reserved for emergency periods and not be squandered on minor peace time situations' (Samuelson, 1981, p. 369).

4. Some Islamic scholars refer to the following verse of the Holy Qur'an to indicate the origin of the *hisbah*: 'Let there arise out of you a band of people inviting to all that is good, enjoining what is right, and forbidding what is wrong; They are the ones to attain felicity' (Qur'an, *Sura* 3, verses 104, 149–50). There are also some supportive *hadiths*, or traditions of Prophet Mohammed.

5. According to Lowry, 'It is true that the Greeks failed to notice the invisible hand of the market and instead, approach efficiency, distribution, economic organization, and individual and public utility from ethical, jurisprudential and ultimately, administrative perspectives. This approach to economic questions was in fact the dominant one throughout most of recorded human history, with market-oriented economic analysis a very recent development.' Further, 'The ascendance of the view of the market' operating 'like any physical system without human interference has tended to obscure the earlier administrative tradition of the political economy followed from ancient Greek times through the Middle Ages to Adam Smith, in which man himself was the manipulator and regulator, the administrator of his economic affairs' (Lowry, 1987, pp. 250, 249). Indeed, Ibn Taimiyah's *hisbah*, though more comprehensive than its antecedents, is part of the administrative tradition that prevailed in medieval Islamic civilization. Lowry further asserts, 'Smith's eclecticism included elements of both systems: his embracing of the nascent market tradition is illustrated by his theory of the invisible hand, while his identification with the administrative tradition is demonstrated by his concern with taxation and trade policy and his view of economics as a branch of jurisprudence' (ibid., p. 249).

6. It is interesting to note that the word *aedile* is also an Arabic word, meaning one who practises and enforces justice. However, in the Islamic tradition this term is not known ever to have been used for *muhtasib*.

7. Foster quotes a French scholar (E. Levi-Provencal) to support his argument; thus, 'L'institution de la hisba dans l'Islam eut, on le sait, à l'origine, à l'origine, un caractère spécifiquement religeux' ('The origin of the institution of hisba in Islam, it is well known, is specifically religious in character') (Foster, 1970, p. 142).

8. Schumpeter argues that St Thomas Aquinas's 'just price' was really the same as 'normal competitive price' (Schumpeter, 1954, p. 93). Gordon says the same: 'to Aquinas the just price of any commodity is its current market price established in the absence of fraud and monopolistic trading practices' (Gordon, 1975, p. 174). And Al-Ghazali had talked in essentially similar terms during the eleventh century – his was the 'prevailing price', one that is determined through market forces, devoid of fraud and deception. Al-Ghazali went on to develop a detailed code of ethics for market behaviour, as did St Thomas Aquinas 200 years later (see Ghazanfar and Islahi, 1990).

9. Incidentally, as with numerous other European scholars (e.g. St Thomas Aquinas, Albertus Magnus, Roger Bacon, Adelaard of Bath, Dominic Gundisilavi, and others) who relied considerably on Arab-Islamic scholarship (especially during the early medieval centuries), Nicholas Oresme was 'noted not only for his translation of Aristotle and Ptolemy but also for his original treatises, which embody ideas traceable to the writings of Ibn Sina, Al-Ghazali, and others' (Myers, 1964, p. 131).

10. It might be noted here that Schumpeter failed to take notice of some other pre-eighteenth century, late or post-medieval European scholars who, according to Barry Gordon, had offered discussions on the interplay of demand and supply forces – such as John Nider (1380–1438), Louis Molina (1536–1600), Navarrus (1493–1586) and Lessius (1554–1632) (Gordon, 1975, pp. 232, 239, 240). However, Gordon himself engages in a mishap similar to Schumpeter's: his otherwise scholarly volume also completely disregards the contributions of Arab-Islamic scholars (including, of course, Ibn Taimiyah).

References

Abu Yusuf (AH 1392), *Kitab al Kharaj* (The Book of Taxation), Cairo: Al-Matba'ah al-Salafiya wa Maktabatuha.

Ali, Basharat (1967), *Muslim Social Philosophy*, Karachi: Jamiyatul Falah Publications.

Boulakia, J. David (1971), 'Ibn Khaldun: A Fourteenth-Century Economist', *Journal of Political Economy*, **39** (5) (September–October), pp. 1105–18.

Daniel, Norman (1975), *The Cultural Barrier: Problems in the Exchange of Ideas*, Edinburgh: Edinburgh University Press.

Dempsey, Bernard W. (1965), 'Just Price in a Functional Economy', in James A. Gherity (ed.), *Economic Thought: A Historical Anthology*, New York: Random House.

Encyclopaed a (1971): see Laoust, Henri (1971).

Al-Farabi, *Abu Nasr (n.d.), *al-Siyasat-al-Madaniyah* (Politics of Civic Society, or Political Economy). Cairo: Nile Press.

Farrukh, Omar A. (trans.) (1966), *Ibn Taimiyah on Public and Private Law in Islam*, Beirut: Khayyat.

Foster, Benjamin R. (1970), 'Agoranomos and Muhtasib', *Journal of Economic and Social History of the Orient*, V.13, April, pp. 128–44.

Ghazanfar, S.M. (1988), 'Scholastic Economics and Arab Scholars: The "Great Gap" Thesis Reconsidered', paper presented at the History of Economics Society National Meeting, Toronto, Canada, June; (1991) *Diogenes*, No. 154, April–June (Paris, France).

Ghazanfar, S.M. and Islahi, A. Azim (1990), 'Economic Thought of an Arab Scholastic: Abu Hamid Al-Ghazali, AH 450–505/AD 1058–1111', *History of Political Economy*, **22** (2) (Spring), pp. 381–403.

Glick, Thomas F. (1971), 'Muhtasib and Mustasaf: A Case Study of Institutional Diffusion', *Viator: Medieval and Renaissance Studies*, **2**, pp. 59–81.

Goldziher, I. (1884), *Die Zahiriten*, Leipzig.

Gordon, Barry (1995), *Economic Analysis before Adam Smith*, New York: Barnes and Noble.

Heaton, Herbert (1948), *Economic History of Europe*, revised edn, New York: Harper & Row.

Hitti, Phillip K. (1951), *The History of Syria (including Lebanon and Palestine)*, London: Macmillan.

Holland, Muhtar (trans.) (1982), *Ibn Taimiyah's Public Duties in Islam: The Institution of the Hisbah*, Leicester: The Islamic Foundation.

The Holy Qur'an, trans. and commentary by A. Yusuf Ali, Brentwood, Maryland: Amana Corporation, 1983.

Ibn Abd al-Hadi (1938), *al-Uqud al-Durriyah*, Beirut: Dar al-Kutub al-Ilmiyah.

Ibn Iyas (1960), *Bada'i al-Zuhur fi Waqa'i al-Duhur*, 4 vols, Cairo: Lajnah al-T'alif wa'l Tarjamah.

Ibn Kathir (1966), *al-Bidayah wa'l-Nihayah*, 14 vols, Beirut: Maktabah Ma'arif.

Ibn Taimiyah (1971), *al-Siyasah al-Shariyah fi Islah al-Ra'i wa'l Ra'iyah*, ed. al-Banna and Ashur, Cairo: Dar al-Sha'b.

Ibn Taimiyah (1971), *al-Siyasah al-Shariyah fi Islah al-Ra'i wa'l Ra'iyah*, ed. al-Banna and Ashur, Cairo: Dar al-Sh'b.

Ibn Taimiyah (1976), *al-Hisbah wa mas'uliyh al-Hukumah al-Islamiyah*, or *al-Hisbah fi'l Islam*, ed. Salah Azzam, Cairo: Dar al-Sha'b.

Koran: *The Holy Qur'an*, trans. and commentary by A. Yusuf Ali, Brentwood, Maryland: Amana Corporation, 1983.

Lane-Poole, Stanley (1925), *A History of Egypt in the Middle Ages*, 4th edn, London: Methuen.

Laoust, Henri (1939), *Essai sur les doctrines sociales et politique de Taki-d-din b. Taimiya*,

Cairo: L'Institut Français.

Laoust, Henri (1971), 'Ibn Taimiyya', in *Encyclopaedia of Islam*, Vol. III, pp. 951–5, London: Luzac.

Levy, Reuben (1962), *The Social Structure of Islam*, Cambridge: Cambridge University Press.

Lowry, S. Todd (1987), *The Archeology of Economic Ideas: The Classical Greek Tradition*, Durham, NC: Duke University Press.

Al-Mubarak, Muhammad (1970), *Ara' Ibn Taimiyah fi al-Dawlah wa Mada Tadakhkhuliha fi'l Majal al-Iqtisadi*, Beirut: Dar al-Fikr.

Myers, Eugene A. (1964), *Arabic Thought and the Western World in the Golden Age of Islam*, New York: Frederick Ungar.

Peters, F.E. (1968), *Aristotle and the Arabs: The Aristotelian Tradition in Islam*, New York: New York University Press.

Polanyi, Karl (1968), 'The Economy as Instituted Process' in *Primitive, Archaic and Modern Economies: Essays of Karl Polanyi*, ed. George Dalton, New York: Doubleday.

Samuelson, Paul (1981), *Economics*, 11th edn, New York: McGraw Hill.

Schumpeter, Joseph A. (1954), *History of Economic Analysis*, New York: Oxford University Press.

Spengler, Joseph J. (1964), 'Economic Thought of Islam: Ibn Khaldun', *Contemporary Studies in Society and History*, VI (3), pp. 264–306.

Suyuti, Jalal al-Din 'Abd al-Rahman (1968), *Husn al-Muhadarah fi Tarikh Misr wa'l Qahirah*, 2 vols, ed. M. Abu al-Fadl Ibrahim, Cairo: Dar Ihya al-Kutub al-Arabiyah.

Tusi, Nasir al-Din (1952), *Akhlaq-e-Nasiri* (The Nasirean Ethics), Lahore: Punjab University.

Umaruddin, M. (1963), 'Ibn Taimiyah – A Thinker and Reformer' in *Usbu al-Fiqh al-Islami wa-Mihrajan Ibn Taimiyah*, Cairo.

Watt, W. Montgomery (1979), *What is Islam?*, 2nd edn, New York: Longman.

Ziadeh, Nicola (1963), *al-Hisbah wa'l Muhtasib fi'l Islam*, Beirut: Catholic Press.

6 Cantillon reconsidered
William D. Grampp

In my music there are good and bad notes; when I conduct it, I can hear only the good ones, but when you conduct it, I can hear all the notes.

Richard Strauss to Toscanini

There are puzzling features in Cantillon's *Essai* and puzzles in what has been written about him. Also puzzling is the fact that these puzzles have not been thought important enough to study if indeed they have been thought about at all. May not one then ask if Cantillon ought to be read again and if what has been written about him should be re-examined? Or, if one is not permitted, I shall presume to ask it. To read the *Essai* again is not a lengthy undertaking, since it is only 160 pages. Reading the people he is said to have anticipated is a longer affair, and still longer is reading what has been written about him. Yet, I suggest, the effort is called for. He is, after all, one of the great names in the history of economics, and among the people who have written about him are economists who themselves are distinguished. If raillery were allowed in the history of economics, I would say Cantillon is an icon among econs who could do with a little econoclasm.

I

Consider, first, the discrepancy between the ideas he is said to have anticipated and what he actually said. Viner claimed Cantillon anticipated the specie flow mechanism of Hume, Schumpeter said the same, and Hayek said Hume's statement was so similar to Cantillon's as to make one think Hume may have seen the *Essai* before it was published, a conjecture for which Viner could find no evidence (Viner, 1937, 74, n.2; Schumpeter, 1954, p. 366, 366, n.9; von Hayek, 1931, pp. lvii, lxii n.1). Antoin Murphy concurred with Viner on the grounds that if Hume had seen the *Essai* he would have improved his description of the mechanism by making changes in cash balances as well as changes in relative price levels a factor that equilibrates trade. What Murphy meant was that Cantillon's description was superior to Hume's, from which a reader may conclude that, chronology apart, Hume anticipated Cantillon. Douglas Vickers said that for both Cantillon and Hume 'there existed international self-balancing and re-equilibrating forces'. Anthony Brewer said Cantillon explained the specie flow mechanism as well as Hume did and as well as anyone else for a century after (Murphy, 1986, p. 271; Vickers, 1959, p. 229; Brewer, 1988, p. 453). Joseph Spengler in his comprehensive study of Cantillon (by far the best I have seen) hesitated to say what others said unhesitatingly, but he did offer the conjecture that if Cantillon had expressly addressed the subject of specie flows, he would have made a complete and satisfactory statement of it (Spengler, 1954, p. 420).

What I find puzzling is that there is nothing in Cantillon that anticipates Hume's specie flow mechanism (Hume, 1955a, p. 63). Its distinctive feature is not that the movement of specie changes the price levels of trading partners, hence changes their exports and imports. That, presumably, is what the economists cited above made of Hume. But he said something more, and it made his description different. He said the movement of specie is itself limited by the changes in the price levels of the trading partners, as well as the movement being initiated by the price level changes, the consequence being that the specie movements equalize the debits and credits of the balance of trade (the current account of the balance of payments). Hence no country can have an unfavourable (or favourable) balance for any length of time. Therefore the balance of trade is non-agenda as a policy objective. That is the point of Hume's description. If he did see Cantillon's work – as he conceivably could have – he said, Quite wrong.

That is because Cantillon made the balance of trade a major objective of policy. He said the nation should acquire a favourable balance in order to amass specie and thereby become a power in the world (Cantillon, 1931, pp. 91, 159, 233). He said the inflow of specie should not become a part of the money stock but should be hoarded by the government. Otherwise the specie would raise prices, reduce exports, increase imports, and the flow would be reversed. This seems to anticipate Hume. But it does not, because Cantillon went on to say – as Hume did not say in 'Of the Balance of Trade' – that an unfavourable balance would bring about a protracted or permanent decrease of output and employment, an emigration of labour, and a loss of population (which along with specie is a requisite of power), to the end that the nation would 'fall into poverty'. To prevent such a condition, the state should secure a favourable balance of trade. If it fails or neglects to do so, it may be able to restore its quondam prosperity by the government's 'encouraging' manufacturers and navigation (Cantillon, 1931, p. 185). There is none of this in Hume, simply because he did not believe specie movements were harmful.

There is more to the puzzle. Hume in 'Of Money', which was written before 'Of the Balance of Trade', said manufactures leave a country where an abundance of money has raised prices and move to where they are lower, the recipient country being thereby enriched. He also said these effects could be avoided if there was a public bank that 'locked up' the excess supply of money (Hume, 1955b, pp. 34–5). On these points Hume certainly does resemble Cantillon, yet, oddly, they are rarely if ever mentioned in what has been written about them. As Hume's argument continues it is unclear because he does not expressly say (as Cantillon does expressly say) that the high-priced countries become impoverished as the low-priced countries prosper. My conjecture is that the movement of manufactures from countries of high to those of low prices is something that enriches all of them, that being 'the happy concurrence of causes in human affairs' which (I believe) the essay is meant to illustrate. But I must report the opposite opinion of Eugene Rotwein, the authority on Hume's economic writings, who understands Hume to be enunciating here a 'law of growth and decay' (Hume, 1955a, pp. lvii–lix). If that is so, the neglect of the law by Cantillon scholars is all the more puzzling. Of course the law is not consistent with the specie flow mechanism. But that cannot explain why they have overlooked the law; the mechanism itself is not to be found in Cantillon.

In what has been said about the influence or precedence of Cantillon, there has been too little attention to Smith. Historians have noted of course the single passage in *The Wealth of Nations* that refers to Cantillon by name and to his explanation of what real wages must be in order to keep the population constant. But there are other passages that recall him, more often allusively than explicitly, although in the matter of specie flows Smith comes near to paraphrasing him. One may not say these passages were suggested to Smith by his reading of the *Essai*. But neither may one say they were not. He was cavalier about acknowledging his sources and was suspiciously sensitive to charges of plagiarism.

There is a passage in *The Theory of Moral Sentiments* that reminds one of how Cantillon censured the rich for their extravagance and accused them of weakening the nation. Smith ridicules rather than censures, is interested in how extravagance affects the distribution of income rather than national power, and here makes everything come out for the best in a Panglossian conclusion that speaks of the 'invisible hand' (words which, students of Smith know, he rarely used even though they are remembered better than any others) (Smith, 1976, p. 304; Cantillon, 1931, pp. 63, 73, 75). Smith here reasons from the same premiss as Cantillon, that the spending of the rich directs the economy and determines the welfare of others.

Cantillon's premiss is more noticeable in *The Wealth of Nations* where Smith describes the literal dependence of retainers on the great proprietors whom they served and how the dependence was altered for the good (again) by its becoming an exchange relation (Smith, 1937, p. 385). One also recalls Cantillon when Smith says the rich colonists of Peru acquired the pernicious habit of luxurious living from the example set by the extravagent reception of a new viceroy (ibid., p. 541). Cantillon is again recalled (and on the same page) when Smith reprobates, in his best anti-clerical manner, the mendicant orders. And again, when Smith deplores the improvidence of landlords, although not (as Cantillon did) because they waste land that could support a larger population but because they reduce saving (ibid., pp. 318–19). But Smith does not resemble Cantillon when he argues for a usury law that would eliminate loans for consumption. Cantillon, although he was not altogether opposed to usury laws, did not approve of them to the extent Smith did (and later regretted) (ibid., pp. 339–40). Then there is the evocation of Cantillon when Smith equates the value of 'a fine piece of cloth...which weighs only eighty pounds [with] several thousand weight of corn', enough to maintain the makers of the cloth and their employers (ibid., p. 383). Smith most certainly did not concur with Cantillon's belief that the nation should exchange its manufactures for foreign food in order to increase its population (Cantillon, 1931, pp. 231, 233). But Smith did say that by exporting manufactures 'a greater quantity of subsistence can annually be imported' than the country itself can grow, from which one may conclude that a nation by exporting manufactures can become more populous (Smith, 1937, p. 383). Cantillon obviously would concur.

The most striking resemblance is between Cantillon's saying an increase in the stock of specie can (though it need not) bring about national 'poverty' and Smith's statement that such an increase 'tends to make everyone poorer', the reason being (according to both) that prices rise, exports fall and imports increase (Cantillon, 1931, p. 185; Smith, 1937, p. 478). Smith did not of course say, as Cantillon did, that the nation should maintain a reserve of specie. The reason was not that Smith was indifferent to the effect of foreign trade on military power. The reason was that he believed that the nation, if it needed foreign resources in time of war, could obtain them by exporting manufactures, which means by acquiring a favourable balance of trade (Smith, 1937, p. 409).

About the effect of specie movements, Smith obviously differed with Hume and was nearer, if not at one, with Cantillon. Yet Jevons did not see things that way. His indiscriminate praise of Cantillon has been described as an understandable expression of the first rapture of discovery. Jevons said Cantillon explained the movement of specie with 'scientific precision' while Hume described it with 'vague literary elegance'. Surely the truth is the other way around. Hume described the matter plainly in 16 lines (by my count) while Cantillon (by Viner's count) used 40 pages and was not always clear (Jevons, p. 353; Hume, 1955a, p. 63; Viner, 1937, p. 74, n.2).

Another of Jevons's raptures was his concurring with Léonce de Lavergne that 'all the theories of the Economists [the Physiocrats] are contained by anticipation' in the *Essai* (Jevons, pp. 353–4). Whatever 'all' encompasses, it ought to include *l'impôt unique*, *le tableau économique*, and *le produit net* of Quesnay, the capital theory of Turgot, and his ideas of the market. Cantillon cannot, in my opinion, be credited (or debited) with any of them.

He is said (by Higgs and others) to have inspired the economic table because he stated that the spending of landed proprietors determines the allocation of resources and composition of output and because he described the transactions between the proprietors and others. What he actually noticed (and correctly) was that people with high incomes have more influence on what is produced than do people with low incomes and what one person spends becomes another person's income. The idea is important, no doubt, but is scarcely recondite and certainly was not the discovery of Cantillon. That purchases are identical with sales must have been noticed at the dawn of exchange. The idea was employed by the writers of the mercantilist period when they proposed various ways to increase spending and thereby to increase income and employment. Petty, from whom Cantillon learned much, employed the idea (Higgs, 1897, p. 37; Schumpeter, 1954, p. 221; Murphy, 1986, p. 258; Petty, 1899, Vol. I, p. 33). There is merit in asking the question: Who anticipated Cantillon? – a novel undertaking since so much has been written about whom he anticipated. That in turn would raise the question: Was he the last of the mercantilists rather than the first of the moderns, or neither? Some of his ideas that have enraptured economists go very far back indeed, such as the idea that owners of resources will direct them to employments that have the highest rate of return, or the idea that prices are fixed by the relation between the amount offered for sale and the amount demanded, or that disorder ensues if prices are set by law and depart substantially from what they would be if set by the market.

Moreover, the ideas he is said (correctly or not) to have anticipated did not alway have the influence claimed for them. The circular flow of income was not what Quesnay's economic table was meant to explain. It is a necessary condition of the table, of course, but it is not the principle the table elucidates (though perhaps 'obscures' would be more accurate). It is meant to show that agriculture is more productive than manufactures and that its development, rather than that of manufactures, should be the object of the state (Kuczynski and Meek, 1972, p. i). He claimed agriculture yielded a net rate of return of 100 per cent (i.e. total revenue was twice total cost). The idea was said by Ronald Meek to have had its origins in the division Cantillon made of the output of agriculture into three equal rents. One was equal to the total cost incurred by the farmer in producing his output, excepting what he paid the landowner, that being the second rent, while the third was the income of the farmer on which he supported himself and his family. According to Meek, the net product that Quesnay described in his *Encyclopédie* article, 'Grains', was the sum of the income of the landowner and farmer, the second and third rents (Meek, 1963, p. 269). The sum is, to be sure, 100 per cent greater than the first which is the farmer's outlay for materials and the like. But that outlay is not his total cost. His total cost is that outlay plus land rent plus the value of his labour, the last being the third rent. This sum is the value of output as well as the cost of producing it. To subtract the latter from the former leaves nothing because they are by definition equal, actually identical. The identity is the foundation of national income accounting. (But no one, so far as I know, has yet said that Cantillon anticipated Simon Kuznets.)

Quesnay did, it is true, refer to the 'fundamental truth' of Cantillon, that everyone is dependent on the proprietors of land. Just what the truth encompassed is unclear. Cantillon could have meant only that the proprietor class being the richest spent more than other classes and so had the greatest effect on total income. But he probably also meant that everyone is dependent on the land because it is the source of all wealth. Yet he did not say, as the Physiocrats did say, that land is the only productive resource. He may have believed it was more important than labour but he did not say, as the Physiocrats did say, that it produced a surplus and that labour not employed on it was unproductive. There were still other ways in which Quesnay differed from Cantillon. Quesnay did not condemn luxuries, did not say the nation should secure a favourable balance of trade, and did not say that the most important form of wealth was specie. He said agricultural goods should be exported in return for manufactures, while Cantillon said the opposite. About population, Quesnay said it would increase as wealth did and remarked that Mirabeau, who had said the opposite on the authority of Cantillon, had gotten the causal relation reversed (Quesnay, 1757-72). Mirabeau wrote *L'Ami des hommes* under the spell of Cantillon before he met and came under the spell of Quesnay. He describes his passing from one to the other in a letter to Rousseau that Ronald Meek very appositely included in his study of physiocracy (Meek, 1963, pp. 16–18). Both Mirabeau and Quesnay believed Cantillon had said that an increase of population would increase the nation's wealth. Actually, what Cantillon said is not clear. He did say labour is the 'form' that produces the wealth that comes from the 'matter' that is provided by the land (Cantillon, 1931, p. 3) – which is consistent with the interpretation of Mirabeau and Quesnay. Also consistent is the title of Chapter 16 of Part I: 'The more Labour there is in a State the more naturally rich the State is esteemed.' But the chapter opens with the statement that the labour of 25 adults is enough to supply 100 people with the necessaries they are accustomed to, which means, he continues, that half the labour force, which is half the adult population, can do all that is needed to support it. Does that imply there would be no change in wealth if half of the workers withdrew from the labour force? Or does it mean there would be no change in the amount of necessaries? If it means the latter, how did Cantillon distinguish between necessaries and wealth (not to be confused with the distinction between necessaries and luxuries)? He did say the unemployed half of the labour force could be set to work making ornaments and toys, for which 'the state is not considered less rich... than it is for useful and serviceable objects'. That makes one ask whether he distinguished between states that were 'esteemed' rich and those that really were. All in all, one sympathizes with Mirabeau and one should with others also, because population was not the only topic about which Cantillon was unclear.

For the single tax of the Physiocrats, Cantillon cannot be held responsible nor can he be said to have anticipated the observations of Turgot about the nature of capital, the rate of return, and usury laws. The two did have similar ideas about how the market operates but Turgot assigned more merit to it and would have given it a wider scope (Groenewegen, 1977, pp. 26–7).

Malthus is another who is said to have been prefigured by Cantillon, if not altogether, then 'almost', according to Jevons (Jevons, p. 347). Cantillon did say, 'Men multiply like mice in a barn if they have an unlimited means of subsistence' (1931, p. 83). The idea suggests Malthus, no doubt, if the language does not, but also suggests numerous other writers who preceded him as he himself acknowledged in later editions of the *Essay on Population* (Malthus, 1807, Vol. I, p. vi). What is distinctive about the *Essay*, especially the first edition, is the checks on population growth which constitute a self-regulating mechanism (Malthus, 1960, ch. ii). There is nothing of this in Cantillon, and he entertained ideas Malthus did not share or would have objected to. Cantillon said that while subsistence determines the population, subsistence is not a fixed amount, that some people choose to live on less than others, that if all people, high and low, preferred less, the population would increase (Cantillon, 1931, pp. 71, 73, 77, 81). That, he implied, is to be desired because the greatness of a nation depends on the size of its population (and its reserve stock of specie) (ibid., p. 233).

These are puzzles of the first sort: the discrepancies between what Cantillon said and what he is said to have said before others said it. There are more discrepancies but those I have described are, in my view, sufficient to call for reading Cantillon again (and, I may say, for reading the people he is said to have anticipated).

II

Another sort of puzzle – a second set within the first – has to do with Cantillon's place in the development of economic theory. His influence on what was written in the eighteenth century is said to have been so extensive that he must be called the economist's economist. At the end of the century he went into eclipse, for some reason, and had to be rediscovered by Jevons, who said the *Essai* was 'the cradle of political economy ... the first treatise on economics' (Jevons, p. 342). Spengler said that a case can be made that Cantillon was the most important of the precursors of classical and neoclassical economics (Spengler, 1954, p. 281).

These of course are statements of what Cantillon anticipated, and so the puzzles they present are related to the first set. But there are two differences. Not all of the ideas Cantillon is said (correctly or not) to have anticipated became a permanent part of economics. Physiocratic ideas did not, and the population theory of Malthus has undergone a sea change into something so strange he would scarcely recognize it. Moreover, to claim Cantillon laid the foundations of modern economics is to claim he stated at least some of its basic propositions. Among them, certainly, are (1) the conception of the market as a method of allocating resources and distributing output; (2) the idea that price is determined by cost and utility; and (3) the belief that self-interest is a, or the, principal motive of behaviour. That of course is not a summary statement of all that economics is but of three propositions that any such statement would contain.

Did Cantillon anticipate them? About the market, he did anticipate several important ideas that were stated later, at times less well than he stated them. He did not say all there is to be said about the market, and that of course in no way diminishes the importance that has been claimed for him. What does diminish it is the uncertain state of his ideas. Just what did he contribute to an understanding of it? Some of his statements are unclear, some are inconsistent with others, some are simply wrong, and a number that impressed later economists were in fact made before his time. That so much has been made of so little that is clear, consistent, correct and original is certainly a puzzle.

To describe just a few of his questionable ideas is quite enough to challenge the claim that he has a principal place in the founding of modern economics. He states early in the *Essai* that the intrinsic and long-run value of a good is determined by its cost of production, cost being measured by the amount of land needed to produce the good including the land needed to support the labour used with the land (1931, p. 29). But he then observes that the 'humours and fancies' of men may induce them to pay more for something than its cost, not because of a temporary difference between market price and cost but as a permanent condition (ibid.). So Cantillon implicitly admitted utility, or demand, to the determination of long-run price, along with cost or supply. That is altogether modern of course but is not consistent with his explicitly stated theory of value (and, incidentally, is not of the same logical order as the exceptions the classical economists made to their cost theory of value). He was even more inconsistent about the price of labour. Beginning with a subsistence theory of wages, he qualified it by saying there are large differences in what a person wants and even in what he needs, then he left subsistence entirely by saying wages vary directly with the trustworthiness of the worker (ibid., pp. 35, 37, 21).

He explains market price, as distinct from intrinsic value, as the outcome of 'altercations' between sellers and buyers. Sellers wonder how much buyers are willing to pay, buyers how little sellers will accept; each wonders if by waiting he will do better, their guesses sometimes being right, sometimes wrong; they higgle and haggle – and out of this a price emerges. One of his present admirers has said Cantillon's description is superior, because more realistic, to the customary explanation of price determination (large numbers, price takers everywhere, mobility, complete information, etc.). Certainly Cantillon's explanation is more detailed. Whether it is informative depends on the value that is placed on the information it provides, some of which, despite its putative realism, is erroneous. It does not lead to a conclusion that is different from that which the familiar explanation provides in markets to which both apply. In the course of his description Cantillon did not always reason consistently from his premisses. One is that market price can be above or below intrinsic value. In his account of the altercation between the sellers of green peas and the *maîtres d'hôtels*, market price rises above intrinsic value, as expected, when the amount demanded exceeds that supplied; but when the amount supplied exceeds that demanded, the price will fall, to be sure, but, for some reason, will not fall below intrinsic value, will not fall even to that amount though it will fall 'almost' to intrinsic value. That may be the peculiar property of *maîtres d'hôtels* or of green peas which he noticed in his quest for realism. In the same chapter (2, Pt. II), there is another odd statement: 'The price of meat will be settled after some altercations, and a pound of beef will be in value to a piece of silver pretty nearly as the whole beef offered for sale in the market is to all the silver brought there to buy beef.' He must have meant more than that one pound of beef will sell for one piece of silver if 50 pounds sell for 50 pieces. Did he mean that the altercations lead to an equilibrium at which the amount all buyers are willing to spend is equal to what all sellers will accept for the entire amount they supply? If that is his meaning, his bargaining explanation of market price leads to the same conclusion as the familiar explanation, as unrealistic as the latter may be.

About the location of firms he was of two minds, and the reader is left to wonder how or if they can be brought together. He said the market is quite able to determine the proper number of stores in a locality, presumably because it sets the rate of profit and because entrepreneurs are directed by profit. But he did not believe the location of factories could be left to the market and he wanted the state to establish them in the proper places, for example, near the source of materials (1931, pp. 53, 155). About the effect of location on prices he could (to say the least) be difficult to follow or (to speak plainly) could be opaque. He subordinated the explanation of price differences to the explanation of why there were differences within the country in what he called the amount of money in circulation (or per capita money holdings). He said prices in the capital are higher because goods must be carried to it at a cost and are higher by no more than the cost of transportation – certainly an objectionable statement. But he also said they were higher because people in the capital had more money, meaning their incomes (hence money holdings) were higher – also unobjectionable but only when unravelled (ibid., pp. 149, 151, 153).

About some of his observations on pricing, one must admire him. He describes what happens when a silver mine having a monopoly is challenged by a new mine with lower costs. A price duel ensues, and the monopoly passes to the challenger at a price (the reader will infer, if he is generous) that is above the challenger's cost and below that of the initial monopolist (ibid, p. 101). True, the description is cluttered with transportation cost and opens with the mistaken notion that monopoly price is 'arbitrary'. Nevertheless it is an early and notable venture into the analysis of duopoly.

But it was a cadenza. On either side, one finds objectionable passages about the market, the price level and the money stock. He said slaves are always more profitable to use than free peasants – which cannot be if, as he elsewhere implies, the market operates to equalize rates of return. Land is a risk-free asset, he said, but he said also that the rent of proprietors is paid in money or kind, either of which is subject to unpredictable changes in value. Given as he was to the little pleasures of the autodidact, he quibbled with Locke over the quantity theory, then admitted Locke's conclusion a few pages on. Cantillon's principal error about money was to open his explanation of its value with the commodity theory and move on to the quantity theory (ibid., pp. 35, 55, 97, 117, 121, 161). The two can be reconciled by assuming decreasing average cost but he made no such assumption.

Then there is the curious remark that a country will benefit more from its exports if an increase in the quantity of money has raised the price level (including the price of exports) (ibid., pp. 159, 235). What he meant, we would describe as an improvement of the terms of trade. In time, he said, exports would decrease and imports increase, so the improvement would not be permanent (ibid., p. 235). Why it would be more than fleeting is a puzzle. Or did he mean the given country's demand for exports and imports was inelastic? That, indeed, was an anticipation.

III

How a country could benefit at the expense of foreigners was a question that attracted, indeed intrigued, him, and what he had to say about it constitutes the third and last set of puzzles. What he said in praise of the market is difficult to reconcile with what he said in praise of departing from it. The difficulty is usually gotten over by making little of his exceptions to it and attributing them to his not having entirely liberated himself from mercantilism.

But that will not do – the exceptions are important. He said the government should accumulate a stock of gold and silver and hold it in reserve for 'bad years, or war' (1931, pp. 89, 91, 185, 233). The specie, he said, is best acquired by a favourable balance of trade. Domestic mining is likely to produce an excessive money stock, although, one may infer, he believed the excess could be avoided by the government's withdrawing it from circulation (ibid., pp. 89, 133). The government must not allow the additional metal to enter the money stock, because (as noted above) that would eventuate in a decline of employment, income, capital and, most serious of all, of population (ibid., p. 185).

The nation in its foreign trade should export labour-intensive goods and import those that are land intensive (ibid., Pt III, ch. i) Making the land support as many people as possible was a major element of his economic policy (just as conserving energy was a major element in the 1980s, which makes one ask why Cantillon has not been said to have anticipated energy economics). He said the population could be increased if the lower orders reduced their consumption, as, he believed, they could do without any detriment to themselves, and if the upper classes adopted a simpler way of living which, he said, they would do if the Prince set an example (ibid., pp. 73, 93). He did, to be sure, decline to say whether a large population with a low average real income was better or worse than a small population with a high income – because the question was 'outside my subject' (ibid., p. 85). To believe he meant that, one also must believe he really did not attach any importance to the size of the population even though he repeatedly said or implied that a nation to be great must be populous (ibid., Pt I, ch. xv).

His reason for advocating a larger population could not have been to increase the supply of labour in those parts of the economy that were directed by the market. This is implied by his proposition (also noted above) that half of the labour force was superfluous in the sense of not being needed to produce necessaries (ibid., p. 87). He said the best use of the excess labour was in manufactures for export or the mining of metals of all kinds (ibid., p. 89).

Not all of his ideas of economic policy have to do with foreign trade. He disapproved of luxurious or extravagant living whether the goods and labour it entailed came from abroad or from the domestic economy (ibid., p. 93). He said proprietors should try to spend no more than their rents (ibid.), and he believed they were more likely to live within their means if their land holdings were small (ibid., p. 73). He implied that loans for consumption were not in the nation's interest (ibid., p. 219), although he did not favour usury laws that fixed rates substantially lower than those of the market (ibid., p. 227). I have mentioned his wanting the state to direct factories to locate near the source of their materials. While he did not believe the state should have an extensive programme for the training of workers he did believe it should train them to produce manufactured goods for export (ibid., p. 25).

Foreign trade nevertheless did get more attention than domestic when he considered what should be left to the market and what should not. What principle did he employ in making the distinction?

That, I submit, is the most important question to be asked about Cantillon. Of course what and whose ideas he anticipated is interesting and merits study. More important is the question of what place he has in the founding of modern economics. Still more important is what principle determined his ideas of economic policy. An argument can be made that the *Essai* is a tract on policy. While the observations of a theoretical nature are interesting, even arresting, they do not comprise a clear and consistent whole and do not, in my opinion, make the work a landmark in the history of economic theory.

Whatever was the purpose of the *Essai* it does call for a reconsideration if only because of what has been said about it and what it says itself.

References

Brewer, Anthony (1988), 'Cantillon and Mercantilism', *History of Political Economy*, **20** (3).

Cantillon, Richard (1931), *Essai sur la nature du commerce en général*, ed. and trans. Henry Higgs, London.

Groenewegen, P.D. (ed.) (1977), 'In Praise of Gournay', in *The Economics of A.R.J. Turgot*, The Hague.

Higgs, Henry (1897), *The Physiocrats*, London.

Hume, David (1955a), 'Of the Balance of Trade', in *Writings on Economics*, ed. with introduction by Eugene Rotwein, Edinburgh.

Hume, David (1955b), 'Of Money', in *Writings on Economics*, ed. with introduction by Eugene Rotwein, Edinburgh.

Jevons, W. Stanley, 'Richard Cantillon and the Nationality of Political Economy', in Cantillon, *Essai*.

Kuczynski, Marguerite and Meek, Ronald L. (1972), *Quesnay's Tableau Economique*, ed. with new material, translations, and notes, London.

Malthus, T.R. (1807), *Essay on the Principle of Population; etc.*, 4th edn, London.

Malthus, T.R. (1960), *An Essay on the Principle of Population, etc.* [1798], New York.

Meek, Ronald L. (1963), *The Economics of Physiocracy*, Cambridge.

Murphy, Antoin E. (1986), *Richard Cantillon: Entrepreneur and Economist*. Oxford.

Petty, William (1899), 'Political Arithmetic', in *Economic Writings*, ed. C.H. Hull, Cambridge.

Quesnay, François (1757–72), 'Grains', in *Encyclopédie, etc.*, Vol. VII, ed. Diderot et al., Berne.

Schumpeter, Joseph (1954), *History of Economic Analysis*, ed. Elizabeth B. Schumpeter. New York.

Smith, Adam (1937), *The Wealth of Nations* [1789], New York: The Modern Library.

Smith, Adam (1976), *The Theory of Moral Sentiments* [1759], Indianapolis: Liberty Classics.

Spengler, Joseph J. (1954), 'Richard Cantillon: First of the Moderns. I and II', *Journal of Political Economy*, **52** (4 and 5) (August and October).

Vickers, Douglas (1959), *Studies in the Theory of Money, 1690–1776*, Philadelphia.

Viner, Jacob (1937), *Studies in the Theory of International Trade*, New York.

von Hayek, Friedrich A. (1931), 'Richard Cantillon', in *Abhandlung über die Natur des Handels im allgemeinen*, trans. Hella von Hayek, Jena.

From the 1970s on, the *Reflections on the Formation and the Distribution of Wealth* has been analysed in historical and sociological perspectives.[1] As a result, commentators have recognized Turgot's contribution to the 'four stages' theory.[2] More specifically, they have wondered about the presence in Turgot's masterpiece of the fourth stage, that is, the 'commercial society'.[3] Thus, even if the historical dimension of Turgot's economics was acknowledged, the capacity of this 'system' to represent the functioning of capitalist society was emphasized much more. Although Turgot's historical perspective deserved some credit when likened to the immutability of 'natural' laws of Physiocrats, it did appear as incomplete compared with Smith's explicit definition of the four 'stages'. Turgot's 'capitalism' suffered from immaturity in relation to Smith's.[4]

In fact, the principal subject of the *Reflections* deals less with the capitalist society itself than with the transition from the agricultural society to the capitalist one. Turgot put forward a genealogy of capitalist behaviours whose purpose was to show how the different conditions of the formation of capital determined its various uses. More generally, Turgot's special concern was to establish the socioeconomic conditions of economic functions. With regard to this genealogy, the *Reflections* gives us the picture of a certain continuity between the society of the 'earliest times' and a society which is not quite capitalist – due to the lack of both capitalist entrepreneurs and 'merchants of money'. Nonetheless, by addressing not only the ways men appropriate and maintain land title deeds but also the formation of capitals in general, Turgot is led to analyse two economic behaviours characteristic of the capitalist society: the lending of money and entrepreneurship.

I. The society of the 'earliest times'
The model of the society of the 'earliest times' takes place just after the stage of pasturage, at the very beginning of the 'state of husbandmen'. Thus, this society cannot be mistaken for the solitary state, which remains a hypothetical situation used in order to describe both the constitution and preservation of landownership. Although the appropriation of land appears as an equalitarian

process based on labour, it is linked with the possession of livestock. As to the maintenance of such capital, it is obviously non-equalitarian.

The appropriation of 'natural' advances and the possession of livestock
The first type of social organization in the agricultural stage, the society of the earliest times, is far from being the most completed one. For instance, the distinction between proprietor and cultivator which corresponds with a 'progress of society' is missing. Only 'industrious classes' – husbandmen and artisans – are to be found. The one who cultivates land becomes the proprietor of its produce. He uses part of its production for his own consumption. As regards the 'surplus of produce', it is exchanged with other produce which the proprietor does not cultivate. The proprietor can also provide the artisans with the raw materials and the consumers' goods, which enable them to produce the other products he needs. This is a particular exchange of produce for labour, and not of produce for products of the 'stipendiary class', for this would mean that the workman himself makes advances. Even though the proprietor fulfils the function of the entrepreneur, he satisfies more his desire for a varied consumption than for enrichment.

Such a conception of society is not merely based on the complementarity of the two classes, as one could conclude from the fact that, once the division of labour is settled, 'everyone gained as a result of this arrangement, for each man by devoting himself to a single kind of work succeeded much better in it' (Turgot, 1766b, p. 121). Actually, 'The husbandman...has the advantage of a greater degree of independence' (ibid.). While facing the need to make advances in agriculture as well as in industry, men who cultivate the land and those who manufacture its produce do not enjoy the same means. The 'cultivating proprietor' has a capital at his disposal, which he has not formed, a free capital in a way, an 'independent and disposable form of wealth, which he has never purchased but which he sells' (ibid., p. 123). The artisan, on the other hand, may gather, only with thrift and patience, the savings which would enable him to finance his investment, as 'the man who pays for his labour...pays him as little as he is able' (ibid., p. 122).

So the question is to find out why some members of the society become artisans when they could enjoy a more abundant subsistence by cultivating the available land.

If advances are necessary in order to produce, then only those which do not result from prior production can initiate cultivation. These natural advances are the work of the land which provides the cultivators with:

> The fruits and plants which it produced of itself...the trees from which men formed their first tools...the stone, the clay, and the wood from which the first houses were constructed; and, *before the separation of occupations*, when the same man

> who cultivated the land provided for his other needs by his own labour, no other advances were necessary. (Turgot, 1766b, p. 151; my italics)

This reference to the solitary state is very interesting. It shows that, in the society of the earliest times, there are other advances than those that nature grants to men in the solitary state. Because they lack such advances, men devote themselves to craftsmanship, and are deprived of natural advances which would make them live more easily. What do these advances consist of? Actually, livestock is the main investment for cultivation. That is why they 'were of all kinds of movable wealth the most sought after in these early times, and the kind which it was easiest to accumulate' (Turgot, 1766b, p. 147). This variety of 'conditions' causes an inequality in the appropriation of land. In some ways, the structure of ownership in the stage of pasturage gives rise to barriers to the entry of new cultivators in agriculture. The hope for a more generous consumption which will balance the worry for the 'more arduous labour of cultivation' (ibid., p. 148) is not enough to allow men to cultivate land. Only those who possess livestock have this possibility. As for the others, they are confined to craftsmanship. Consequently, the situation of artisan is not the result of an inclination, even though Turgot sometimes refers to a choice.

Now, we can understand the 'pre-eminence' of agricultural labour in a different way. On the one hand, the husbandman has at his disposal a capital (made of livestock) which contributes to the progress of agricultural methods; on the other hand, he supplies the goods which constitute the most important part of consumption in the agricultural society. This pre-eminence stems from 'physical necessity' in the sense that it does not disappear little by little, as the model of society gets closer to reality by integrating its social data. Therefore, this pre-eminence does not necessarily correspond to the primacy of one class. It is rather embodied in several labours which represent the mode of subsistence characterizing the evolution of society. If, as the description of the solitary state implies, only the labour which provides for the subsistence (see Turgot, 1766b, pp. 121–2) is pre-eminent, then rearing can be a pre-eminent labour in the stage prior to the agricultural one, as well as hunting in a society of hunters. The common characteristic of all these labours is obvious. Whatever the stage – hunting, pasturage or agriculture – the relationship with wealth is always conceived as the access to goods whose increase is guaranteed by nature through the process of 'generation' (this does not mean that labour is ineffective). Thus it was only natural that Turgot had trouble associating industrial labour with other types of labour, according to the generation criterion. The conceptualization of man's relationship with nature is less obvious when it deals with activities in which man-operated transformation of nature is more essential than the transformation due to time. Furthermore, the dominant mode of subsistence did not suggest the pre-eminence of a new kind of labour.

Eventually, access to natural advances is possible provided that other advances (livestock) are achieved. This accounts for the distinction between cultivators and artisans. A second criterion of inequality makes possible the distinction between landlords themselves.

'Causes of inequality' and modes of appropriation of land

According to Turgot, there are different 'causes of inequality': the cultivator's working capacities; the fertility of land; the dispersal of possessions through inheritance and the 'most powerful one of all', the 'contrast between the intelligence, the activity, and above all the thrift of some with the indolence, inactivity, and extravagance of others' (Turgot, 1766b, p. 125). This last opposition implies that the cultivator can either take advantage of natural advances so that 'this primary fund gr[ows] little by little' (ibid., p. 147) or consume them for the satisfaction of his personal wants. The cultivator's thrift may be a secondary criterion for the distinction from the artisans. However, it is essential in order to understand the disparities in landowners' wealth.

> The negligent and improvident Proprietor, who cultivates badly, and who in abundant years consumes the whole of his surplus in frivolities, on the occurrence of the slightest accident finds himself reduced to asking for help from his more prudent neighbour, and to living on loans. (ibid., p. 125)

The land not only affords gratuitously to the husbandman the first advances which are essential for any productive activity but also gives him back the 'physical result of the fertility of the soil, and of the correctness, much more than of the difficulty, of the means he has employed to render it fruitful' (ibid., p. 123). The 'pure gift' does not explain everything: 'It is by labour that the land produces' (Turgot, 1770a, p. 169). Between the stage of capital advances and the returns of advances, not only the 'generation' effect but also the combined action of labour and capital is operative. Advances are likely to make variable profits. This has effects on the structure of property. Inasmuch as 'negligent and improvident' proprietors are unable to form and maintain capital, the division of landed property suffers from inequalities – whether or not there is available land. In fact, Turgot emphasized the second origin of the formation of capital, namely, thrift. From this point of view, society of the earliest times represents a transitional period, an 'epoch' of agricultural society, which gives rise to the inequalities of property ownership characteristic of the full ownership.

The process leading to the full ownership of land, with the clear-cut distinction between proprietors and those who are not[5] takes three different forms: 'lending proprietors' monopolize land which was badly managed by other proprietors; landed estates become objects of commerce; land is cleared for cultivation.

The circulation of land depends on its capacity to discharge debtors. The insolvent proprietor must sell part of his funds in order to meet his commitments. The wise landowner helps the one who is thriftless. This loan turns to his advantage each time his debtor

> finds that he is not in a position to pay [...so that] there will in the end be nothing left for him to do but abandon a part or even the whole of his estate to his creditor, who will take it as an equivalent; or to part with it to another in exchange for other assets with which he will discharge his obligation to his creditor. (Turgot, 1766b, pp. 125–6)

The commerce of landed estates exists before full ownership,[6] and gives rise to a simple evaluation, 'in accordance with the current price which is established by the competition of those who want to exchange land for livestock and those who want to part with livestock to get land' (Turgot, 1766b, p. 149). By considering the inequality in the endowments both of land and livestock, one can understand that some proprietors are ready to give up part of their land in exchange for livestock. Thus, the 'lack of men's labour is made up for with that of cattle' (ibid., p. 130) so that the productivity of the remaining land is improved. Yet the opposite is also true: 'In a time when a large amount of land was still uncultivated and belonged to no one, it was possible to possess livestock without being a Proprietor of land' (ibid., p. 148). Consequently, it is possible that possessors of livestock would rather give up part of their 'movable wealth' in exchange for arable land instead of clearing new land.

As long as there is available land, those who want to become landowners may clear it for cultivation, since 'everyone was gifted with the land' (Turgot, 1753–4, p. 439; my translation).[7] The comparison between the cost of clearing and the price of arable land creates the decision to clear. Nevertheless, clearing land is not necessarily the best way to appropriate it, especially if land is for sale. Preparing land for cultivation is necessary since, without prior labour, land gives only a low income. Yet Turgot considered that improvement of land already cleared was less expensive than the expenditures incurred when clearing. Furthermore, cleared lands are likely to give more certain revenue (see Turgot, 1770c, p. 316). In addition, 'in the course of time all the best land came to be occupied. There remained for the last comers only the infertile soils which had been rejected by the first' (Turgot, 1766b, p. 124). Clearing, therefore, becomes less and less worthwhile as land is appropriated.

As far back as society of the earliest times, the main economic functions (uses of capital) that Turgot draws up in the monetary economy are to be found. The 'cultivating proprietor' makes advances, he is at the origin of loan transactions, and he purchases landed estates. However, full ownership and the introduction of money give these functions a different meaning.

II. The evolution in landowners' behaviour

Full ownership – which implies that laws perpetuate inequalities in the division of property (see Turgot, 1766b, p. 124) – and the introduction of money are the two most important changes to affect society of the earliest times. Among landowners, only those who commit their land to a farmer have time for public affairs. The change in the forms of wealth induces some landlords to fulfil the function of moneylender.

Full ownership does not mean complete freedom

Once all land is occupied, property no longer necessarily ensues from labour, for some men are prepared to cultivate the land which belongs to others. Thus a social division of labour is drafted, which enables one to make a distinction between the working classes ('productive' and 'stipendiary') and the 'disposable class'. This division is not limited to the 'distinction, between the rich and those who are not... which at any rate·does not precisely divide the society into two classes' (Turgot, 1771, p. 521; my translation). At this point not only the artisans but also the cultivators work for the landowners. The latter commit the cultivation of their land to agricultural workers, invest (seed, livestock, implements, consumption goods), and recover the produce of the land. Due to this evolution, the landowner seems to have more free time. Yet we should not grant him too quickly an exemption from productive tasks. 'That instead of employing all his time in arduous labour he should prefer to give a part of his surplus to people who will work for him' (Turgot, 1766b, p. 126) can be easily understood: the landowner only wants to maintain his level of consumption and 'enjoy his wealth in pace' (ibid.) Yet this is not enough to set him totally free from labour. Actually, his degree of freedom depends on the different options he has to get his land cultivated.

Let us look at the first method: to shift labour to wage-earners. The landowner who made that choice is not fully free to do as he wishes:

> This first method (to derive revenue from land) has the drawback of requiring a great deal of labour and attention on the part of the Proprietor, who alone can direct the workmen in their labours, and keep an eye on the use of their time and on their trustworthiness so that none of the product is misappropriated. (Turgot, 1766b, p. 129)

Of course, the landowner 'may also pay a man of greater intelligence, and with whose trustworthiness he is familiar, to direct the workmen and keep an account of the product in the capacity of overseer or manager; but he will always run the risk of being deceived' (ibid.). Thus it is clear that the landowner will not really be free when employing wage-earners. In any case, he may not remain free from responsibility for a long time because of the loss of income which might result from badly managed labour or embezzlement of his products.

As regards cultivation by slaves, we learn that 'the management of a property cultivated by slaves is an arduous task which involves close attention and an irksome restriction on one's place of abode' (ibid., p. 131). Here again the 'master' is only partially free. '[He] ensures himself of a freer, easier, and more secure enjoyment of his property by interesting his slaves in cultivation and giving up to each of them a certain area of land, on condition of their rendering to him a portion of its fruits' (ibid.). This leads to a third method of getting land cultivated, by giving up landed property for claim ('alienation of the estate subject to the payment of dues'). Here it becomes difficult to evaluate the degree of the landowner's freedom, for this operation merely consists in a transfer of property. The responsibilities of land management are not eliminated, they are passed on to the new landowner. Apparently, only tenant-farming or the *métayer* system (share cropping) would make freedom actual. Moreover, Turgot stressed these two methods of turning land to account.[8] The others have too many disadvantages:

> The first is too expensive, and is very rarely put into use; the second can find a place only in countries which are still ignorant and barbarous; the third is less a method of turning one's property to account than a surrender of one's property in return for a debt claim on the estate, so that the old Proprietor, properly speaking, is no more than a creditor of the new one. (Turgot, 1766b, p. 134)

In fact, the *métayer* system does not spare the landowner labour worries since he goes on investing and cannot determine his income *a priori*. His situation is directly linked to the *métayer*'s productive efficiency. The sharing of production guarantees a certain proportion in the distribution of the land produce but not a specific amount of produce. The landowner cannot be really free if his income is uncertain. Here again, the link between the landowner's personal exertion and the income he expects is important:

> [Share cropping] demands continuous care and permanent residence from the landlord. So, as soon as the proprietor either experiences troubles in his business or must be away from work, his property stops producing anything. (Turgot, 1766b, p. 134, my translation)

In addition to the above, Turgot pointed out that landowners must provide their *métayers* with subsistence, when crops are insufficient (see Turgot, 1770f, p. 243).

Full freedom thus only occurs when a rich landowner meets a rich farmer who can both secure him a fixed annual money rental and take in charge the entire agricultural labour. In this case, there is no longer a link between the landowner's own exertion and the revenue he receives. Hence one can assume Turgot introduces a new kind of behaviour. Here we encounter a problem, for this situation is only possible in a society where money is put into use.

However, Turgot refers to the 'disposable class' before he even alludes to this hypothesis. So it is not clear what the content of this class might be, at least if we accept Turgot's definition of it as 'The only one which, not being bound by the need for subsistence to one particular kind of work, may be employed to meet the general needs of the Society' (1766b, p. 127). As long as there are no rich entrepreneurs, landowners cannot be completely free. Hence we may wonder whether the 'disposable class' is only an empty shell.[9] Under such conditions, one would waste time by trying to justify membership of this class according to land ownership. The impoverished landowner, for instance, must devote all his time and attention to the cultivation of his land. It is better to explain the behavioural logic of people who belong to the 'disposable class', for it includes not only landowners but also rich people who, without working, live on the revenues of their money.

> Wealthy though they be, the cultivating proprietor, the entrepreneur in agriculture, the manufacturer, the merchant cannot get involved either in warfare or magistracy without giving up the works which enable them to live and consequently diminishing the nation's revenues.–Only the proprietor who enjoys his revenue without working and the lender of money who draws interest on it can... engage in all kinds of occupations... listen to elevated motivations, such as glory, the desire for esteem, and the love of the public good. (Turgot, 1766a, p. 524, my translation)

The analysis of the effect the introduction of money has on the role played by landowners in economic activity may help us to clarify the vagueness regarding the content of the 'disposable class'. Although freed from productive activity and enjoying a constant income, landowners still have their place in Turgot's economics.

The introduction of money, lending at interest and landowners
The use of money produces a new acceleration in favour of the development of society (see Turgot, 1766b, p. 145). Indeed, the introduction of money contributes to the multiplication of sources of savings and the emergence of moneylenders.

In the first place, we wish to explain Turgot's statement – which appears just before the introduction of the hypothesis on the use of gold and silver in commerce – that 'there is another way of being wealthy without working and without possessing land' (ibid, p. 134). This way is undoubtedly to possess money and lend it at interest. Turgot made a distinction between, on the one hand, the means 'to be wealthy', that is, the different forms of possessing wealth (landed estate, working capital and capital in the form of money), and, on the other hand, the means 'to become wealthy', that is, the appropriation of land and thrift. Nevertheless, after the full occupation of land and the introduction of money, thrift becomes the only way to become wealthy, since all land has an owner and thus natural advances have a price:

> In the present state of things, *when all the land is occupied*, there is only *one way to become wealthy*, and that is to possess or to obtain for oneself, by whatever means, a revenue or annual profit over and above what is absolutely necessary for one's subsistence, and to put this surplus into reserve each year in order to create a capital, by means of which one may obtain an increase in revenue or annual profit, which may again be saved and converted into capital. (ibid., p. 169; my italics)

So, when Turgot set out to analyse the origin of this other way of being rich and its link with the 'system of the distribution of wealth', his purpose was first to explain the origin of the 'possessors of money or capitals' and the decision some of them made to lend their money at interest instead of buying land or investing in enterprises; then, to emphasize the similarities between lending at interest and the purchase of land, when compared with investment; finally, to point out that the introduction of money did not really question the social division between the working classes and the 'disposable class'.

Now that they receive their revenue in the form of money, landowners can save part of it more easily. At any rate, they no longer need to invest this surplus in the form of advances in order to give it a 'more durable nature', as they did in society of the earliest times. The monetary form of savings gives more freedom as far as their use is concerned. Besides, the working classes are able to save due to imperfect competition (see ibid., p. 146). When dealing with the savings process, Turgot never alluded to anyone but the landowners and the working classes. This implies that both the possessors of money and moneylenders come from the model of society previously described, that is, from one of its associated socioeconomic classes (landowners, cultivators and artisans). Turgot clearly explained this process:

> Anyone who, whether in the form of revenue from his land, or of wages for his labour or his industry, receives each year more value than he needs to spend, can put this surplus into reserve and accumulate it: these accumulated values are what is called *a capital*. (ibid., p. 150)

On the other hand, he stated: 'Today, loans can only be placed in large quantities. An artisan is inconvenienced by his small savings; they are sterile for him until they become large enough to be placed on loan' (1770e, p. 162).

Due to the fact that the banking system is not very well organized, wage-earners cannot give their low savings to borrowers. Moreover:

> Those who are industrious and like work but have no capital at all, or who do not have enough for the enterprises which they want to establish, have no difficulty in deciding to give up to the Possessors of capitals or money who are willing to entrust them with it, a portion of the profits which they expect to get in over and above the return of their advances. (Turgot, 1766b, pp. 159–60)

Wage-earners are more interested in investing in enterprises than in lending at interest. Only landowners may become moneylenders, therefore. Another idea strengthens this latter point. Turgot described moneylenders as free as far as their person is concerned.[10] However, there seems no reason why they would not work. Turgot even sounds paradoxical when he asserts that the 'capitalist lender of money ought to be considered as one who trades in a commodity which is absolutely necessary for the production of wealth'.[11] Nonetheless, this makes sense, for Turgot considered that lenders' resources did not result from labour (the 'trade in money'), but from an exclusive right – similar to a title deed on land – to possess and dispose of money. Thus the most appropriate way to reveal the nature of lending at interest is to compare the purchase/sale of the use of money with that of the use of a leased estate (see ibid., p. 160). This results in establishing the point that their two incomes are equivalent (ibid., p. 150).[12] Behind the purchase of land and lending at interest there is not only a similar reality – the title deed which guarantees a fixed money income – but also the same behaviour which favours the preservation of capital more than its increase. This is why, 'among the wealthy, all those who are sensible limit themselves to spending their revenue, and take great care not to break into their capitals' (ibid., p. 169). Besides, Turgot considered moneylenders to be free because, unlike the working classes, the effort they may make is not required to sustain and nourish them. Being rich, lenders of money are not subject to the rigours of life.

Moreover, freedom is the main motive which drives landlords when their level of consumption is satisfactory. As far as landowners' well-being is concerned, lending at interest always represents a better solution than any methods of drawing a revenue from the land. Indeed, 'the man who lends his money at interest enjoys it even more peaceably and freely than the possessor of land' (ibid., p. 171).

In addition to the above, we know about Turgot's *political geography* which contrasted the poor French provinces and the rich ones. The interest rate is higher in the poorest part of the kingdom, where capital available for loan transactions is very scarce, just where landowners are the poorest, their income the least assured, the making of advances their fate. In these regions the shortage of moneylenders is related to the lack of wealthy landowners.

Although analytically moneylenders come from the class of landowners, it is quite obvious that, after a while – when most of their wealth consists of claims – they become a different socioeconomic class, like those 'merchants of money' whose absence the *Paper on Lending at Interest* (Turgot, 1770e) pointed out with regret. For proof that Turgot does not exclude the idea that the formation and the distribution of wealth might affect the social structure, we can recall the question he asked of two Chinese people about their country:

> It is asked whether the wealth of most [families enjoying their wealth without working] consist either of landed estates or money lent at interest. (1766a, p. 525; my translation)

Furthermore, the interest drawn by the moneylender 'is not disposable in this sense, that the State can without any disadvantage appropriate part of it for its own needs' (Turgot, 1766b, p. 178). This point is crucial, for it emphasizes the main difference between the landlord and the moneylender. Due to the origin of his capital (thrift) the moneylender, just as the other 'possessors of money' (in fact, those who possess capital in the form of money), cannot be burdened with taxes because the interest on his loan is 'the very condition of the loan' (ibid., p. 179). In a society where the constitution of capital lies only in the efforts people make to save on their consumption, no one will accept the abandonment of part of the income the use of one's capital is supposed to yield. That not only landlords but also the working classes are able to amass savings by their own exertions means everyone considers the 'exchanges of Commerce from a new point of view' (ibid., p. 144). From now on, there is no longer room for any form of wealth that one has never purchased but can sell. The society of the earliest times and capitalist society are worlds apart. Nonetheless, the fact that thrift only reproduces in a different form the social division between the working classes (capitalist entrepreneurs and workmen) and the 'disposable class' (moneylenders and landowners) suggests that commercial society is still a long way off.

III. The capitalist entrepreneur's behaviour
As society evolves, capitalist entrepreneurs take over from proprietor-entrepreneurs. The ability the former have to make advances and the landowners' desire to be freer give rise to this evolution. Capitalist entrepreneurs' aptitudes ('intelligence') contribute both to the constitution of their capital and to the management of the enterprise.

From the proprietor-entrepreneur to the capitalist entrepreneur
In the society of the earliest times, the proprietor's investments, both in agriculture and industry, were modest. The amount of these investments was related to the proprietor's needs. In other words, the landlord invested enough to make possible a level of outcome which was not intended to be sold on the marketplace. The emergence of capitalist entrepreneurs is the effect of an important innovation – the introduction of money – on a secular process, 'the economy of the centuries which have followed one another since man began to cultivate the land' (Turgot, 1766b, p. 181). This process takes time, at least as much time as working classes need in order to constitute savings which can be changed into capital. It is very well described in the *Sixième Lettre*

sur le commerce des grains, wherein Turgot tried to measure the effect of free market on the *métayers'* propensity to save. First, Turgot gave some explanations of the situation of poor provinces. In so doing he specified the conditions under which the transition from 'small-scale cultivation' to 'large-scale cultivation' is possible:

> In those provinces [of small-scale cultivation], cultivation never was lucrative enough to enable poor *métayers* ... to amass enough capitals and make the advances involved in cultivation. (Turgot, 1770b, p. 310; my translation)

By increasing the revenue of land, the free trade of grain will contribute to changing *métayers* into capitalist entrepreneurs:

> They [*métayers*] will progressively form a small capital (made of livestock) which, while increasing, will enable them to make the advances involved in cultivation and thus to cultivate land for their own sake.... As a result, *métayers* will end up farmers.... This revolution might be slow. (ibid., p. 311; my translation)

Yet once this revolution has started, things can only quicken because the higher the number of farmers, the keener the competition between them. So landowners will more easily find farmers to turn their land to account, and tenant farming will progressively gain on the *métayer* system. The enrichment which stems from the increase of the surplus must necessarily benefit industrial workers. Some of them will save money on their wages and become capitalist entrepreneurs. So the 'possessors of large capitals' who become entrepreneurs are the *heirs* to the working-class members who have succeeded in amassing capital, thanks to their thrift and labour. Their emergence can logically be explained on the basis of Turgot's first model of society. That the entrepreneur function exists from the earliest times is unquestionable. Nevertheless, Turgot thinks that the landowner only fulfils it because his needs compel him to. Consequently, he does it imperfectly:

> [T]he proprietor does not obtain profits from his enterprise comparable to those of the *farmer*. The *farmer* controls cultivation himself with care and skill; the proprietor is forced to trust his whole stock to a person who can be negligent or a cheat and who can never make a suitable return. (Turgot, 1767a, p. 29).

Turgot's comparison helps us understand better the contrast between the capitalist entrepreneur's behaviour and that of the proprietor-entrepreneur. The entrepreneur can only fulfil his function well when he is totally involved in the management of his business. Participating in public affairs and overseeing one's own interests are incompatible. Consequently, landowners are not good entrepreneurs, as compared to capitalist entrepreneurs, 'devoting themselves exclusively to their enterprises, occupied in increasing their fortunes and diverted by their work from costly amusements and passions' (Turgot, 1766b, p. 181). Moreover, capitalist entrepreneurs remain in contact with the actual conditions of business so that they can manage their enterprises more efficiently. Turgot's 'maxim, that in general every man knows his own interest better than another to whom it is of no concern' (1759, p. 26) does not really apply to the proprietor-entrepreneur whose interest is divided between public affairs and the management of his business. Furthermore, the landowner's decision to quit cultivating land is irreversible. It entails that he can no longer master the *savoir-faire* which is the prerequisite of any work. Now, the knowledge the proprietor-entrepreneur possesses is not enough to guarantee that the best decision will be made. The lowness of his investment is the expression of a dilemma. The making of advances involves management and supervision. It is reasonable not to expect landowners to invest a lot, since they want to free themselves from productive tasks. Otherwise, they would have to pay more attention to the allocation of their expenses of production. In the provinces of small-scale cultivation ' [l] andlords...only make advances because they cannot do otherwise' (Turgot, 1767a, p. 30).

Because of the distinction between the landowner and the cultivator, a significant modification takes place in agricultural society: the 'net product' no longer directly or exclusively depends on the husbandman's labour. Nothing guarantees that those who are in charge of agricultural labour will do it with as much zeal as those who take account of their interest in the appropriation of produce. As soon as the landowner no longer directly controls the execution of work, he must formulate instructions on its conditions and oversee their application. Consequently, the function of instruction appears, with a double meaning: the passing on of the knowledge needed for carrying out the work; the command which comes from the necessity to obey the landowner's or his representative's directions. This function proceeds from a more general one which is the formation of advances. However, it must not be assimilated to it, for the entrepreneur may entrust the land to a worker who will act as overseer. Once again, one must point out that the more the entrepreneur is involved in public affairs, the less he will check on the application of his instructions.

Actually, Turgot distinguished between two opposite capitalist behaviours which referred respectively to capitalist entrepreneurs and landowners. The latter want to stop working and still receive a fixed income which guarantees a certain level of wealth. The former try to manage the enterprise with 'intelligence' so that they get richer, even if its income is uncertain.

The capitalist entrepreneur's 'intelligence'

'Intelligence' does not only apply to one class of economic agents. In general, it is associated with intellectual abilities, and it contrasts with 'indolence'. In the first place, the opposition is between those who are able to learn by experience and those who 'usually cannot read nor write, and who cannot be relied on as far as their intelligence and their probity are concerned' (Turgot, 1764, p. 336; my translation). However, as intelligence represents a body of abilities inherited from specific experience, it is more or less efficient, depending on whether it adapts more or less correctly to the manner in which society operates. The intelligence of the capitalist entrepreneurs consists of the *savoir-faire*, calculation abilities and the capital they possess.

Due to the fact that he belongs to the working classes, the capitalist-entrepreneur can accumulate both the information and the *savoir-faire* which are necessary to manage the enterprise. This process of learning is the condition of the knowledge of one's own interest. This *savoir-faire* is the product of a 'long experience which is acquired only by working continuously and on a great quantity of materials' (Turgot, 1766b, p. 120). All enterprises need *savoir-faire*. This is why Turgot put forward objections to the *corvée*. This system is inefficient, at least as regards works which require some specific knowledge. People used in the *corvée* are not stupid: they simply have occupations whose rules are different. Accordingly, the productivity of their labour is very low.

The second ability the capitalist entrepreneur possesses comes from his experience as a wage-earner. Then his wage was limited to what was necessary for his subsistence. Having to survive during bad years, the workman had to be thrifty. Without savings, he could not satisfy his basic needs.[13] Both the uncertainty of his future income and fear of 'accident' urged him to evaluate what he could rely on (calculation). Similarly, the certainty of future needs induced him to limit his everyday consumption to the bare essential needs. So the capitalist entrepreneur's aptitudes for thrift and calculation originate in his fear for the future. This economic agent applies indifferently these aptitudes to the expenses of production of the enterprise, thereby contributing to its success. According to Turgot, the more 'intelligent' the management of the enterprise, the higher the profitability of the capital.[14] This implies both the preliminary calculation of costs and profits and thrift – which takes part in the realization of the entrepreneur's expectations. Although necessary, the calculation is not infallible. It is necessary because the entrepreneur will only invest when he is sure of the profitability of his activity. Besides, all capitalist entrepreneurs make calculations, that is, farmers, industrial entrepreneurs and merchants.[15] The calculation may be erroneous. Experience guarantees its correctness only if the entrepreneur makes his evaluations according to information he learned from past experience. Entrepreneurs integrate into their speculations only foreseeable risks. They fear investing in enterprises for which they lack references.[16] In spite of imperfect calculations, the farmer-entrepreneur has the advantage when negotiating with the landowner:

> [The farmer] precisely knows the outgoings and receipts of his concern. Consequently, he knows what share of his benefit he can give up to the landlord without putting in danger his capital nor the interest on his advances nor the profit he wants to keep. However, he will not let the landlord into the secret and the latter has no means to find out about these details with some certainty. (Turgot, 1770b, p. 305; my translation)

At last, the possession of capital is the expression of the entrepreneur's aptitudes. This is why Turgot considered that enterprises which were financed on borrowed funds were less likely to be successful:

> The majority of agricultural entrepreneurs borrow little, and scarcely any of them seek to turn to account anything but their own funds. The entrepreneurs in other fields of activity, who want to consolidate their fortunes, also try to achieve the same position; and, unless they are very able, those who base their enterprises on borrowed funds run a great risk of failing. (Turgot, 1766b, p. 181)

Turgot did not mean that capitalist entrepreneurs did not borrow at all. He simply stressed the fact that the larger the capital the entrepreneur possessed, the more efficient his enterprise. This capital shows the entrepreneur's ability to save on his expenses and to manage the enterprise. Conversely, those who have no capital at all (and who, therefore, are unable to save and calculate) cannot be successful in their enterprise. Within the working classes, intelligence has degrees. The possession of capital is the expression of the capitalist entrepreneur's ability to confine himself to commitments based on his estimates. Moreover, this capital creates a social effect. The larger the capitalist entrepreneur's personal credit, the more easily he can borrow money. His personal credit depends on capital he possesses. On the one hand, this capital may be used as real guarantee; on the other hand, it is a 'sign' lenders of money can use in order to estimate the capitalist entrepreneur's solvency.[17] This brings about disparities in borrowing conditions:

> Money on loan does not have the same price, either for all men or at all times, because in lending, money is paid for with a *promise* only, and because, if the money of all buyers looks the same, the promises of all the borrowers are not the same. (Turgot, 1770e, p. 161)

By showing his title deeds as if they were titles of nobility, the capitalist entrepreneur not only accesses more easily the capital market but also obtains lower rates than other borrowers. Capitalist entrepreneurs possess capital because they are successful. They are successful because they possess capital.

Conclusion
By analysing the transition from society of the earliest times to a society which is not quite capitalist, Turgot tried to shed light on the social conditions of

economic functions. These functions constitute the stable core from which the working of the society can be understood at a certain time. On the other hand social progress results from the evolution in the forms of wealth, from landed wealth to monetary wealth. Nonetheless, Turgot did not consider the relationship between the formation and distribution of wealth, and the social structure as a one-way relationship. He was interested not only in analysing the economic determinants of social change but also in integrating deterministic elements regarding social relations – the different relationships people have with needs – in the explanation of economic behaviours. This is why, despite the emergence of both the capitalist entrepreneurs and moneylenders, Turgot maintained the social division between the 'disposable class' and working classes. No doubt, social progress took time.

Historically speaking, Turgot's analysis refers to a shift of the 'balance of power' in French society. Turgot had perfectly understood that in the society he described the opposition was between those who were attached to the preservation of their capital and those who wanted it to increase, between capitalists themselves. It was no longer an opposition between landed and moneyed interests. It was not yet an opposition between the owners of the means of production and workers. It was simply an opposition between rentiers and capitalist entrepreneurs. Perhaps we should consider it differently from a temporary form of social relations just before the capitalist society. In this case, Turgot gives us a very penetrating analysis of the relationships between the uses of capital and the conditions of its formation.

Acknowledgements

I thank André Lapidus for encouragement, advice and criticism. Thanks go as well to Joël Ravix and Arnaud Berthoud for their thorough comments on an earlier draft, and to the anonymous referee. This paper is part of a larger research for which the author has received the support of the French Ministry of Foreign Affairs (Lavoisier programme). Any errors are mine alone.

Notes

1. Ronald Meek perfectly illustrated this reading: 'This system [of economic theory] cannot be fully understood...without an appreciation of the way in which its leading propositions were connected with Turgot's historical and sociological theories' (1973, p. 15).

    Peter Groenewegen confirmed this view: 'The systematic attempt to explain general progress by stages from hunters, shepherds, farmers to a commercial society to a large extent provides the basis on which Turgot constructed his analysis of the production and distribution of wealth in the *Reflections*' (1987, p. 709).
2. This theory describes the development of society as a series of 'stages', each of which is linked to a mode of subsistence (hunting, pasturage, agriculture and commerce). On this topic, one may refer to R. Meek (1971).
3. Roberto Finzi (1982, p. 116) expressed the most sceptical judgement as to the existence of an analysis of commercial society in the *Reflections*. According to R. Meek (1973, p. 20): 'What Turgot did, in effect, was to accept the view...that after the hunting, pastoral, and agricultural stages society proceeded to a fourth stage – the so-called "commercial" stage'. Joël Ravix and Paul-Marie Romani (1984, p. 116) observed that the '*Reflections* deals mainly with the analysis of this fourth "stage"' (my translation).

4. See R. Meek (1973, p. 33).
5. Turgot wrote: 'In the natural constitution of society, there are only two really distinct orders, the distinction of which is clear, definite and leads to different rights: the order of proprietors and the non-proprietors' (1771, p. 521; my translation).
6. Finzi notes that the inequality in the division of land is a 'fact which is both anterior and posterior to the institution of property' (Finzi, 1981, p. 12; my translation).
7. This argumentation reminds one of Locke, who expressed the concept of an initial divine gift: 'God gave the world to men in common' (1946, p. 18).
8. According to Turgot, '[These] two last methods of cultivation are those most generally used: that is, cultivation by *Métayers* in poor countries, and cultivation by Farmers in more wealthy countries' (Turgot, 1766b, p. 134).
9. Jean-Paul de Gaudemar proposed an original interpretation of the concept of 'disposable class' in Turgot. He suggested that this class 'might have a mainly symbolic content'. The consequence would be that this 'class is primarily that of power, for it takes the place of power' (1983, p. 195; my translation).
10. There is no doubt as to the moneylenders' freedom. Many statements attest it. For example, 'Of all the employments of money, that which requires the least effort on the part of the capitalists, is lending at interest' (Turgot, 1767b, p. 116). Or, 'The lender of money . . . has nothing to do' (Turgot, 1766b, p. 178).
11. Turgot, 1766b, p. 178. Likewise, 'The loan at interest is nothing at all but a trading transaction in which the Lender is a man who sells the use of his money, and the Borrower a man who buys it' (ibid., p. 160).
12. J. Ravix & P.-M. Romani emphasized the fact that the 'five methods of employing capital (purchase of a landed estate, capital advances in agricultural, industrial and commercial enterprises, and lending at interest) led to the appearance of a dichotomy as 'both the purchase of a landed estate and lending at interest neither induce the transformation of "capitals" into "advances" nor even, more generally, the purchase of commodities' (1985, p. 157; my translation). Hence they identified two different circulations, 'The first is obviously that of the commodities which Turgot calls the 'circulation of money', where money is only used as a means of payment. The second is what Turgot calls the 'trade in money', and corresponds to financial circulation. It does not only include lending at interest, that is, the financing through credit, but also the purchase of land' (pp. 157–8; my translation).
13. Turgot drew his reader's attention on what is necessary for subsistence: 'It should not be thought . . . that this necessity is thus reduced to the essentials for avoiding starvation to such an extent, that nothing remains outside it, which these men may have at their command either to obtain some little luxuries, or, if they are thrifty, to create a little movable fund which becomes their resort in unforeseen cases of sickness, or times of high prices, or unemployment' (1770a, p. 168). To be more specific, 'It is necessary that the workman should draw a certain profit in order to meet unexpected expenses and raise his family' (Turgot, 1767c, p. 663; my translation).
14. Regarding cultivation, 'The expenses of agriculture consist in giving the soil such preparation as is most likely to make it fruitful. Now, the outcome of these preparations, which determines the product, is by no means proportioned to the expenditure: *the knowledge of the cultivator renders the same amount of expenditure more or less productive*, depending on the extent to which his method of applying it is appropriate to the nature of the soil and all the seasonal factors' (Turgot, 1767b, p. 11; my italics).
15. See Turgot, 1766b, pp. 153–4 and 157.
16. Turgot considered that the 'entrepreneurs, when dealing with a new business which scope they do not know about yet, are particularly afraid of making agreements' (Turgot, 1765, p. 424; my translation).
17. Indeed, Turgot wrote: 'Although the interest cannot be the same in all situations, there is however an interest which very little varies – at least in a short period of time – namely: the interest on money placed with nearly full guarantee, such as a sound mortgage, or the solvency of some merchants whose wealth, wisdom and probity are widely acknowledged' (Turgot, 1770d, p. 192; my translation).

References

Turgot's writings

1753–4. *Sur la géographie politique*, in Schelle (1913–23), Vol. I.

1759. *In Praise of Gournay*, trans. in Groenewegen (1977).

1764. *Lettre au Contrôleur général (L'Averdy) exposant en détail le plan de rachat [de la corvée des chemins]* (30 July), in Schelle (1913–23), Vol. II.

1765. *Lettre au contrôleur général (L'Averdy) sur l'abolition de la corvée pour le transport des équipages* (19 April), in Schelle (1913–23), Vol. II.

1766a. *Questions sur la Chine adressées à deux Chinois*, in Schelle (1913–23), Vol. II.

1766b. *Reflections on the Formation and the Distribution of Wealth*, trans. in Meek (1973).

1767a. *Des Caractères de la grande et de la petite culture*, in Schelle (1913–23), Vol II, trans. in Groenewegen (1983).

1767b. *Observations on a Paper by Saint-Péravy on the Subject of Indirect Taxation*, trans. in Groenewegen (1977).

1767c. *Lettre à Hume* (25 March), in Schelle (1913–23), Vol. II.

1770a. *Fifth Letter on the Grain Trade* (14 November), extracts trans. in Groenewegen (1977).

1770b. *Sixième Lettre au contrôleur général (abbé Terray) sur le commerce des grains* (27 November), in Schelle (1913–23), Vol. III.

1770c. *Septième Lettre au contrôleur général (abbé Terray) sur le commerce des grains* (2 December), in Schelle (1913–23), Vol. III.

1770d. *Mémoire sur les prêts d'argent*, in Schelle (1913–23), Vol. III.

1770e. *Paper on Lending at Interest*, extracts trans. in Groenewegen (1977).

1770f. *Ordonnance imposant aux propriétaires de nourrir leurs métayers jusqu'à la récolte* (28 February), in Schelle (1913–23), Vol. III.

1771. *Lettre à Condorcet* (16 July), in Schelle (1913–23), Vol. III.

1776. *Édit de suppression [des corvées]*, in Schelle (1913–23), Vol. V.

Secondary sources

Finzi, R. (1981), 'Turgot, l'histoire et l'économie: "Nécessité" de l'économie politique? "Historicité" des lois économiques?', in C. Bordes and J. Morange (eds), *Turgot, économiste et administrateur*, Paris: PUF.

Finzi, R. (1982), 'The Theory of Historical Stages in Turgot and Quesnay: a Few Comparisons', *Keizai Kenkyu*, 33 (2) (April), pp. 109–18.

Gaudemar, J.-P de (1983), 'La Régulation despotique – Un commentaire du Tableau économique de Quesnay', *Revue d'économie politique*, 93 (2) (March–April), pp. 177–96.

Groenewegen, P.D. (1977), *The Economics of A.R.J. Turgot*, The Hague: Martinus Nijhoff.

Groenewegen, P.D. (ed.) (1983), *Quesnay, Farmers 1756 and Turgot, Sur la grande et la petite culture, 1766*, Reprints of Economics Classics, Sydney: University of Sydney.

Groenewegen, P.D. (1987), 'Turgot, Anne Robert Jacques, Baron de L'Aulne (1727–1781)', in J. Eatwell, Murray Milgate and P. Newman (eds), *The New Palgrave: A Dictionary of Economics*, Vol. IV, New York: Stockton Press.

Locke, J. (1946), *The Second Treatise of Civil Government and a Letter concerning Toleration*, ed. J.W. Gough. Oxford: Basil Blackwell.

Meek, R.M. (1971), 'Smith, Turgot, and the "Four Stages" Theory', *History of Political Economy*, 3 (1) (Spring), pp. 9–27.

Meek, R. (ed.) (1973), *Turgot, on Progress, Sociology and Economics*, Cambridge: Cambridge University Press.

Ravix, J. and Romani, P.-M. (1984), 'L'Idée de progrès comme fondement des analyses économiques de Turgot', *Économies et Sociétés*, 18 (1), pp. 97–118.

Ravix, J. and Romani, P.-M. (1985), 'Argent, "capital" et reproduction chez Turgot', in R. Arena et al., *Production, circulation et monnaie*, Paris: PUF.

Schelle, G. (1913–23), *Œuvre de Turgot et documents le concernant*, 5 vols, Paris: Alcan.

8 *Noli me tangere*: Platonic ideas in Quesnay's *Tableau Economique*
S. Zin Bae

Introduction
The Marquis de Mirabeau, in his eloquent *Eloge*, compared his Master to Socrates and placed the father of economics even higher in heaven than the father of philosophy, because the philosopher had left only doubtful sayings whereas the economist had handed down many thoughtful writings to posterity. To this devoted pupil the Physiocrat was another Confucius and Prometheus. However dithyrambic it may seem, all economists – from Smith to Marx, from Walras to Leontief – look up to François Quesnay as one of the greatest figures of their science. Yet the full force of the *Tableau Economique* has been concealed until today, as Linguet already avowed with cynicism, under the 'metaphysical hieroglyphic'.

In the conviction that the meaning and significance of Quesnay's economic thought can best be interpreted via a comparison with the pre-Physiocratic vision of the world, not with contemporary theories which have proliferated from an obscurity of the founder of economics, the present paper explores the *physis-kratos* as a continuity of ancient ideas, and in the light of what Professor S.T. Lowry calls the 'administrative tradition' (1987, especially pp. 16–29).

It is concluded that, as opposed to the market-oriented interpretations considering Physiocracy in the framework of biological circulatory liberalism and of scholastic *lex naturalis jus naturale*, Quesnay's *Tableau Economique* is based on a ground plan of Plato's *Republic*. Not only is its famous zigzag congruous with the Euclidean reconstruction of the Pythagorean *ancien régime* being demolished by the alogical relativism of mercantilistic exchange, but the Physiocrat's hostility towards the bullionism can also be compared with the Philosopher's repugnance to the chrematistic, or money-maker's, oligarchy.

I *Bon prix* and the Platonic theory of proportion
There is a constitutional myth in economics that François Quesnay's political economy is that of Madame de Pompadour's doctor; that economic science sprang from a physiologist's head greatly inspired by Harvey's discovery of blood circulation; and that, therefore, the *Tableau Economique* is no more than an anatomical chart defending the free circulation of goods in the political body. To let the organism be in a healthful state for which 'the wisdom of

nature has fortunately made ample provision' (*Wealth of Nations*, Bk. IV, ch. 9, p. 638), it would be the perfect liberty, or the *laissez-faire* policies coloured in the *Tableau*, which encourage merchant-manufacturers' natural drive for gain and the natural progress of a nation towards wealth and prosperity. This naturalistic optimism, laying more stress on individual economic activities than those of the State, returns to Aristotle's biological concept of the household, or *oikonomia*, removed from the setting of *politeia*. And why did the Physiocrat call his doctrine the *Œconomie politique*?

In so far as Quesnay's political economy is considered as a revolutionary synthesis of *politeia* and *oikonomia*, it should be asserted that the Physiocratic economy no longer stayed in the world of the Aristotelian-Scholastic cosmos – the world of qualities and of differentiated place-continuum, which was the dominant ideology in feudal society – but disappeared, destroyed by the revived Platonic world of quantities and of geometric coherence.[1] The economic problem henceforth does not concern a prince's treasury nor a merchant's business. That is just a matter of the State, *the* subject of study for the Guardians. And the Thomist's incomprehensible justification of deistic market functions, based on the Aristotelian *locus naturalis*, shall be thrown up for the sake of the physical science of economy.

It is in this sense that Dupont de Nemours edited Quesnay's works under the title of *Physiocratie*, agreeably to his teacher's epigraph, *Ex natura jus ordo & leges*. He did not translate *natura* as *nomos*, but transliterated it into *physis* – the nature of material things, not the spontaneous order of nature.

One of the anti-naturalistic concepts of the economy is Quesnay's theory of the *bon prix*. In his formulation we can see a Platonic transcendental method, a unique method which deserves to be called 'theory', in contrast to a mere collection of the 'fact' of demand and supply. The following table presents the 'empirical data' of the variation in corn price drawn by Quesnay (*Grains*, INED, p. 462).

Price of corn

Year	Quantity	Price	Income	Cost
Abundant	7 setiers	10 livres	70 livres	60 livres
Good	6	12	72	60
Normal	5	15	75	60
Poor	4	20	80	60
Bad	3	30	90	60
Total	25	87	387	300

From this table, we know that the income per arpent (a French land measure)

(r) is a function of two variables, the quantity of production per arpent (q) and the price per setier (French measure for grain) (p), so that we have $r = p \cdot q$. When we choose the *nominal* value of the income as a measure of wealth, the relation (r,(p,q)) directly contradicts what we believe and expect: if we have a good harvest thanks to our great effort, its return as a social measure *should be* good or better, otherwise, why should we work harder?

Contrary to common belief, the table tells another paradoxical fact. Considering the cost terms (c) in the table above, we can rewrite the income function as follows: $n = p \cdot q - c^*$, where (n) indicates the net money income. It should be noted that the cost terms given by Quesnay are *invariable*, though measured in a monetary unit which must be variable corresponding to the relative quantity of money. So the table appears to be simply fallacious. However, the invariability of cost in the Physiocratic production has an interesting facet which could be explained as follows: (1) The production cost is strictly composed of the products measured in a physical unit. To produce 5 units of corn, one needs 2 units of seed corn, not 2 units of silver. Consequently, in the agricultural mode of production where the metamorphosis of money (and of capital) is restricted, the input-product should be reserved in the first place (Quesnay called it 'reprise', *Analyse*, INED, p. 798). (2) It follows that this reserved seed corn, or *reprise*, should not enter the market price mechanism; only the *produit net* could participate in price determination. Quesnay distinguished these two, contrasting 'a half which enters into trade' with the other half of products, 'which is not traded...and which should not enter into the calculation of price changes' ((*Premier*) *Problème économique*, INED, pp. 680–2). Since this part should not enter the market nor affect the price, Quesnay thought the cost to be invariable as opposed to the variable price. He had to suppose then two prices (all measured in a monetary unit) for the same product.

Quesnay's adoption of two different measures in the same calculation shows that he was no more able to explain how the *avance* measured in monetary terms was transformed into the *reprise* in physical terms. Nonetheless it shows the fact that 'a quantity of silver cannot *per se* produce a quantity of corn'. The silver must be exchanged with the labour, a direct productive power. But Quesnay's truism did not consider this delicate problem of the production subject susceptible to a long controversy (in Smith–Marx's theory of labour value).

What the Physiocrat devoted himself to by analysing market prices, and that is succinctly expressed in his famous words: 'Abundance & valuelessness does not equal wealth. Scarcity & dearness equals poverty. Abundance & dearness is opulence' (*Extrait*, MK, p. 9), is a fatal contradiction in the market price mechanism, in which all products are compulsorily measured in *nominal* values. But when we take the *physical* quantity of agricultural production as a measure of wealth, the economy will have another aspect closer to reality. So the table above does not present a *relation* between variables, but rather *images* of a variable projected differently: a nominal value of income gives a deformed *image* of the economy, while the physical quantity of production is thought of as the *form* or *idea* of the true economy. Which unit of measure should a 'true economist' rely upon?

Such a contradiction in exchange mechanism, which reveals not only an epistemological ambivalence but an ideological antagonism too, had already been stated in Plato's dialogues. He remarked on the failure of Pythagorean arithmetic equalization in exchange life: 'The arithmeticians do precipitously the same calculation of two units quantitatively unequal, for example, of two arms, two cows, or two things one of which might be the smallest and the largest thing in the world' (*Philebus*, 56d).[2] In the *Republic*, Plato was confronted with the problem of inequity in exchanges, which would be the problem of justice in general, and described how 'civilized society' with its structurally complicated economy becomes 'luxurious and fevered' in contrast to the 'primitive society' which is 'true and healthy' (372a–374d). He asserted that the 'simplest form of society' as such is 'truly just', for it is constituted by 'men's mutual needs'. However, as far as society is concerned with only men's natural insufficiency, i.e., physical subsistence, it is 'not a society but a community of pigs' (372d). In response to Glaucon's hedonistic protest, the historical Socrates had to introduce 'gold and ivory' into the standard of living of society. But inevitably 'justice and injustice' arise from this non-subsistential need for 'luxury' and from its exchange with subsistence (371e). The equalization of not easily equalizable elements, 'food, ivory, and gold', is then required. 'With our new luxuries we shall need doctors too, far more than we did before' (373d).

A solution to this dilemma is, of course, subjective evaluation in exchange, and an ontological importance must be accorded individually to the evaluator rather than to the evaluated. This means that things have no predetermined value *before* they are brought into the evaluation process, i.e., exchanges. Yet if they are conceivable only in the realm of Becoming, then a science of Being will be impossible; there will be but a conjecture of Protagorean relativism or Peripatetic probabilism that Plato's *noesis* repudiates.

Like Plato, Quesnay could not content himself with uncertain price formation in the relativistic market. Rather he supposed a variety of the 'fixed price', predetermined outside the market. To evaluate it from the view of the State's necessity, he did not forge a stochastic equation between the form and the image, like a modern model, $p = f(q) + \epsilon$, that might be replaced for the 'true price' unknown.[3] Neglecting the error term which is but a probabilist's ignorance, the author of the *Evidence* established the *bon prix*, the parametrized average price by dividing prices *in toto*. Being a parameter, this invariable ratio (p*) must not distort the 'form and idea' of economic activities, and then, the work yields the fair crop, *proportional* to its productive effort (i.e., $n = p^* \cdot q - c^*$, whatever the quantity and the cost of production may be).

The values obtained from arithmetic operations such as summation and division are not numbers properly said in the Pythagorean immanentism of numbers. Though *every* number arrayed in the table may represent the things enumerated and reserve in itself a certain particularity which determines the things as they are, *the* value of the mathematical mean, transcending the particularities by totalization, will not permit arithmetic properties for each number. Inversely, every individual number stemming from the value of the mean appears to be diversified, according to its situation, but without changing its essence. Quesnay was convinced that intelligence could find such essential proportions, or *rapport essentiel*, submitted to the 'immutable law of all social phenomena' (cf. *Evidence*, INED, pp. 397–426).

II   *Tableau Economique* and distributive justice

Quesnay's *Tableau Economique* is another example of the Platonic reconstructions of political economy. The development of segments here, called 'zigzag', could be appreciated as a synthesis of two contradictory conceptions of economy: the one at first glance is geometric, which shows that the segment in every step is exactly proportional to the previous one, making a geometrical series as a whole; the other arithmetic, by which the segment in any step is perfectly equal to the corresponding one. The latter may describe the exchange between two parties, *as if* this phenomenon could be analysed to the infinitely small quantity of exchange between the *classe productive* and the *classe stérile*. It could be thought, conversely, because the total is a simple aggregation of the parts, that it is such an *infinitesimal exchange* between individuals that determines the economy as a whole. But the geometric development of the zigzag comprises in fact these individual exchanges, and demonstrates that exchanges are not independent (or natural) economic behaviour of individuals, but dependent on the 'primary behaviour' of the *classe des propriétaires*.

By geometric illustrations, Quesnay intended to show the evidence that '*all* economic activities are derived from *one* primary axiom'. This Euclidean axiomatic method though tautological does not mean a static view of the world. It expresses the constructiveness of the method. The proposition, 'A Nation is reduced to three classes of citizens: the productive class, the class of proprietors, and the sterile class' (*Analyse*, INED, p. 793) is a definition just in the same way as this mathematical example: 'A triangle consists of three sides'. But in contrast to Aristotelian syllogistic propositions, Euclidean definitions may be functional. If one believes an equilateral triangle or a triadic society to be 'ideal', one can *make* any copy congruent with 'the best' by using such and such a theorem.

The theorem or basic premiss in Quesnay's *Tableau* is the distinction between two orders of reality, and it is from this premiss that his economic analysis starts. His distinction, however, on the grounds of both dualism and dichotomy, is not categorical but hypothetical. That is why, in spite of its taxonomic presentation and the fact that Quesnay himself was a doctor, the *Tableau Economique* remains axiomatic, and says nothing about a syllogistic statism based on biological discrimination. Lacking categorical distinction drawn from nature, Quesnay's demarcation of 'productive' and 'sterile' would be obvious in hypothetical meaning only, but it has often proved to be an obscure problem, from Smith and Marx until the present day. So far as economics is considered as *lex parsimoniae*, of course, all problems should be reduced to this one: '*what is productive?*' There must be something productive and something that is not. Yet, '*how* can the productive be demarcated from the unproductive?'

Like Plato's dichotomy which reduces all things to oppositions, the Just and the Unjust, Good and Bad, the Soul and the Body, etc., Quesnay, by means of definition, divided economic men into two: the *classe productive* and the *classe stérile* as its opponent, and economic behaviours into the *dépense productive* and the *dépense stérile*. But since a distinction of one reality from others is impossible by reference to its intrinsic quality, a definition of externalized reality would imply an indefiniteness of this quality, which must not be inherent in itself but necessarily shifted on to outer realities. From this inner indefiniteness arises the conception of *interdependence*, which means, because indefiniteness is meaningless, a closedness of the global definition. Let us divide an economic activity into two, say productive expenditure (Cp) and non-productive or sterile expenditure (Cs). Then clearly, if and only if the global definition is closed, we will have a relation $C = Cp + Cs$, which, though merely definitional, appears to describe some functional interdependent relations, $Cp = C - Cs$, $Cs = C - Cp$, or more simply but meaningfully, $\alpha + \beta = 1$, where $\alpha = Cp/C$ and $\beta = Cs/C$.

This *prima facie* interdependence more importantly appears when the relation of exchange is associated with that between production and consumption. As the zigzag traces it, money expenditure (or purchase) for 'productive goods' *at a moment* (Cp_t) is determined by previous money income (C_{t-1}). Considering that only the production and the sales of products realize the income (in the Physiocratic economy, no stock is presupposed), consumption will be naturally connected to production. By definition, the revenue of the landlord *in a period* (R), uniquely composed of the rent, is the total sum of sales or productions made by the farmer during the period. It can be also represented by the summation of a geometrical series, $R = \Sigma C_t$, from which a 'solution' or a simplified equation in terms of the initial 'productive expenditure' can be formulated, i.e., $R = 1/(1 - \alpha) \cdot Cp^*$. Such an algebraic form of Quesnay's zigzag could demonstrate an obvious effect which anticipates very strikingly the Keynesian multiplier advocating the anti-*laissez-faire* policy that 'the happiest economic welfare could be attained only by the government's meticulous interventions'.

As always, such equations rest upon some *ad hoc* assumptions: (1) A specific production function is supposed, with its unlimited production possibility. That is, in contradiction to the definitional dichotomy, the space of economy must be *open-ended* and thus indeterminate; (2) There is a unique functional relation between production and 'productive expenditure', suggesting that the 'sterile class', though its existence is necessary, does not contribute to the 'real production'. There is no interdependence, but a strict dependence of the 'sterile class' on the 'productive class'; (3) The existence of the solution of equations which requires a *timeless* conception of Time, because the equations involve time-lagged variables not simultaneously resoluble. All these assumptions are implied in the zigzag, giving a picture of the economy self-adjusting harmoniously, though zigzagging temporarily, but progressing infinitely. One of Quesnay's ingenious contributions to economic analysis is that he rendered complex economic movements into one static *Tableau*.[4] By such simplification, he found that *a* solution of the equations would exist when $\alpha = 1/2$ (satisfying $Cp = Cs = 1/2 \cdot C'$, and $C = R = 2 \cdot Cp'$). In other words, when the proprietor spends 'half' of his revenue on 'food' and the other half on 'luxury', the Physiocratic system seems to have not only a unique solution with economic meanings but also an *equilibrium* which stabilizes the system.

By totalizing all exchange activities infinitely seriated, then by rendering them into a single function of the proprietor's wise economy, Quesnay could negate the oligarchic interdependence, and neglect the chrematistic exchange. Interdependence is eliminated mathematically and then annihilated socially. But it remains in figures, in the famous zigzag. these 'puzzling patterns of flows' suggest nonetheless a complete vision of the 'economic machine', not only a confusion which glorifies the achievement of Physiocratic theories as if all of them were founded upon empirical observations of the most fundamental phenomenon in economy, i.e., the flows of money and goods, but also an illusion of equilibrium that the total sum of the one side of the zigzag coincides perfectly with that of the counter side.

However, it is arguable that equilibrium is not a numerical identity endorsed by accounting: (1) As this is a *dynamic notion*, and an identity obtained by totalizing variables, annihilating the evolution of time, cannot be an equilibrium; (2) Equilibrium in exchange presupposes above all a *democratic process* respecting the 'invisible force' of participants, and to be realized concurrently between them. If, therefore, these criteria for validating the notion of equilibrium are acceptable as a method of approaching it, we can assert that Quesnay's dichotomy, and the solution inferred from it, is not the 'equilibrium analysis'. His conclusion that 'the medium situation in which the reproductive expenditure renews the same revenue from year to year' would take place 'when one-half of the proprietor's revenue has passed into the productive expenditure... and the other half is distributed to the sterile class' (*Explication*, MK, pp. i–iii), cannot have any logical validity. This is a repetition of the postulate, and a reduction of all analyses to that postulate, inferred by linguistic confusion, but in which the definitional dichotomy of qualities between 'productive' and 'sterile' has changed to the functional dichotomy of quantities that 'one-half of the productive expenditure' and 'one-half of the sterile expenditure' would make the 'best and most just' set of the unity.

The *Tableau Economique* is thus bound to reassert the idea of an ancient proverb, even in neutral language, the idea of the 'Happy Golden Mean' that Plato admired (*Republic*, 466b–c; *Laws*, 690d–691a): 'if [the Guardian] tires of the stability and security of the ideal life... and is impelled by extravagance into using his power to appropriate the wealth of the city, then surely he must learn the wisdom of Hesiod's saying that "the half is more than the whole".' Plato's warning against the misuse of prerogatives by the ruling class was revived by Quesnay, who repeated the words to the class of proprietors: 'It is also to ignorance that we should attribute the imprudent behaviour of proprietors who abuse the ascendancy of their farmers... by ruining their farmers, they destroy themselves, devastate their land' (*(Premier) Problème économique*, INED, p 869).

The first of all economic problems for Quesnay as for Plato crystallizes in an essentially ethical form, a deontology imposed on the ruling class, not that of every individual who constitutes society. Again, since these passages show clearly a negation of Mandeville's 'Grumbling Hive', where the 'Private Vices' are unconsciously metamorphosing into 'Public Benefits' through an amoralizing exchange mechanism, Quesnay's ethical equilibrium reveals his negation of the effects of economic interdependence in society. The Physiocratic version of the Hesiodean 'Happy Golden Mean' is not a Stoic prescription for atomic happiness; this is rather a Platonic politics geometrically calculated, which compels the class of proprietors to obey the 'laws of nature', or the 'economic laws'.

Quesnay's quotation from the *Republic*, 525b–c, manifests his aspiration for Platonic *logos*, or knowledge, concerning the idea and role of political sciences. 'It is thus required that we impose a law upon those who hold positions of responsibility in our Republic, by which they devote themselves to the science of calculation, to study it not superficially' (*Second Problème*, INED, p. 977). It is no more the vulgar *techne* of merchants' naturally given experience, but the *episteme* of 'the ministers guided by superior education' (*Extrait*, MK, p. 10n(b)) – like that of the Duc de Sully (1560–1641) under the reign of Henri IV – that can direct economy to opulence. 'This science is not confused here,' said Quesnay, 'with the trivial and specious science of financial operations whose aims are but the money stock of the Nation & the monetary movements resulting from traffic in money' (*ibid.*, p. 21). As Plato had emphasized the importance of training in geometry for the Guardians,[5] Quesnay did so by conferring on economics the status of the fundamental knowledge for administration.

Economics as *the* 'art of well-governing' is the main idea of Physiocracy. Its subject matter is how to establish distributive justice in society. Its study demands that the ruling class not only observe the best given order of distribution, but also submit all political interests to administrative efficiency in distribution, which entirely depends on a fatherly ruler's virtue. At this point the 'art' shows the Platonized influence of Confucianism (or that of patriarchal bureaucratism) on Quesnay. He was in fact greatly fascinated by Confucian patriarchism (*Despotisme de la Chine*, Oncken, p. 592 ff.; *Le droit naturel*, INED, p. 737). Furthermore, he substituted for the 'eldest member' of the Confucian patriarchy (and of the 'autocracy' that Plato called 'the obedience to accepted usage and "ancestral" law', *Laws*, 680a–b) the 'wisest member' of more complex society, and elaborated the elite despotism based on the aristocracy of personal talent (cf. *Despotisme de la Chine*, Oncken, pp. 638–9; Mercier de la Rivière, *L'ordre naturel et essentiel des sociétés politiques*, Daire, p. 471). To these elites who administer the State, like the Guardians in the *Republic*, the 'fundamental knowledge about the laws of the order of regular and annual reproduction and distribution of wealth are needed far more than ever' (*Le droit naturel*, INED, pp. 740–1).

III Friendly property and autarchy
Platonic 'distributive justice', which could be more rhetorically justified by geometry than arithmetic, backs up the main idea of the *Tableau Economique*. Emphasis on this kind of justice arises mainly from the frustration of social harmony. No conflict between subdivided factors, no justice in distribution would be required; the economy could be self-regulated and self-justified by forces immanent in individuals operating intersubjectively. Yet for Quesnay as for Plato, neither individuality nor interdependence could harmonize the chrematistic, or money-lover's, oligarchy. Such being the case, 'how can the economy work?'

However quasi-unanimously Quesnay's 'neglect of money' has been received, in sympathy with his extreme hostility towards mercantilistic bullionism, money was, *de facto et de jure*, the most important and the unique constituent of the Physiocratic economy. Even the exclusion of metal-money from Physiocracy could be interpreted as the reverse side of a theory of symbol-money. Only by symbolizing money, could Quesnay substitute the verbal equilibrium of the exchange system, and attain the stability of the distribution system. Already Plato had sterilized money in calling it *symbolon* (*Republic*, 371b) and strictly limited its role as the medium of exchange. Perhaps, as Schumpeter notes, 'such an occasional saying' does not justify the attribution to Plato of any definite view on the 'nature of money' (1954, p. 56). Nevertheless, in so far as money is an *invention* for fulfilling a need in the *Republic*, like the 'market' and the 'class of retailers', it has no nature but an assigned *function*. It is thus important to understand the *idea* and *role* of money rather than its ahistorically forged *nature*. The question: 'who runs the economy?' should thus be reformulated: 'what is the economic role of the class of proprietors?'

In contradistinction to the total inhibition of economic activities of the Guardians in Plato's *Republic*, Quesnay's *propriétaires* appear to play a decisive role as participants in the process of production. He speaks not only of Hesiod's virtue of parsimony, but also of the landlords' positive contribution to the economy. However, in fact as in theory, their role or position in the *Tableau* is not to act as 'land lenders' by whose 'land supply' production can be determined;[6] they are essentially a group of 'pure consumers' (or 'parasites' in Marxist terminology). It should be noticed here that a non-producer's consumption in the so-called 'exchange system', where appropriation by physical coercion is institutionally inhibited, can only be done via his dispensation of purchasing rights represented by money. But if it were possible to eliminate the interference of money from this process, then a 'pure relation' between exploitation and production would be exposed. It could be asserted that it is the structure of exploitation (or of consumption) that determines the structure of production rather than vice versa. This is a truism that can be proved simply: if a closed economy has a *produit net*, i.e. if it realizes more production than required for subsistence, the surplus must be at the proprietors' full disposal, so the transformation of subsistence surplus into non-subsistence goods depends entirely upon the final consumers' preference. A relative quantity of money paid for a particular non-subsistence commodity in this view is an index showing proprietors' actual preference for that commodity; the total quantity of money represents the maximum possibility of exploitation, or in a more moderate but misunderstandable term, the 'purchasing power'.

In order to keep the maximum power over all the *produit net* in the hand of the proprietors and, therefore, to keep the stability of the State against oligarchic sedition, the quantity of money should be rigorously fixed at the level of the *produit net*. Quesnay noted: 'the total money stock of an agricultural nation is only about equal to the *produit net* or annual revenue of its landed property, for when it stands in this proportion it is more than sufficient for the nation's use' (*Extrait*, MK, p. 17n(a); *Analyse*, INED, p. 797, p. 800n(5), p.-809; cf. also Plato's proposal in the *Laws*, 743d: 'the citizens' wealth should be limited to the products of farming'). Furthermore, 'money should have no value when it is in the hands of others', especially of merchants, manufacturers and foreigners, suspected of concealing money, accumulating capital, and consequently, of jeopardizing the proprietors' politico-economic hegemony. 'Thus money should not remain in sterile hands', said Quesnay. 'So it is not a matter of such indifference to the State as people believe whether money goes into Peter's pocket or into Paul's, for it is essential that it should not be taken away from the man who employs it to the benefit of the State' (*Extrait*, MK, p. 18).

To prevent all these politico-economic diseases, but without damaging the 'civilization which the invention of money has brought' (Mirabeau, 1764, Vol. I, ch. 2, p. 52; the passage is also quoted in *The Wealth of Nations*, Bk V, ch. 9, pp. 643–4), the role of money should be restricted to 'an intermediate gauge between sale and purchase'. Quesnay thought the use of metal-money need no longer be indispensable in exchange; he did even develop a modern concept of credit money (*Analyse*, INED, pp. 809–10). Yet this 'modernism' is based on an ancient idea of the Treasury of Egypt embraced by Plato and on the paper money of Cathay noted in John Mandeville's *Voyages*, the idea that is set forth both in a mature, industrial society and an authoritarian, hydraulic community, without the existence of which money has no value.

Quesnay's symbolism of money can be well elucidated in the light of what Plato meant by saying that 'no private person shall be allowed to possess any gold or silver, but only coinage for day-to-day dealings' (*Laws*, 741e–742a). Such a repudiation of the use of gold and silver may agree with logical and historical consequences of the fact that metal-money, even though nominalized, has an immanent and independent value which is not determined by physical relations, but which becomes by itself the *determinant* of all social relations. Money in the fetishistic mercantile system could come into the possession of anyone who desired it, whether prince or merchant, indifferently giving them the same oligarchic power. As Plato warned in the *Republic* (550c–555b), 'once gold and silver towards iron and bronze, iron and bronze love gold and silver', that is 'the beginning of all corruption'.

It is to rescue 'happiness and goodness' from the 'money-lovers and money-makers', to restore the justice of a perfect society, that money as the symbol of sovereignty, of property, and of all economic activities, should be revertible to the State. 'Speaking rigorously,' concludes Quesnay, 'money which is assigned to this use has no owner at all: it belongs to the needs of the State, which cause it to circulate for the purpose of reproducing the wealth which enables the nation to subsist and provides contributions to the sovereign' (*Extrait*, MK, p. 18n).

The absence of a self-proliferating monetary and capital theory in Quesnay reveals in this context a (quasi-) negation of the 'private property' of products and land. The value of things, being of an intrinsic nature whether imposed or inherent, the negation of value removes from economic things all qualities except the quantity. Economic things become the objects of immediate consumption, not of permanent possession. Even the 'possession' of things of no value in themselves, though permanent, has no reason to be called 'property'.

Quesnay has generally been considered one of the defenders of 'private property' in Locke's tradition, that is, in the Aristotelian and Scholastic conception of property as a human natural propensity or natural right.[7] Yet Quesnay's notion of property fundamentally differs from this view. It seems to have originated from Plato's so-called 'agricultural laws', legislated under a theological conviction that 'moving the immovable is inhibited' (*Laws*, 842e–843b; 736c–737d). Property in this sense does not mean 'natural right' but a 'legal duty' imposed on citizens. Once 'perfect constitutional laws' have distributed the land to them and marked by 'stone' the boundary of their land, they must obey these laws, otherwise 'terrible wars break out'. To ensure the social stability of such 'distributed properties', Plato had to promulgate the *Laws* (913a): 'Ideally, no one should touch my property or tamper with it, unless I have given him some sort of permission; and if I am sensible, I shall treat the property of others with the same respect.' Property, then, is not 'having' but 'being just' in economic life, or 'keeping what is properly one's own and doing one's own job' (*Republic*, 433e).

Although Quesnay's *droit naturel* (INED, p. 732) – 'what is proper to men's enjoyment in the order of justice... is determined by an effective possession naturally right, acquired by labour, without usurpation of other's right of possession' – involves somewhat misleading expressions like 'natural right', his intention is far from those of natural law philosophers. For the Physiocratic Platonist, 'property' is the result of functional distribution, not of natural acquisition: 'by this distribution of works, each man can best perform his own completely... each man can enjoy the whole of his natural right, in conformity to the benefit which results from the cooperative labours of society' (ibid., p. 737; cf. also *Despotisme de la Chine*, Oncken, pp. 647–8).

Property as 'justice in performing one's proper function' had been further developed by Quesnay, with two economically significant consequences: (1) In pursuing effectiveness of specialized skills, it gave rise to the concept of 'expert', from which the 'entrepreneur' or the 'administrator' were derived. In a similar way to that in which Plato accentuated the importance of the expert (*Laws*, 741d; for Plato's view of 'expert', cf. Lowry, 1987, pp. 118–21, p. 278n(25)), Quesnay introduced the concept of the 'entrepreneur': 'It is the entrepreneur who administrates and makes valuable the enterprise by his intelligence and his wealth' (*Grains*, INED, p. 483). The entrepreneur, or *fermier* in Quesnay's general nomenclature, as an intermediate between proprietors and workers, emancipates them from a *vis-à-vis* class antagonism.

(2) The introduction of this concept is also a prelude to the definite end of the controversy on value. Since all economic decisions professionally made by the entrepreneur appear to be based on the monetary cost-benefit analysis along with the development of bookkeeping techniques, which may be objective and thus independent from any particular interests, this neutralism is easily convertible to the foundation of the 'value free' theories. The advent of entrepreneurs with emphasis on the efficiency of the system, however, results from and contributes to the bureaucratization and centralization of the economy (cf. Schumpeter, 1950, pp. 123–4, 133–4).

This functionalistic notion of property, when extremely extended, will necessarily meet the notion of the community. Or perhaps, in centralized community, bureaucratic property might be born. Anyhow, these two modes of possession are not different in the 'ideal state'. Because, as Plato put it, 'Our citizens are devoted to a common interest, which they call *my own*; and thus entirely share each other's feelings of joy and sorrow' (*Republic*, 464a; cf. also 412d, 'the deepest affection is based on identity of interest'). The 'identity of interest' comes after all from 'community of property', the form of the society, towards which all imperfect societies should evolve. Yet an ideal is not always real. Plato had to content himself with a 'second-best' transitional state:

> You will find the ideal society and state, and the best code of laws, where the old saying, 'friends' property is genuinely shared', is put into practice as widely as possible throughout the entire state...I do not know whether the perfect community exists or will ever exist, but at any rate in our state the notion of 'private property' will have been by hook and by crook completely eliminated. (*Laws*, 793b–c)

Plato's 'friendly property' echoed in the salon of the French pre-revolutionary communists. On the notion of *partage amical*, Mirabeau – Quesnay's companion and his most brilliant pupil – wrote the *Ami des Hommes*. Another follower, the Abbé Baudeau, annotated this precious word: 'To be Friend of Men, that is all moral philosophy and all political economy' (*Introduction à la philosophie économique*, Daire, p. 821). Mercier de la Rivière came to the same conclusion: 'we have found, in the relation of the social order and the physical order, all essential laws which concern this co-property, and which make its interest inseparable from those of the nation' (*L'ordre naturel et essentiel des sociétés politiques*, Daire, p. 447).

If 'private property' is merely one of the legal forms of society, 'community of property' or 'co-property' is never impossible either in theory or in history. Quesnay was the first who clearly recognized that property and markets are specific institutions by which the social *produit net* is produced and distributed. Throughout his studies on the political systems of the Inca Empire of Peru and despotism of China, he advanced the theory of a perfect society – the 'ideal state' once existed (*Gouvernement des Incas du Pérou*, Oncken, pp. 557–8): 'no money, no writing, no speculative science, no foreign trade have they...but no idler, no poor, no robber, no mendicant'. This economic verse reminds us of Homer's account of the household of the Cyclopes (*Odyssey* IX, 112 ff.) quoted by Plato (*Laws*, 680b).

> No laws, no councils for debate have they:
> They live on the tips of lofty mountains
> In hollow caves; each man lays down the law
> To wife and children, with no regard for neighbour.

In consequence, we have a necessary and sufficient reason to refute the classical interpretation of the famous maxim, *laissez-faire*,[8] attributed to Physiocratic liberalism. This is the most powerful propaganda that men have ever heard. This too is the most influential motto which glorifies the ideal of all 'liberal' moralists, economists and politicians. So much as the liberalists pronounced this categorical imperative, it is interpreted as signifying strict non-interventionism, i.e., anti-protectionism. And no one could object to the identity: Physiocracy = anti-mercantilism = *laissez-faire* = the origin of economic liberalism.

Nevertheless, the basis of Physiocratic liberalism can be found only in the policy of free commerce, not in the morality of individualistic liberalism. In fact, Quesnay never represented by 'free commerce' a system of 'perfect liberty as the only effectual expedient for rendering this annual reproduction the greatest possible', as Smith freely interpreted (*Wealth of Nations*, Bk V, ch. 9, p. 642). Differentiating two modes of exchange, 'commerce' and 'traffic', Quesnay identified the latter with foreign trade and placed it within a narrow limit (Beer, 1939, p. 59). He also declared: 'foreign trade is the *worst way* for nations where home trade does not suffice as an outlet for their production' (*Du Commerce*, INED, p. 849; cf. also *Analyse*, INED, pp. 809–12. This passage is parallel to that of Plato in the *Laws*, 949e: 'A state which does not go in for trading and whose only source of wealth is the soil is obliged to have some settled policy regarding foreign trade.')

The reason for such asymmetry in the Physiocrat's liberal mood is mainly to attack the bullionist doctrine of the balance of trade. But 'more liberty at home, less liberty abroad' may disclose a Physiocratic favouritism no better than mercantilist protectionism. Political ambivalence is total when Quesnay calls the merchants *commerçant régnicole*, a very Platonic word obviously translated from *metoikos*. It should here be remembered that Plato's isolation of 'the retailers who serve the public by buying and selling in the home market' from 'the merchants who travel abroad' (*Republic*, 371d) stemmed from his theory of *autarkeia*, or self-sufficiency of the State. The metics (aliens living in Greek city generally engaged in commerce), undoubtedly, cannot contribute anything to this autarchy; their existence itself not only impairs the autonomy of the state, worse than ever, it produces 'a medley of all sorts of characters... in a healthy society living under sound laws', which is 'an absolute disaster' (*Laws*, 949e–950a). Quesnay, in a Platonic voice, reproached mercantile multinationalism:. 'Our merchants are the merchants of other nations, the merchants of others are also ours... the communication between their commerce penetrates and spreads everywhere, always and finally aiming at money-making' (*Analyse*, INED, p. 812).

Autarky or economic autarchy, in the view of Plato and Quesnay, designates more than a political type of protectionism. It is the Form of the best society, because only this type of economy can assure a self-sufficient, never perishing, thus immortal and eternal movement *par excellence*, that is, the ideal of *autokineton*.[9] If then, the world of the economy were ideally self-moving, in the sense of what Mirabeau meant by 'Il mondo va de se' (1764, Vol. I, ch. 7, p. 417), there would be nothing to do. The maxim *laissez-faire* hence signifies a pure negativism, as Quesnay himself put it into a succinct metaphor, *Noli me tangere* (*Explication*, MK, p. xi), or 'Never touch the economic machine moving by itself.'

Conclusion

The resurrection by Quesnay of the sublime idea of Plato's *Republic* was received rather ironically as the discovery of scientific truth. Apart from Linguet's *Réponse aux Docteurs modernes* (1771; also quoted by Higgs, 1897, pp. 147–50), in which he compares side by side Quesnay's *Tableau* with Confucius' 'holy table' – the *Y-King*, of 64 terms, also connected by lines – to satirize the 'anabaptism of philosophy', even Adam Smith presented an Aristotelian eulogy to the economics of the Platonic Physiocrat: 'This system, however, with all its imperfections, is, perhaps, the nearest approximation to the truth that has yet been published upon the subject' (*Wealth of Nations*, Bk V, ch. 9, p. 642).

Yet this glorious, if not glorified, foundation of a physics of economy is not due to its own scientific achievements. It is more or less a *produit net* of the mood of the Enlightenment, a revival of Plato's simile of the Sun and Shadows (*Republic*, 515a ff.). In the Cave of mercantile obscurantism, Quesnay draws up 'royal economic maxims' for the government,

> the essential principles of a perfect system of Government, in which authority is always a benevolent protectress and a beloved guardian... which maintains everywhere the interests of the Nation, good order, the rights of the public, and the power and domination of the Sovereign. (*Extrait*, MK, p. 22)

Not a word of Quesnay seems to evolve or even escape from the ideas once recited by Plato, but it comes two thousand years and more too late. So how could we revere the *Tableau Economique* as a 'scientific revolution'? Is it only in the meaning of 'revolution' that the movement of thoughts should revolve to the very beginning of thoughts, initiated by Plato's *episteme*, and that the Physiocracy has marked the re-commencement of the history of economic thought? Is it just because Quesnay has exaltedly paraphrased the Philosopher-King into the Economist-King?

To these questions, one answer is possible. For François Quesnay and his disciples, for those who are later called 'economists', Plato's *Republic* is not a *utopia* – just as the Platonic cosmology in the *Timaeus* is not a *mythos* for Galileo and for the founders of 'modern physics' (cf. Koyré, 1965, p. 220). The story of the 'perfect', 'best', and 'ideal' is the 'model' or 'original' of all existing States; it is a 'scientific truth' for the 'political economy', a 'scientificated faith' upon which economics is constituted.

Notes

* I wish to express my gratitude to Professor D.Y. Chung of Sungkyunkwan University, Seoul, and to Professor Jacques Wolff of the Université de Panthéon-Sorbonne, Paris, for helping me to develop my Physiocratic study. Among the participants to the seminar, particular thanks are due to Professor Emeritus A.I. Bloomfield of Pennsylvania University for his suggestions. I am most indebted to Professor S.T. Lowry for his encouragement and comments on an earlier draft.

1. For the significance of the disappearance of Aristotelian cosmos, see Koyré, 1965, especially pp. 7–8.
2. A fuller discussion of the mathematical meaning of this passage may be read in, for example, Brunschvicg, 1929, pp. 49–51.
3. Quesnay did not calculate the mean value without considering the weight or frequency of each value. The average given here (cf. also *Hommes*, INED, pp. 532–3) is that of the current prices over five years, but it is not weighted by the quantities produced and sold each year (i.e. Quesnay's average price is $p^* = (\Sigma p_t)/T$; logically, it should be $(\Sigma p_t \cdot q_t)/\Sigma qt$). With these statistical errors, it was inevitable that Quesnay assumed a difference between the 'price of the buyer' and the 'price of the seller', which are in reality identical. Of course, there may be a difference between the 'consumer price' and the 'producer price' if the existence of 'trade profit' is assumed. However, this case of mercantile system was not admitted by Quesnay.

   Professor Vaggi also notes Quesnay's strange calculation of the average price (1987, pp. 65–6). But, without pointing out such statistical errors, Vaggi accepts the difference in prices and asserts that 'the notions of current and retail price provide the analytical basis for one of the most important physiocratic contentions: the establishment of free competition in foreign trade' (ibid., p. 71). In my opinion, Vaggi's interpretation resides fundamentally in the naturalistic idea of the market price (which originates in the Aristotelico-Scholastic 'just price', and is subsequently developed in Turgot and Smith's theory of the 'natural price'), that 'it is competition... that plays the dominant role in determining the market value of commodities' (ibid., p. 71). So he draws a comparison declaring that Quesnay's *prix fondamental* is the 'analytical category', which throws 'a bridge linking pre-physiocratic price theories and Smith's concept of natural price' (ibid., pp. 93, 165).

   However, seeing that Quesnay disapproved the probabilistic idea of approximation (*Evidence*, INED, p. 408), the *bon prix* cannot be identified with the market price. It is the supposition of a price *predetermined* 'by the causes anterior to the operations of commerce'. This a-priority differentiates conceptually the *bon prix* from the 'just price' or 'natural price' which is formed in the market *tâtonnement*.
4. Although Marx is considered to be the first who clearly analyses the *Tableau* with some

dynamic notions (see his sketch of the *Tableau* in *Theories on the Surplus-Value*, MS. p. 422), its dynamization is, it appears to me, at least as old as the reformulation by the Marquis de Mesmon in 1775. Cf. 'Eloge de François Quesnay' in Oncken, pp. 73–114, especially his 'Tableau' at p. 104.

5. Some helpful comments on the ideological importance of geometry can be found in Popper, 1966, p. 248(n.9); and in Lowry, 1987, p. 85 ff.

6. See for example, Phillips, 1955, pp. 137–44.

7. Max Beer affirms: 'The Scholastic influence, particularly that of Aquinas, on the leading physiocrats is striking... [Quesnay's] works read in the light of *ius naturale* and Aristotelian and Schoolmen's ethics' (1939, p. 59); cf. also Schumpeter, 1954, pp. 228–32; Steiner, 1984, pp. 139–59.

8. As a matter of fact, the maxim *laissez faire* appears only once in the whole works of Quesnay (*Le langage de la science économique*, INED, p. 940). The maxim was used in the quotation to render preposterous the mercantilistic liberalism of Forbonnais (who had published a *Lettre* in the *Journal d'agriculture* in 1767 criticizing the 'nouvelle science économique'), not in the properly Physiocratic expression. Oncken's study, *Die Maxim laisser faire et laisser passer, ihr Ursprung, ihr Werden* (Berne, 1886), makes it clear that the maxim is really due to Legendre, a merchant who attended a deputation to Colbert around the year 1680 to protest against excessive state regulation of industry. Turgot already noted it in his *Eloge de Vincent de Gournay*, 1759 (1913, Vol. I, p. 620). Cf. Editor's note in Oncken, pp. 671–2; and Higgs, 1897, p. 67.

9. The concept of *autokineton* or 'self-moving', with the concept of *aeikineton* or 'eternal-moving', are employed by Plato in order to demonstrate the immortality or 'eternal-living' of the Soul (*Phaedo*, 103e ff.; *Republic*, 608c–612a; *Theaetetus*, 153a ff.; cf. also Bernhardt, 1971, pp. 221–8). Quesnay reproduced this Platonic conception 'Of the immortality of the Soul' in *Essai physique sur l'oeconomie animale*, 1747, Vol. III, pp. 373–82 (cf. Oncken, pp. 758–63; *Evidence*, INED, p. 418 ff.). Whether Platonic *autokineton* is biological or physical, it implicates a strict *closedness* of the universe. Indeed, Plato's saying: 'the same souls have always existed. Their number cannot be decreased, because no soul can die; nor can it increase, because any increase in the immortal must be at the expense of mortality' (*Republic*, 611a), describes a *stationary* state of the universe. This may explain why autarchy, an economic interpretation of the *autokineton*, is constitutionally a closed, stationary economy, and why this system lays more emphasis on the repartition of the given assets than on the generation or production of value.

References

1. The following editions of François Quesnay and the Physiocrats' works are referred to:

Dupont, *Physiocratie ou constitution naturelle du gouvernement le plus avantageux au genre humain*, edited by Dupont de Nemours, Leyde: Merlin, 1768.

Daire: *Physiocrates: Quesnay, Dupont de Nemours, Mercier de la Rivière, L'abbé Baudeau, Le Trosne*, edited by Eugène Daire, Paris: Guillaumin & Cie, 1846.

Oncken: *Œuvres économiques et philosophiques de F. Quesnay*, edited by Auguste Oncken, Frankfurt: Joseph Baer & Cie; Paris: Jules Peelman & Cie, 1888.

INED: *François Quesnay et la physiocratie*, edited by Institut National d'Etudes Démographiques, with notes by Louis Salleron, Paris: Presses Universitaires de France, 1958.

MK: *Quesnay's Tableau Economique*, edited, with new material, translations and notes by Marguerite Kuczynski and Ronald L. Meek, London: Royal Economic Society and Macmillan; New York: A.M. Kelley, 1972.

Mirabeau (1756): *L'Ami des Hommes ou Traité de la population*, by the Marquis de Mirabeau, Victor de Riqueti, Avignon, 1756–1760.

Mirabeau (1764): *Philosophie rurale ou Economie générale et politique de l'Agriculture*, Amsterdam: Les Libraires Associés.

2. For the Platonic dialogues, the Budé series (Paris: E. des Places and A. Diès, 1951–6) are used, following the traditional mode of reference given by the numbers of the pages in the edition of Stephanus (1578).

3. Secondary sources:

Allix, Edgar (1911), 'Le physicisme des physiocrates' in *Revue d'Economie Politique*, no. 2.

Beer, Max (1939), *An Inquiry into Physiocracy*, London: George Allen & Unwin.

Bernhardt, Jean (1971), *Platon et le matérialisme ancien*, Paris: Payot.

Bloomfield, Arthur I. (1938), 'The Foreign trade doctrines of the Physiocrats' in *American Economic Review*, no. 4.

Bourthoumieux, Charles (1936), *Essai sur le fondement philosophique des doctrines économiques: Rousseau contre Quesnay*, Paris: Rivière.

Brunschvicg, Léon (1929), *Les étapes de la philosophie mathématique*, Paris: Félix Alcan.

Fowler, D.H. (1987), *The Mathematics of Plato's Academy*, Oxford: Clarendon Press.

Heath, Thomas L. (1921), *A History of Greek Mathematics*, Oxford: Clarendon Press.

Hecht, Jacqueline (1986), 'Une héritière des lumières, de la physiocratie et de l'idéologie: la première chaire française d'économie politique (1795)' in *Economies et Sociétés*, no. 6.

Higgs, Henry (1897), *The Physiocrats*, London: Macmillan.

Koyré, Alexandre (1965), *Newtonian Studies*, London: Chapman & Hall.

Lowry, S. Todd (1987), *The Archeology of Economic Ideas: The Classical Greek Tradition*, Durham: Duke University Press.

Meek, Ronald L. (1962), *The Economics of Physiocracy: Essays and Translations*, London: George Allen & Unwin.

Phillips, Almarin (1955), 'The Tableau Economique as a simple Leontief Model' in *Quarterly Journal of Economics*, no. 1.

Popper, Karl R. (1966), *The Open Society and its Enemies*, London: Routledge & Kegan Paul, 5th edn.

Schumpeter, Joseph A. (1950), *Capitalism, Socialism and Democracy*, New York: Harper & Row, 3rd edn.

Schumpeter, Joseph A. (1954), *History of Economic Analysis*, ed. E.B. Schumpeter [ren. M.L. Severn, London: Allen & Unwin, 1982.]

Shackle, G.L.S. (1973), *Epistemics and Economics: A Critique of Economic Doctrines*, Cambridge: Cambridge University Press.

Smith, Adam (1937), *An Inquiry into the Nature and Causes of the Wealth of Nations*, ed. E. Cannan, introd. M. Lerner, New York: The Modern Library.

Steiner, P. (1984), 'Locke et Quesnay: une conception politique de l'économie', *Economies et Sociétés*, no. 1.

Turgot, A.R.J. (1913), *Œuvres de Turgot*, ed. G. Schelle, Paris: Félix Alcan.

Vaggi, Giovanni (1987), *The Economics of François Quesnay*, London: Macmillan.

Weulersse, Georges (1910), *Le mouvement physiocratique en France de 1756 à 1770*, Paris: Alcan.

Wolff, Jacques (1973), *Les grandes œuvres économiques*, Paris: Editions Cujas.

9 Equality and social differentiation in *The Wealth of Nations*
Françoise Duboeuf

Smith's theory of value appears complex, open to many interpretations. The different elements which constitute it (the problems of the measure and of the constitution of value) suggest a rather questioning relation between the principle of equality of all men and social differentiation. In my opinion this is to be linked to Smith's real conception of wealth, against the mercantilists' view where real wealth consists of the goods which suit the needs of all people. Social differentiation is then only a piece of the social mechanism that is best fitted to achieve real wealth.

I want to show that the theory of value in *The Wealth of Nations* answers several questions. The never-varying value of labour that permits an accurate measure of wealth should be related to Smith's moral and philosophical views of man. It provides the necessary link between ethics and economics. At this level Smith appears as an egalitarian. Meanwhile, his approach to natural price borrows from the Physiocrats the conception of a differentiated order;[1] this differentiation is not the result of merit, but a necessary social structure.

This interpretation is opposed to the Marxian approach in terms of exploitation, as well as to the ultra liberal one, which views Smith as an unconditional advocate of individual liberty. In my view, Smith does not consider social differentiation as opposed to justice in so far as it is a necessary framework for efficient individual action. At the same time, individual liberty of economic action, far from being a social value in itself, is essentially advocated as a means to public welfare.

I

The Wealth of Nations is presented as a whole. But we know Smith's economic work was first conceived as part of his moral philosophy. Indeed, in the *Lectures on Jurisprudence* economic thinking appears as the application of the principles emerging from ethics. These are largely developed in *The Theory of Moral Sentiments* as a basis for the positive action of government. Smith's aim is to show how government should behave to achieve public opulence. In *The Wealth of Nations*, Smith clearly develops the knowledge that is necessary for accurate choices in the field of economic policy.

The well-known conclusion is an anti-mercantilist position: the state should not interfere in the action of the free market; free individuals seeking their selfish satisfaction do better for the general welfare than any benevolent statesman. In this way, Smith establishes the superiority of liberal individualistic organization above any centralized system. He appears then both as the father of political economy as a science of an autonomous, self-regulated economic process and as the father of the liberal doctrine stating the superiority of a system of individual freedom. Meanwhile, *The Wealth of Nations* seems to owe much in its elaboration to the Physiocratic thought Smith encountered, particularly on his journeys to France.

From the *Lectures on Jurisprudence* to *The Wealth of Nations*, an enormous amount of thinking is elaborated, clearly marked by the influence of the Physiocrats. In a paradoxical way, it is not so much the *laissez-faire* doctrine which makes its way into Smith's preoccupations, as the rather holistic conception of economics of the Physiocrats: that is, their conception of a class-structured economic system.

We will examine two points:

1. We will try to see how the economic thinking in *The Wealth of Nations* can be considered as a logical application of Smith's moral thinking, particularly as far as the problem of equality is concerned.
2. We will try then to interpret the Physiocratic influence in this framework, specifically on the question of social differentiation.

The first economic texts left by Smith (*Lectures on Jurisprudence*, Early Draft) are characterized by great ambiguity and lack of precision as far as social differentiation is concerned. When Smith tries to define 'opulence', or to explain the role of the market, he refers to the 'labourer',[2] most often as if an independent one, just alluding here and there to the fact that the whole product does not go to him. Profits are not clearly distinguished from wages. Meanwhile, economic inequality is far from absent from Smith's reflection. Although it does not play a prominent role in the economic texts, it receives a whole section in *The Theory of Moral Sentiments* (*TMS*, Part I, section III). The famous text on the 'Invisible Hand' is a proof of the importance and impact of the question: inequality in riches is not contrary to the views of Providence. If wealth is pure illusion, 'it is well that nature imposes on us in this manner. It is this deception which arouses and keeps in continual motion the industry of mankind.' The demonstration goes further: 'It is to no purpose that the proud and unfeeling landlord views his extensive fields, and without a thought for the wants of his breathren, in imagination consumes himself the whole harvest', but the rich 'consume little more than the poor . . . they are led by an invisible hand to make nearly the same distribution of necessaries of life which would have been made, had the earth been divided into equal portions among all its inhabitants' (*TMS*, Part 1, ch. 2, p. 303). Remarkably enough, this text does not concern the merits of the market order, as will be the case with the second allusion to the Invisible Hand in *The Wealth of Nations* (*WN*, Book 3, ch. 4). Here it is purely social inequality through the possession of land, giving in turn unequal access to the produce of the land which generates the best social effects, no matter what the social mechanism may be through which the produce is distributed among people.

So here individual selfishness shows its aptitude for social efficiency in its purest form.

Two remarks should be made concerning the normative content which comes out of the text:

First, providence appears as more concerned by collective than by individual wealth: it is the perspective of social welfare which renders individual selfishness and the illusory search for riches acceptable. Clearly Smith does not approve of selfish individual motives in themselves.

Second, there is a double implicit reference to the equality of men as a norm: providence aims at wealth for all men; considering the stomach of a poor person is about the same as that of a rich person, it intends to satisfy the fundamental needs of everybody. Moreover, Smith refers to equality in the possession of land as a model of justice,[3] the normal basis for economic equality. So it appears that differentiation in possession is only acceptable if it gives the same or better results as an incitement to individual action, than equality.

So social differentiation, generated and reinforced by the mechanism of sympathy,[4] does not appear as an order which is legitimate in itself. It is acceptable only because it is the best path to public welfare. I would interpret Smith's moral position here as reversing the traditional view.

The social end which imposed itself through moral sentiments was a materialistic and egalitarian one.[5] The main aim of society was the satisfaction of the material needs of man, of all men.

We can confirm this view when reading the *Lectures on Jurisprudence*, where Smith defined opulence, the aim of government, as the quantity of goods a labourer can afford.

He also insisted that the merit of the division of labour was that it enriched even the poorest labourer by giving him power over the labour of so many of his fellow citizens. So the English workman was richer than the Indian prince, whilst the general interdependence through the market ensured that no one got any hierarchical power over the others: the more division of labour there was, the more riches there were for everybody and the more independence there was for equal citizens.

So, social differentiation was legitimate in that it was the best means to achieve such a norm. As it was a necessary framework for selfish individualistic action it was not a source of social disorder, but on the contrary the best means for the achievement of collective wealth. Smith's first economic thinking started with a collective norm but he saw individual freedom was going to be its best instrument.

It is this norm which underlies the rejection of the mercantilists' position on wealth. For Smith, wealth is *real* wealth – wealth for all men, not only for princes and merchants. Hence Smith's endeavour to distinguish wealth and money entirely, and finally to produce a theory of value, that is a means of quantification of wealth which is different from its monetary form.

II

It is in this context that I want to appreciate the results of the encounter of Smith with Physiocratic thought.

In the Physiocrats and especially Quesnay, Smith also found a normative conception of economic activity, a conception that opposed social interest and individual interest, and made the despot the depository of the general interest.

In a very similar way to Smith, the Physiocrats developed a conception of real wealth composed of consumable goods satisfying fundamental human needs; they too rejected the mercantilists' conception. Although Smith did not share the Physiocratic view on the origin of surplus, we know that he reflected the influence of the Physiocrats' agrarian model. Smith found something new in Physiocratic thought which he incorporated in his own way into a theory of value and accumulation in *The Wealth of Nations*.

It was the first theoretical economic approach to social classes, an imperfect approach indeed, since the classifying principles used by Quesnay for instance were not homogenous; his social classes were characterized by the fact that they play a different role in the economic order. They constitute the necessary structure for economic reproduction through which the whole mechanism can function. Social differentiation was, in Physiocratic thinking, a necessary constituent of the natural economic order.

The reasons are not the same as in Smith's view: for Quesnay and the other Physiocrats, social differentiation and inequality in possessions were not the necessary incentive for individual action. On the contrary, in Physiocratic thought, the search for individual wealth, in the sterile class for instance, was socially dangerous. Classes were considered a part of the necessary general structure implementing divine purpose.

But what is essential as far as the influence upon Smith is concerned, is that for the Physiocrats, economic regulation required definite economic relations between the different classes, and the respect of the conditions which permit the maintenance of this social structure.

It is in the framework of this social structure that the Physiocrats proposed a first analysis of capital. Wealth was an annual flow of riches produced from advanced stocks which had to be reconstituted at the end of the period. The classes were characterized by the role they played in this process.

Smith borrowed the principle of capital reproduction in a class structure. He added the profit-earning class to the scheme and extended the notion of productivity to all sectors. He specified the principle of the economic differentiation of classes in a more accurate form: they are defined by the means of production they possess, and by the specific revenue they get from these. Smith extended the problematics of reproduction with a systematic approach to the accumulation of capital.

But through this borrowing, Smith carried out a fundamental rebuilding of the Physiocratic approach. The conditions for the regulation of the economic system were to be achieved not through the equilibrium of flows under the surveillance of the despot but through the operation of the competitive market. In the same way as in the moral sphere, sympathy assured the realization of the necessary moral conditions of social life. In the economic sphere it is exchange and individual action which ensure the appearance and the respect of the rules that are necessary for general economic order. So, from a theoretical point of view, the laws which govern exchange are substituted for the natural proportions between the flows in Quesnay's *Tableau Economique*; general economic interdependence is realized through exchange.

Hence the crucial position of the theory of value in *The Wealth of Nations*. Value and natural prices express the necessary logic which lead a nation to opulence, once we know that free competition can enforce this logic on individuals without any outside intervention.

So the theory of value (real and natural prices) constitutes, in my view, first the bridge between ethics and economics,[6] and then the realm of expression and realization of the conditions of the natural order, that is, the order most appropriate to the wealth of the nation. Exploring the theory of value in *The Wealth of Nations* is the best way to see how Smith conceived the relation between the principle of equality and of social differentiation, from the perspective of national enrichment.

The laws of exchange as elaborated by Smith opened the way to a vast debate and a great deal of criticism. I propose to interpret their complexity as a consequence of the fact that they had to answer and explain several questions. They provide the link between ethics and economics and constitute the space of realization of the conditions of the economic order.

If the economic system is regulated through exchange by the laws of value, then once the main economic aim of society has been defined as the materialistic satisfaction of the needs of all men, the laws of value will be confronted with two problems. The first problem is of being accepted by all individuals constituting the nation; the second is of achieving the chosen collective end.

The social nature of value

If wealth is defined as real, it is by nature heterogeneous. The problem of its quantification appears as soon as wealth is distinguished from money. Indeed, Smith considered metallic money as a good measure of value in his early economic texts, because of the precision and permanence of its physical qualities.

There was then some confusion about the qualities of a good standard of value in Smith's mind (see Duboeuf, 1990), a confusion he later clarified in *The Wealth of Nations*.

But, more importantly, he distinguished the 'value' of wealth from its monetary expression, and he then attempted to propose a sort of quantification of wealth as the objective of the state, as an answer to the question: What is the nature of opulence? Opulence is positively related to the purchasing power of labour, and inversely related to the labour cost of goods. The more opulent a nation is, the cheaper are the goods it obtains, the dearer is labour (under the crude assumption that 'labour' receives all its produce as a recompense).

So the level of wealth, the aim of a good government, is appreciated by the rate of exchange between labour and goods. As productivity increases the real wage improves and the labour price of goods diminishes. Significantly this relation, in the *Lectures of Jurisprudence*, was not linked to the question of value or of its measure. It is clearly in the context of a normative attempt to define wealth that Smith established an initial quantitative relation between labour and its produce (a relation based on the effects of the division of labour)[7]; whilst the problem of measure is mainly treated from a technical point of view (the necessity for merchants to dispose of a good standard).

We know why Smith explicitly rejected gold as a standard of value in *The Wealth of Nations* when he wanted a theoretical standard permitting comparisons through time: the value of gold varies like that of any other good.

We also know that Smith pleaded for a radical distinction between real wealth and money, contrary to the mercantilists' views.

What is interesting is that when Smith says that in the real measure of value the real price of goods is the quantity of labour they can purchase, he gives an answer to two different questions, or rather fuses these two into a single question. The theoretical problem of a good measure of value is solved together with the more fundamental problem of the conditions under which heterogeneous goods can be socially considered as homogeneous and quantifiable. Or, to put it in another way, if value appears as the social quantitative dimension of wealth, the problem is to know what the nature of this social dimension is. If money is neither wealth nor a good measure of it, it is only an approximate expression of value which is the true quantitative dimension of real wealth. The problem, however, is to clarify the nature of value. The question of its measure is directly linked to that of its nature. This might explain why Smith, in *The Wealth of Nations*, brings up the problem of the measure of value just after the fourth chapter devoted to the question of money.

We saw earlier how Smith established an initial relationship between labour and opulence in the *Lectures on Jurisprudence*. Significantly, it was this relationship that came back as a solution to the problem of the measure of wealth and of value. Smith turned to the normative approach to wealth for a solution. Value is the social representation of wealth and quantifies it in respect to its deeper and normative significance. All men's needs can be satisfied through man's labour; when value is measured by such a real price, namely labour, it is expressive of the fundamental nature of wealth. That is to say, real goods that are apt to sustain men, or rather labourers, when labour became the source of all production under the Lockean influence.

We shall refer to *The Theory of Moral Sentiments* to precisely delineate this interpretation. Smith shows how sympathy creates a space of social relations between individuals. Through these relations, moral values are constituted and imposed as principles of action in society. Indeed these values are not a given of human nature; they are social creations, social points of view which permit social cohesion. So I propose to interpret the value dimension of wealth in the same way, as a social representation, a purely social point of view about wealth; the way all men agree to interpret wealth. So the real price of goods, in terms of labour, is both the expression of the necessity of a moral consensus on the significance of economic grandeur, and a good measure of value.

Here, Ricardo's criticism falls short, because labour is not a good like any other and, according to Smith, its value does not vary.

Contrary to Ricardo, Smith does not identify the value of labour with its purchasing power in terms of wage goods. So, when the quantity of corn given to the labourer varies, it is the real price of corn which is changed, not the value of labour (see *WN*, Book I, ch. 5, p. 50).

This invariability should not, in my view, be interpreted as an error on the part of Smith. It points out the fact that labour does not belong to the world of produced goods and that its 'value' is outside the general definitions and rules of exchange. The value of labour is not its power to purchase other goods except in the 'popular sense' (ibid., p. 52). It is the standpoint from which all other values assume their meaning. So Ricardo's criticism is based on a misunderstanding about the real theoretical function of what in Smith's view is the real standard. The meaning of this never-varying value of labour is to be found in the fact that here the term 'value' should not be given an economic content. The economic value of labour is its real wages, the never-varying value of labour is its intrinsic moral content from a social point of view. In a world where all men are considered as morally and therefore legally equal, and in which labour is the means through which men achieve their natural rights, their equality finds its economic translation in the idea of a constant 'value' of human labour at all times and in all places.[8]

The reason why Smith used such a theoretical device to give a content to the nature of value is linked to the fundamental importance for him of an ethical basis for the functioning of the economic system.[9]

In *The Theory of Moral Sentiments* Smith endeavoured to show how the sentiment of sympathy between men is the framework for the constitution and acceptance of the moral and social norms which are necessary to ensure social cohesion.

The never varying value of labour was one of these moral norms, the moral norm that was fundamental in allowing economic cohesion. Linked to the real wage by an approximately constant relationship through the competition between masters and labourers in the labour market, the constant 'value of labour' provides the necessary theoretical bridge between ethics and economics. At the same time, it constitutes the real measure of values.[10]

This is confirmed by the fact that, from a strictly economic point of view, the real wage, corn for instance, could just as well play the role of a correct standard of measure (see Duboeuf, 1989, 1990). Smith himself proposed corn as a possible measure of value (in *WN*, Book I, ch. 5) and in fact used it when he studied the formation of rent (see ibid., ch. 11; see Duboeuf, 1989).

But for Smith the question of the nature of value cannot be treated from a strictly economic point of view. Value is a social representation of wealth to which all individuals must adhere. So it must belong to the social sphere of moral consensus before it can function as a strictly economic quantity.

So Smith's conception of the relation between value and labour is very far from Ricardo's, as it refers not to the conditions of the production of goods, but to the social link that is necessary to support the economic order.

Natural prices

On this moral basis, the economic order can develop its rules legitimized by their efficiency in the task of achieving the social norm of welfare.

Here the second question emerges: what are the conditions under which individual action can most efficiently achieve the desired results?

Smith then introduced the necessity of a differentiated order as the best framework for accumulation and social enrichment. And, logically, it is through the principles that determine natural prices that the necessary social differentiation is imposed.

From this point of view, the development from the primitive situation, in which the whole produce belongs to the labourer, to the 'civilized' stage, in which he is forced to share with capitalists and landowners, does not constitute a change in the theory of value. From the perspective of accumulation, the labourer has to give up some of his 'natural recompense' because this is the most efficient way to achieve opulence, so natural prices must enforce social differentiation.

Natural prices give an account of the way the surplus created by the increasing productivity of labour must be appropriated. They incorporate the rules of the repartition of the physical produce between the owners of land, capital and labour, rules that must be respected if they are to lead to the best level of accumulation. So Smith never proposed a concept of value that is regulated by the quantity of labour necessary for the production of goods. The levels at which the natural prices of goods should be established are never simply dictated by the conditions of production in a Ricardian way – they must also ensure the permanence of the social structure which is most appropriate to accumulation.

Smith, contrary to the Physiocrats, proposed a clear economic definition of classes, directed by differentiated access to the means of production, labour, land and capital. Each access gives a right to a specific revenue which constitutes an incentive to their most efficient use.

Market competition ensures at all times that the rate of revenue is equal for every individual in each class. Fundamentally, this determines the best allocation of labour, land and capital in respect to the demand for goods. The individual search for gain is a tool for an optimal use of the existing resources at any moment.

In the long run, the evolution of the rates of the distribution of revenues to classes is the result of both accumulation and the incentive to further action. From Smith's perspective, accumulation presupposed the existence of a demand; except for one good, that is corn, the principal food of labourers. The existence of a positive and sufficient rate of profit is a clue to the fact that wealth has not yet reached its maximum level; and accumulation will go on so long as there is a demand for goods, that is for the produce of labour. When this demand is satiated, accumulation has achieved its social purpose; so has the capitalist class, which then only obtains the lowest possible rate of profit and ends both accumulation and demand for labour.

The differentiated order or class inequality has played its role. It has, at every moment and in the long run, constantly induced the owners of land and capital to use them in the most productive way, by allocating them in the way most appropriate to the demand for goods that shows on the market, and the process of enrichment in the long run stops by itself when the possibility of the expansion of demand no longer exists.

Meanwhile, in the long-term process, we have to distinguish between two different sorts of demand: the demand for wage goods,[11] which has no limit, and the demand for non-wage goods, which is satiated in the long run. Clearly the development of the working population depends on the accumulation of capital but this in turn depends on the existence of markets for non-wage goods.

In this way also, social differentiation assures the greatest possible development of the working population by promoting a demand for manufactured and luxury goods.

Social differentiation may therefore have a role to play in the enlargement of markets that in the long run ensure a further development of capital and labour. From this point of view, the theory of the 'component parts' of the price of commodities is not simply to be interpreted as a cost of production theory of prices. Up to a certain point, they rather announce Sraffa's conception of 'production prices', in the sense that natural prices, according to Smith, should both technically and socially reproduce a specific system.

Meanwhile, natural prices are necessary prices, but not in the sense that they should obey the logic of the reproduction inherent in a differentiated order (a capitalist one for instance). They should reproduce this order in so far as it is necessary for the achievement of a general objective norm. So they do not represent a class society logic, but a normative holistic point of view.

Conclusions

Smith's system of natural liberty involved social inequality as the framework necessary to achieve public opulence, opulence is the norm. Natural liberty, in a context of social differentiation, was only the mechanism through which it could be attained in the best possible way.

It should be remembered that Smith himself pointed out the illusion inherent in confusing a beautiful mechanism and the reality of its performance; admiring its beauty instead of concentrating upon the essential, that is, the purpose of the machine.

In the same way, from Smith's point of view, social differentiation is socially legitimized by the fact that it permits natural liberty to give its best results, but this should not lead us to believe that such a remarkable social mechanism is desirable for its own beauty. It is only advocated against the mercantilist policy because it is better adapted to the aims of a good society, that is, because it is after all the least bad system. That Smith is not an unconditional advocate of individual interest is clear enough in the way he qualifies it. The essential free individual in the market mechanism should be the capitalist who freely directs capital, but

> the interest of the dealers . . . is always in some respects different from, and even opposite to that of the publick. . . . The proposal of any new law or regulation of commerce which comes from this order, ought always to be listened to with great precaution, and ought never to be adopted till after having been long and carefully examined, not only with the most scrupulous, but with the most *suspicious* attention. It comes from an order of men . . . who have generally interest to *deceive and even to oppress the publick*. (*WN*, Book I, ch. 11, p. 267, my italics)

Everybody knows how Smith describes the conditions in which real wages are established on the labour market, and how he complains about the consequences of the division of labour on the labourers. Meanwhile, we cannot interpret Smith's suspicion of capitalists as an effect of his preferences for a precapitalist order or as complacency about landed interests: 'The landlords, like all other men, love to reap where they never sowed' (*WN*, Book I, ch. 4, p. 67) and

> they are the only one of the three orders whose revenue costs them neither labour nor care.... That indolence, which is the natural effect of the ease and security of their situation, renders them too often, not only ignorant, but incapable of that application of mind which is necessary in order to foresee and understand the consequences of any publick regulation. (ibid., ch.11, p. 265)

We can be certain that if in Smith's mind inequality is a necessary correlative of natural liberty, it is not the result of merit. It is difficult in Smith's vision to see an advocacy of natural liberty in itself: the individual desires of wealth are the product of illusion and the owners of wealth are either ignorant, indolent or suspect.

In this way Smith's ethics remain entirely anti-chrematistic, and individual freedom is not a social value or a social aim in itself. A holistic point of view remains clearly pre-eminent, in which the fundamental equality of men keeps its place through the necessity of satisfying the fundamental needs of all men. The distance between the fundamental aim of accumulation and social differentiation as its means opens the way to the legitimacy of state intervention. Smith's anti-mercantilist position has led many interpreters to the idea that, for him, the state has no other function than the protection of property, contracts and national defence.

In fact what Smith clearly opposes is the direct intervention of the state in the process of land and capital allocation. This is far from avoiding any sort of economic intervention.

Indeed there are many clues in *The Wealth of Nations* that point to the fact that the Invisible Hand is partly that of the state. If the market mechanism is apt to convey profitable social results, it implies that general conditions are respected. Some patterns of social differentiation are more appropriate than others. Some individual interests are more appropriate than others.

It is clearly the role of the state to operate the accurate selection between different possible patterns of inequalities in property, through taxation for instance. In this light state property, for instance, is opposed to the general interest according to Smith, not because it belongs to the state, but because it is too large, in the same way as feudal property. The role of the state should be to discourage the ownership of property in excessively large holdings by appropriate taxes and limitations on inheritance.

This indirect conception of economic intervention by the state is illustrated by Smith's position on the rate of interest and the regulation of banking. The government should impose a legal rate of interest, just a little above the lowest market rate. This is meant to discourage all the prodigals, 'projectors' and other free individuals whose selfish conceptions clearly do not contribute to social welfare in Smith's mind (see *WN*, Book 2, ch. 4, p. 355).[12]

In the same way, bankers can trade 'perfectly' freely under some conditions; for instance they should not issue banknotes for less than a certain sum:

> To restrain private people it may be said, from receiving in payment the promissory notes of a banker, for any sum whether great or small, when they themselves are willing to receive them; or to restrain... is a violation of natural liberty which it is the proper business of law, not to infringe, but to support. Such regulations may, no doubt, be considered as in some respect a violation of natural liberty. But these exertions of the natural liberty of a few individuals, which might endanger the security of the whole society, are, and ought to be restrained by the laws of all governments; of the most free as well as of the most despotical. (ibid., ch. 2, p. 324)

So it seems that the state has a very important economic role. It should impose a framework for individual action to achieve its best results. This goes along with encouraging the expression of 'sober' as opposed to imprudent behaviour and socially profitable inequalities in possessions as opposed to discouraging disproportions. There is room for the intervention of the state, which will eliminate both the imprudent and the indolent from the market through clever regulation.

In conclusion, Smith's position on social differentiation appears to be subject to a holistic conception of social welfare. The aim of accumulation is the satisfaction of real human needs on the basis of an egalitarian conception of man. This conception should be linked to Smith's moral thinking; the economic field was not to be conceived as an entirely closed one. Economic actions and relations must be coherent with and related to the set of moral values prevailing in a 'civilized' society. Among these, the equality of men and their needs acted as a normative reference for the interpretation of the economic functioning of society.

In this perspective, social differentiation is necessary and legitimate only in so far as it constitutes the efficient framework for individual action.

Individual economic liberty is preferred because it is more productive than direct state intervention in the field of land and capital allocation. Probably, in Smith's mind, the fundamental natural liberty of man should not be confused with his selfish economic liberty.

So the system of free individual economic action conceived by Smith does not reject the existence of a collective norm. On the contrary, it rests on the acknowledgement that society aims at public welfare, as distinct from individual ends. It is this normative general point of view that gives sense to market efficiency. This is why Smith can use a structural conception of the natural functioning of the market order, an order in which individuals, in the framework of the economic classes to which they belong, have to play a role which is defined by the aims of society as a whole.

Notes

1. Social differentiation is linked here to unequal access to land and capital. It implies different revenues and, therefore, material inequality and difference in social status.
2. See the description of the market process in the *Lectures on Jurisprudence* where the labourer appears as a central figure, while in other parts of the text Smith allows that he has to share a part of his produce with his master.
3. A model of justice which seems to be based on the idea that men have an equal right to land. Here we remember Locke's discussion of private property, first seen as an equal right for all men, linked with their aptitude to work.
4. In *The Wealth of Nations* Smith stated that men were naturally equal in talents. The differences in capacities were the result not the cause of the division of labour. The mechanism of sympathy, described by Smith in *The Theory of Moral Sentiments*, reinforced social differentiation as individuals sympathized more easily with richness than with poverty. The poor were ashamed while material wealth appeared as a desirable end. For Smith, this bias in sympathy was not based on any real difference in merit but it seemed to support a necessary social order; sympathy for the wealthy prompted men to industry.
5. We consider here the 'materialistic' approach as related to an egalitarian view of society: the 'real' conception of wealth, consisting in consumable goods fit for all men, is opposed to a conception of wealth as a basis for the Prince's power. This conception shows the material necessity in which all men live as the aim of the government's action and the basis of the social order. This can be related to a view in which all men are equal in rights through their needs and their labour.

   Nevertheless, Smith is very ambiguous about what really is the wealth of nations; moral and juridical equality of men does not go along with their material equality, not even with the improvement of the material situation of all of them: indeed the long run is characterized by the lowest possible rate of wages. At the same time, Smith constantly stresses the advantages of the English poorest, compared with the Indian Prince's possibilities. It looks as if Smith had to cope with a contradictory view of the aim of the nation: workers have a moral and juridical right to material satisfaction while economic logic can only lead to general improvement.
6. About the 'bridge' between ethics and economics: in our sense, the theory of value belongs to the process of constitution of the set of social values, that is social representations that are necessary to social order; it also belongs to the constitution of the elements which are necessary to understand economic relations. I think that the theory of value can be interpreted as an attempt to articulate ethics and economics, that is, to start economic thinking on the basis of a complete moral theory.

   In particular, the theory of real prices should be interpreted both as an explicit expression of the social nature of wealth and as a theory of the economic measure of wealth. This is why, in my view, the theory of value plays a crucial role, because the laws of exchange are supposed to rule economic relations as a whole, and they must also be related to and consistent with the logic of social cohesion as it is developed in the ethical field.
7. Labour should not be considered as a 'production factor', but, in the frame of a normative question, as a reference to a conception of wealth; as the wealth for all men, relating their needs to their efforts. Smith, like Locke, is opposed to conceptions in which land, for instance, is a source of wealth; that is, to conceptions which are marked by the traditional views about property and power.
8. Smith copes with a fundamental question: how to articulate equality of rights with material inequality? The constant value of labour is typical of the necessity of considering the two aspects within a single proposition: there is no 'value' of labour if labour does not appear

as a commodity, which implies social differentiation. At the same time, this value is constant and expresses the fundamental equality of men.

9. Smith's theory of value was quite different from Ricardo's as he inquired both into the social nature of value and its quantitative dimension. Ricardo was not interested in the first aspect of a theory of value; from our perspective he misunderstood the meaning of Smith's approach to the relation between labour and value. Marx on the contrary came back in his own way to the problems stated by Smith.

10. So the moral norm implied by the 'real' prices articulates the juridical and moral equality of men with their material inequality, owing to the differentiation in property.

11. Wage goods were the goods that constituted the real wage of labourers, namely corn, which was the cheapest food. Food being the main expense of the labourers, all the other goods are non-wage goods.

12. The legal rate of interest is low enough for 'sober' entrepreneurs to employ capital in a profitable way. A higher rate would be accepted only by speculators apt to destroy the real national capital through imprudent business. Smith supposes that owners of capital would prefer to lend it to reliable men first, at a given rate of interest.

References

Blaug, M. (1962), *Economic Theory in Retrospect*, London: Heinemann Educational Books.

Cartelier, J. (1976), *Surproduit et Reproduction*, Maspero: Presses Universitaires de Grenoble.

Duboeuf, F. (1985), 'Adam Smith, mesure et socialité', *Oeconomia*, **3**, 73–107.

Duboeuf, F. (1988), 'Le Processus de formation économique du taux de la rente et du taux de salaire chez Smith, *Oeconomia*, **10**.

Duboeuf, F. (1990), 'Espace économique, espaces moral et politique', *Cahiers d'Economie Politique*, **19**.

Halévy, E. (1900–3), *La Formation du radicalisme philosophique*, Paris: Alcan.

Hirschman, A.O. (1980), *Les passions et les intérêts*, PUF.

Macfie, A.L. (1976), *The Individual in Society*, London: Allen & Unwin.

Marx, K. (1969), *Theories of Surplus Value*, London: Lawrence & Wishart.

Meek, R. (1973), *Studies in the Labour Theory of Value*, London: Lawrence & Wishart.

(1958) *François Quesnay et la Physiocratie*, INED edn, Paris.

Ricardo, D. (1951), *On the Principles of Political Economy and Taxation*, in *The Works and Correspondence of David Ricardo*, Vol. I, ed. P. Sraffa, Cambridge: Cambridge University Press.

Schumpeter, J.A. (1976), *History of Economic Analysis*, New York: Oxford University Press [1954].

Skinner, A.S. and Wilson, T. (1975), *Essays on Adam Smith*, Oxford: Clarendon Press.

Smith, A. (1976), *Essays on Philosophical Subjects*, edited by W.P.D. Wightman (*The History of Astronomy, The History of Ancient Logics and Metaphysics, Of the External Senses*); *An Inquiry into the Nature and Causes of the Wealth of Nations*, edited by R.H. Campbell and A.S. Skinner; *Lectures on Jurisprudence*, edited by R.L. Meek, D.D. Raphael and R.G. Stein; *Lectures on Rhetoric and Belles Lettres*, edited by J.C. Bryce (*Considerations concerning the first formation of languages*), Oxford: Clarendon Press.

Smith, A. (1976), *The Theory of Moral Sentiments*, Indianapolis: Liberty Classics.

10 Adam Smith on value in use and value in exchange: a counterrevolution which eventually failed
John C. Winfrey

Introduction

Adam Smith's treatment of the water-diamond paradox, where he reaffirmed that 'nothing is more useful than water...' and that 'a diamond...has scarcely any value in use...' has caused no small amount of controversy. I will base much of my argument on an interpretation of Smith's value theory which credits him with a consistent theory, but one which recognizes the tension between individual preferences, as expressed in market demand, and the social value of goods and services. Smith mounted a counterrevolution against the conflation of these two meanings. Value theory prior to Smith seemed to be leading inexorably to acceptance of the idea that value in use is nothing more than the usefulness, or utility, of a good to consumers. It follows that if market demand accurately reflects consumer preferences, then market prices; i.e. exchange values, accurately reflect values in use. The social norm advocated by Smith is economic growth. The wealth of a nation, according to him, is represented by the nation's capacity to employ labour in productive pursuits. Thus, the value in use of a commodity is defined in terms of its ability to sustain productive labour. Exchange values, by contrast, depend on market demand, which may include conflicting, sometimes even 'frivolous' goals. I will maintain that the theme of value in use as productive capacity runs through all of Smith's arguments. This allows us to see the consistency in Smith's use of labour as a standard of value, his contrast between productive and unproductive labour, and his evaluation of various economic institutions.

The focus of this essay will be on how Smith's definitions of value in use and value in exchange, his 'counterrevolution', were received and treated by those who followed him in the classical tradition. To anticipate, I will argue that Smith successfully delayed the acceptance of the idea that consumer preferences are the only source of value; but the consistency of his theory was undercut as his ideas were reinterpreted.

Smith's treatment of the water-diamond paradox eventually follows not from a failure to appreciate the role of diminishing marginal utility, as some critics argue, but from his rejection of the implicit assumption that value in use is expressed simply by summing consumer preferences.

Smith would have us accept another theory of value, one which is in conflict with the more familiar versions of the utilitarian approach. Although he doesn't include Smith in their number, Matthew Stephenson argues that some classicists use 'value in use' in two ways: (1) to describe how individuals subjectively evaluate goods for their personal use and (2) to describe the value of goods to society as a whole.[1]

Most modern economists see no subtle normative content to the mechanics of demand and supply. We see the water-diamond paradox as an interesting pedagogical illustration of how prices account for scarcity. With little hesitation we would take as given that water is more useful to mankind than diamonds. That point being made, we would be willing to proceed to the next; namely, that market values do in fact reflect values in use, but of course, in marginal rather than total terms. But this step is one step that Smith is unwilling to take because of his belief that it contains an unacceptable normative statement. The normative implication is that market prices, or 'values in exchange' actually reflect 'values in use' and that the resolution of the water-diamond paradox somehow legitimizes market allocations as being the 'best' or 'most useful' attainable for society as a whole. But Smith has another societal norm from which his definition of value in use is derived. Moreover these values often differ from market-determined 'values in exchange'.

As the title of his book so aptly announces, Smith's choice for a social priority is economic growth: a nation's accumulation of wealth. He is not so much a utopian that he thinks it possible or appropriate to design a society where an ideal growth path will be followed. However, he is willing to use an ideal growth path as a norm. The 'usefulness' of a good is derived not from its utility, in the now familiar sense of satisfying consumer tastes, but from its capacity to enhance economic growth.

Thus 'value in use' is interpreted in terms of societal norms while 'value in exchange' reflects individual subjective wants.

My argument depends on an appreciation of the context in which the water-diamond paradox is presented. Smith makes this context clear in his 'Introduction and Plan of the Work' (1976, p. 10). The economic activity to be analysed is the 'annual labour' that supplies the nation with all the 'necessaries and conveniences of life which it annually consumes'. The focus is on labour as it is being employed as a productive agent. The productivity of labour depends on how 'labour is generally applied' and the 'proportion' of productive (or 'useful') to unproductive labour. Interpreters of Smith do not always appreciate just how pervasive is the theme of productive versus unproductive labour. The distribution of income, the composition of goods and services consumed, and the nation's institutional structure, are all analysed in terms of how well they channel the employment of labour into productive rather than unproductive uses.

Smith's first three chapters are devoted to an explanation of how the 'Division of Labour' makes for 'improvement' in its productive powers. The division of labour is a consequence of man's 'propensity to truck, barter, and exchange one thing for another' (p. 25). Chapter 4 explains how the division of labour is enhanced as the introduction of money increases the potential of exchanging. It is in this context that the word 'value' is explained as having two different meanings, 'value in use' and 'value in exchange', and the water-diamond paradox is employed. Smith immediately announces that he will 'investigate the principles which regulate the exchangeable value of commodities' (p. 46). Before that, however, he introduces labour as a standard of value.

Productive labour as an index of productive capacity
Smith ends Chapter 6 of *Wealth of Nations* with a summary. He also draws the distinction between productive and unproductive labour:

> As in a civilized country there are but few commodities of which the exchangeable value arises from labour only, rent and profit contributing largely to that of the far greater part of them, so the annual produce of its labour will always be sufficient to purchase or command a much greater quantity of labour than what was employed in raising, preparing, and bringing that produce to market. If the society were annually to employ all the labour which it can annually purchase, as the quantity of labour would increase greatly every year, so the produce of every succeeding year would be of vastly greater value than that of the foregoing. But there is no country in which the whole annual produce is employed in maintaining the industrious. The idle everywhere consume a great part of it; and according to the different proportions in which it is annually divided between those two different orders of people, its ordinary or average value must either annually increase, or diminish, or continue the same from year to year to another. (p. 71)

In the annual productive process a surplus is created which would be sufficient to employ or 'command' a far greater quantity of labour in productive activity than is actually employed. Note the use of the subjunctive: 'If the society *were* annually to employ [in productive work] all the labour which it can annually purchase... the produce of every succeeding year *would be* of vastly greater value than the foregoing.' Smith is clear that economic growth – the wealth of a nation – is directly a result of more labour being productively employed. An implicit assumption is that the supply of potentially productive labour is very elastic. Obviously the institutions which determine income distribution also determine the path of economic growth. In those societies where the 'idle' are able to claim and consume a larger proportion of production, growth will be diminished.

Smith argues that it is important how the surplus of production is spent. It can be spent on frivolous consumption by idle guests and menial servants or it can provide subsistence for 'labourers, manufacturers, and artificers, who reproduce with a profit the value of their annual consumption' (p. 338). Thus to the extent that a greater portion of the surplus goes to the idle rich, capital accumulation and the nation's wealth will suffer.

Smith's tone is obviously moralistic. Some countries have 'command' over vast resources which could be put to better use. He is comparing what could be accomplished with what in fact is being accomplished. But, again, Smith's analogy does not refer to the division of a static 'pie'; it is referring to the possibilities of growth through time. The more labour that is allocated to productive employments the greater will be the increase in wealth.

One of Smith's main purposes in developing labour as an index is to use it to measure a nation's capacity for growth. Smith concludes that if a country's economic institutions were so oriented that its surplus was spent on frivolous consumption, such as that of a landowner's idle guests or the services of menial servants, its real wealth would diminish. On the other hand, if its institutional structure were accommodating, its wealth, even that in the form of 'labour commanding' vendible commodities, would have the potential of enabling productive labourers to be put to work. The index then, represents *potential*, just as we estimate how much real GDP could be raised by lowering the unemployment rate by one or more points.

Schumpeter complains that Smith had three incompatible labour theories of value (Schumpeter, 1954, pp. 188–9). The first follows the famous beaver-deer example, demonstrating that the relative prices of each depend on the quantity of labour involved in the hunt. As Schumpeter points out, 'Smith confines this proposition only to that "early and rude state of society" in which there are no other distributive shares to take into account' (p. 188).

A second labour theory which Smith describes as the 'toil and trouble', which is 'the real price of everything', is related to more complex markets and, as we shall see, is complementary to Smith's major theme. Schumpeter is correct in stating that Smith 'made no effort to develop the theme of disutility' as an explanation for value in exchange (ibid., p. 189).

Smith's third 'labour theory of value' also fails as an explanation of how the 'value in exchange' of a commodity is derived from the labour expended in its production. This third theory is nothing more than Smith's assertion that labour would make an excellent *standard* of value. Schumpeter and others are quick to point out that, although Smith goes to some lengths to promote labour as a standard of value, he makes no attempt to show how it *explains* the market prices of commodities. But, of course, if our central theme is correct, Smith has no intention of making such a link. On the contrary his purpose is to *contrast* the 'real' values of goods and services with their values in exchange. We are left not with the problem of linking labour to 'value in exchange' but of linking it to 'value in use'. That is precisely what Smith does. He uses labour, or at least 'productive labour', to explain a nation's capacity for economic growth.

Smith's effort is not altogether successful. He is not convincing when he attributes value to commodities simply because they can potentially be used to 'command' productive labour. This would imply that at any point in time all of these values could immediately and simultaneously be transformed into productive labour. But perhaps we are being too critical of Smith. We, like him, can envision no such wholesale transformation. But we would certainly acknowledge the possibility of marginal reallocations of labour to more productive pursuits.

This question of the allocation of labour is one of Smith's central themes; and if market prices reflect an unproductive allocation, they cannot reflect true 'values in use'. If we follow Smith's definitions, there is no possibility of resolving the dichotomy between 'values in use' and 'values in exchange'. His definition of 'value in use' is related to whether the good or service directly or indirectly enables labour to be employed productively; that is, in a way that enhances economic growth. The criticism that Smith somehow failed to link individual subjective evaluations or 'utility' to demand and thus to the interaction of supply and demand is mistaken. Smith does in fact link individual subjective evaluations to effective demand and he presents a very complete explanation of the price mechanism as it functions in both the short run and the long run. But Smith looks elsewhere for an explanation of a commodity's 'usefulness' or 'value' to society as a whole. Thus Smith would resist the normative element in utilitarian interpretations of social welfare which focus only on summations of individual subjective wants. This brings us to the question of whether there could be some right set of free market institutions under which Smith could envision a resource allocation occurring that would satisfy his norms concerning productivity and economic growth. Is there a configuration of institutions that would allow the 'unseen hand' to guide society along an ideal path of growth? Of course there can be no definitive answer to this question. However the question itself provides very useful perspectives for understanding Smith's basic themes in *Wealth of Nations*. Smith is aware that with free consumer choice, which inevitably allows for waste on frivolous luxuries, such a path may not be attained. Nevertheless much of Smith's analyses and evaluations can be understood from using the norm of a favourable path of economic growth. This includes not only our present concern – Smith's rejection of the link between 'value in use' and 'value in exchange'. It also includes his choice of labour as a standard of real value, his definitions of productive and unproductive labour, and, very generally, the nature of his critiques of practically all of the economic institutions of his day.

The proportion of funds going to support productive or unproductive hands determines the growth path of the country:

The proportion between these different funds necessarily determines in every country the general character of the inhabitants as to industry or idleness. We are more industrious than our forefathers; because in the present times the funds destined for the maintenance of industry, are much greater in proportion to those which are likely to be employed in the maintenance of idleness, than they were two or three centuries ago....

Wherever capital predominates, industry prevails: wherever revenue, idleness. Every increase or diminution of capital, therefore, naturally tends to increase or diminish the real quantity of industry, the number of productive hands, and consequently the exchangeable value of the annual produce of the land and labour of the country, the real wealth and revenue of all its inhabitants. (1976, pp. 335–7)

Very briefly a nation's economic institutions and their influences on behaviour determine whether labour will be employed in productive pursuits. Institutions are evaluated on the basis of how income is distributed between that 'destined for replacing a capital, and that which is destined for constituting a revenue, either as rent or as profit'. Whereas some funds flow directly back into 'capital' (the stock that supports productive labour), revenue in the forms of 'rent' or 'profit' may or may not maintain 'productive hands' (p. 334). Moreover spending that is 'laid out' in durable commodities usually gives maintenance to productive hands whereas spending directed towards 'frivolous objects, the little ornaments of dress and furniture, jewels, trinkets, gewgaws, frequently indicates, not only a trifling, but a base and selfish disposition'. The former 'expense' is 'more favourable to private frugality, and consequently, to the increase of the publick capital, and as it maintains productive, rather than unproductive hands, conduces more than the other to the growth of public opulence' (pp. 348–9).

Although it is not possible to present all the available evidence here, a survey of value theory prior to Smith reveals an evolution towards interpreting individual subjective preferences expressed in market demand as the necessary and sufficient explanation of all economic value. The dichotomy between value in use and value in exchange had been explored in Greek thought and had remained in tension over the centuries. This tension was in danger of being superseded by the utilitarian theory which explained value as a summation of individual preferences. Value in use was becoming conflated with individual preferences, which in turn were the basis for value in exchange.

Direct challenges to Smith's thinking came from his Scottish predecessors Gersham Carmichael and Francis Hutcheson.[2] Much of the discussion of the Scottish Enlightenment had been sparked by the work of Hugo Grotius (Hugh de Groot, 1583–1645; Grotius, 1646) and Samuel von Pufendorf.

When Pufendorf defines the 'natural Ground' of a good's value he emphasizes its fitness for supplying the 'Necessities of Humane Life' although 'rarity' and 'Scarceness' are also important (Pufendorf, 1724, Ch. 14).

But both Carmichael and Hutcheson are clear that a good does not have to be a necessity to have value. Carmichael describes usefulness in terms of whether a good is thought to 'add to the utility or pleasure of human life'. Moreover this aptitude can be real or imagined (Carmichael in Pufendorf, 1724). Hutcheson goes further. Usefulness is 'Not only a natural subserviency to our support, or to some natural pleasure, but any tendency to give any satisfaction, by prevailing custom or fancy, as a matter of ornament or distinction.' (Hutcheson, 1755, p. 53).

As his critics point out, Smith, in his *Lectures on Jurisprudence*, shows that he is familiar with the relationships among demand, scarcity, wealth, and value in exchange and the resolution of the paradox of value. There Smith describes the determinants of market price as:

> First, the demand, or need for the commodity. There is no demand for a thing of little use; it is not a rational object of desire.
>
> Secondly, the abundance or scarcity of the commodity in proportion to the need of it. If the commodity be scarce, the price is raised, but if the commodity be more than sufficient to supply the demand, the price falls. Thus it is that diamonds and other precious stones are dear, while iron, which is more useful, is so many times cheaper, though this depends principally on the last cause, *viz.*:
>
> Thirdly, the riches or poverty of those who demand. (Smith, 1978, p. 497)

Smith's treatment of supply and demand in his *Lectures* is extensive. In another example he explains:

> A thing which is hardly of any use, yet if the quantity be not sufficient to supply the demand, will give a high price; hence the great price of diamonds. . . . Abundance on the other hand such as does more than supply all possible demands, renders water of no price at all and other things of a price the next thing to nothing. (p. 358)[3]

Smith's clarity in his *Lectures* as to the link between individual utility estimates and exchange value supports my argument that his change in emphasis in *Wealth of Nations* is purposeful. Smith fully intends to 'derail' the train of economic thought in its progress towards a utilitarian theory of value. Several of his critics certainly give him 'credit' for creating this result.

Smith's concepts as interpreted by other classical economists

Although Smith's influence on other classical economists was profound, all departed in significant ways from what I describe here as his concept of value in use and its integration with the major themes of his work. We will briefly consider the ways David Ricardo and John Stuart Mill responded to Smith's treatment of the paradox of value, his definitions of value in use and value in exchange, and his use of labour as a standard of value.

As I have argued, Smith had no difficulty in resolving the paradox of value; and as Hollander and others have argued, Ricardo and Mill also had no such difficulty.[4] Ricardo followed Smith in differentiating between 'value in use' and 'value in exchange'.[5] But Ricardo, unlike Smith, attempts to explain 'values in exchange' in terms of labour. Smith's explanation of market prices anticipated neoclassical analysis by explaining short-run market prices in terms of demand and supply and long-run prices in terms of costs (in modern terms, the low point of the long-run average cost curve). As noted, Smith's use of the labour theory of value is restricted to his model of that 'early and rude state of society'. Ricardo agrees that Smith 'so accurately defined the original source of exchangeable value' but expresses disappointment at his failure to extend the theory further. In Ricardo's theory the exchangeable values of goods depends not only on the labour 'applied immediately' to their production, 'but the labour also which is bestowed on the implements, tools, and buildings, with which such labour is assisted' (Ricardo, 1951-73, Vol. I, p. 22). Ricardo notes that even in Smith's 'early state' the hunters of beaver and deer worked with 'capital' in the form of weapons they had previously made. Thus the exchangeable value produced 'would be in proportion to the labour bestowed in their production; not on their immediate production only, but on all those implements or machines required to give effect to the particular labour to which they were applied' (ibid., p. 24). In a running discourse with Jean Baptiste Say over several years and editions of their books,[6] Ricardo claims that Say,

in his account of value and riches...has confounded two things which ought always to be kept separate, and which are called by Adam Smith, value in use and value in exchange. If by an improved machine I can, with the same quantity of labour, make two pair of stockings instead of one, I in no way impair the utility of one pair of stockings, though I diminish their value.... Utility then is not the measure of exchangeable value. (ibid., p. 280, citing editions 1 and 2)

One objection to using labour as an invariable standard of value is that improvements in labour productivity necessarily change its value relative to all other goods. Ricardo's answer to this objection was simple: if labour productivity increases it causes the value of all other goods to decrease. Ricardo opens Chapter 20 by quoting Adam Smith:

'A man is rich or poor,' says Adam Smith, 'according to the degree in which he can afford to enjoy the necessaries, conveniences, and amusements of human life.'
    Value, then, essentially differs from riches, for value depends not on abundance, but on the difficulty or facility of production. The labour of a million of men in manufactures, will always produce the same value, but will not always produce the same riches. By the invention of machinery, by improvements in skill, by a better division of labour, or by the discovery of new markets, where more advantageous exchange may be made, a million of men may produce double, or triple the amount of riches, of 'necessaries, conveniences, and amusements', in one state of society, that they could produce in another, but they will not on that account add anything to value....(ibid., p. 273)

Here we see similarities with Smith but at the same time important differences; differences which, I argue, tend to focus attention away from the Smithian dichotomy between value in use and value in exchange.

Smith's 'value in use' is based on the efficacy of a good in supporting the productivity of labour and ultimately in enhancing a nation's wealth. Ricardo continues: 'By constantly increasing the facility of production, we constantly diminish the value of some of the commodities before produced, though by the same means we not only add to the national riches, but also add to the power of future production' (ibid., p. 274). Like Smith, Ricardo links economic growth with the employment of productive labour. According to Ricardo:

> The wealth of a country may be increased in two ways: it may be increased by employing a greater portion of revenue in the maintenance of productive labour, – which will not only add to the quantity, but to the value of the mass of commodities; or it may be increased, without employing any additional quantity of labour, by making the same quantity more productive, – which will add to the abundance, but not the value of commodities. (ibid.)

Thus among the similarities two striking differences appear. First, as we saw earlier, Ricardo insists on explaining exchange values of goods in terms of the labour employed in their production. Secondly, while Ricardo agrees that a nation's wealth may be 'increased by employing a greater portion of revenue to the maintenance of productive labour', he doesn't see, as Smith does, that greater output per labourer also adds to growth potential. According to Smith that 'abundance' always has the potential of being transformed into support for productive labour. While it is true that some goods have high exchange value and little immediate value in use, they have some implicit value in that they can be sold and the proceeds used to support productive labour. Although Smith realizes that the wealth of a nation will never be utilized fully in support of productive labour, within certain limits such transformation is feasible and the availability of potentially productive labour is completely elastic. Ricardo by contrast downplays the possibility of using a country's wealth or 'abundance' to employ productive labour. Ricardo's focus is on the question of just how the mass of commodities was produced rather than on their potential in the growth process. If they were produced by greater quantities of labour they have greater value. If they were produced by the same quantity they have greater 'abundance' but not greater value. Finally, then, it becomes clear that Ricardo's focus on labour as the source of all value necessarily obfuscates Smith's dichotomy between value in use and value in exchange.

Mill's treatment of Smith's value theory

Mill discredits Smith's idea of 'value in use' but clearly recognizes that Smith meant his labour theory to be used as a standard rather than an explanation of exchange values.

Adam Smith, in a passage often quoted, has touched upon the most obvious ambiguity of the word value; which, in one of its senses, signifies usefulness, in another, power of purchasing; in his own language, value in use and value in exchange. But (as Mr. De Quincey has remarked) in illustrating this double meaning, Adam Smith has himself fallen into another ambiguity. Things (he says) which have the greatest value in use have often little or no value in exchange; which is true, since that which can be obtained without labour or sacrifice will command no price, however useful or needful it may be. But he proceeds to add, that things which have the greatest value in exchange, as a diamond for example, may have little or no value in use. This is employing the word use, not in the sense in which political economy is concerned with it, but in that other sense in which use is opposed to pleasure. Political economy has nothing to do with the comparative estimation of different uses in the judgment of a philosopher or a moralist. The use of a thing, in political economy, means its capacity to satisfy a desire, or serve a purpose. Diamonds have this capacity in a high degree, and unless they had it, would not bear any price. Value in use, or as Mr. De Quincey calls it, *teleologic* value, is the extreme limit of value in exchange. The exchange value of a thing may fall short, to any amount, of its value in use; but that it can ever exceed the value in use, implies a contradiction; it supposes that persons will give, to possess a thing, more than the utmost value which they themselves put upon it as a means of gratifying their inclinations. (Mill, 1965, pp. 456–7)

This passage demonstrates that Mill has missed Smith's point that individual preferences as realized in effective demand are unlikely to result in a resource allocation which takes account of social goals such as economic growth. As Hollander points out, 'Mill [is] unfair in his complaint that Smith by his formulation [has] introduced an irrelevant moralistic dimension' (Hollander, 1985, p. 280). There is, I have argued, a social norm embedded in Smith's 'value in use' but Smith's concern is more one of efficiency in resource allocation than simply the moral depravity of consumers. Mill and De Quincey would be correct if all final commodities and the resources used in their production had no purpose other than consumer 'gratification'. But if social goals conflict with the resource allocation determined by market prices, then 'value in use' may well conflict with 'value in exchange'. We may interpret De Quincey's *teleologic* value to be the highest price a given group of consumers would pay, perhaps including any consumers' surplus. But it is certainly not the limit of 'value in use' if, as I argue, there are societal goals that may not be expressed by consumers as values in exchange.

Mill also criticizes Smith's choices of corn or labour as standards of value. The problem of comparing prices over time or from country to country, which we attempt to solve with price indices, Mill declares to be insoluble. But his criticism of Smith goes deeper:

Adam Smith fancied that there were two commodities peculiarly fitted to serve as a measure of value: corn, and labour. Of corn, he said that although its value fluctuates much from year to year, it does not vary greatly from century to century.

> This we now know to be an error.... With respect to labour as a measure of value, the language of Adam Smith is not uniform. He sometimes speaks of it as a good measure only for short periods, saying that the value of labour (or wages) does not vary much from year to year, though it does from generation to generation. On other occasions he speaks as if labour were intrinsically the most proper measure of value, on the ground that one day's ordinary muscular exertion of one man, may be looked upon as always, to him, the same amount of effort or sacrifice. But this proposition, whether in itself admissible or not, discards the idea of exchange value altogether, substituting a totally different idea, more analogous to value in use. If a day's labour will purchase in America twice as much of ordinary consumable articles as in England, it seems a vain subtlety to insist on saying that labour is of the same value in both countries, and that it is the value of the other things which is different. (Mill, 1965, pp. 579–80)[7]

When Mill relates Smith's use of the labour standard to the idea of a 'value in use' he is supportive of my argument that Smith intended to link the two. But Mill either does not understand or, more likely, does not approve of Smith's purpose to use the labour standard to evaluate economic institutions in terms of the social norm: economic growth. Although Ricardo and Mill, like Smith, develop models which feature stationary states, they, like Smith, also believe that economic growth is possible and advocate public policies aimed at enhancing growth. But Smith ultimately fails in his attempt to forestall the acceptance of consumer preferences (as expressed in effective demand) as the norm to be maximized. And one reason for his failure is that, as his contributions to economic theory are modified and elaborated upon, the integrity of his general theme is lost. This integrity requires that 'value in use' be distinct from 'value in exchange' and that the accepted norm for evaluating a nation's 'wealth' be its potential for employing labour in productive pursuits.

Some modern criticisms of Smith's treatment of the water-diamond paradox

Emil Kauder outlines the inheritance given Smith from the utility theorists and characterizes his treatment of the water-diamond paradox in *Wealth of Nations* in the following way:

> Yet it was the tragedy of these writers that they wrote in vain, they were soon forgotten. No scholar appeared to make out of these thoughts the new science of political economy. Instead, the father of our economic science wrote that water has a great utility and a small value. With these few words Adam Smith had made waste and rubbish out of the thinking of 2,000 years. The chance to start in 1776 instead of 1870 with a more correct knowledge of value principles had been missed. (Kauder, 1953, p. 650)

H.M. Robertson and W.L. Taylor, while not so critical as Kauder, still agree that 'there can be only regret for Smith's new emphasis given with such vastly influential consequences in *The Wealth of Nations*, which led on to at least a serious underemphasis on, and, at times, to the almost complete eclipse of, these ideas in British political economy for nearly a hundred years' (Robertson and Taylor, 1957, p. 190).

Smith's critics are in disagreement as to whether he changed his own thinking in some fundamental way or whether he simply lapsed and became slipshod in his treatment. Robertson and Taylor point out that we can hardly make use of the bluff Johnsonian riposte, 'Sir, it was pure ignorance' (1957, p. 190). But their answer to the riddle is unsatisfactory: 'He used few words because he was merely echoing something he regarded as traditional, trite and obvious' (ibid., p. 191).

Samuel Hollander is one of the few interpreters who sees Smith's failure to link individual subjective utility and 'value in use' as intentional. He argues that in Smith's 'unhappy contrast' between 'value in use' and 'value in exchange' the term 'value in use':

> must be understood in the narrow sense of biological significance and not in the economist's broad sense of desirability. The proposition amounts to an insistence that physical properties of commodities are quite irrelevant in the determination of exchange value. From his observations in this regard we can learn nothing of his position regarding the relationship between price and utility in the sense of desirability. (Hollander, 1973, p. 136)

According to Hollander: 'The "paradox of value" was not formulated as a *problem* requiring a *solution*; it was rather a statement of fact regarding the irrelevance for exchange value of the physical (biological or cultural) properties of commodities' (ibid., p. 137).

Paul Douglas, like Mill, attributes Smith's reluctance to link individual subjective utility and 'value in use' to his moral values (Douglas, 1928). This explanation, although incomplete, fits well with our present line of argument. We have already noted the moralistic tone to the pejoratives Smith uses to describe 'frivolous objects' whose purchase indicates not only a 'trifling, but a base and selfish disposition'. If some individual choices lack moral standing, it is obvious that the summation of the individual estimates of value in the forms of effective demand cannot aspire to moral legitimacy in the broader sense of a social norm. My argument takes this line of reasoning one further step. I argue that 'value in use' can be defined in normative terms in the context of Smith's larger societal norm, economic growth. Thus some of the values individuals place on things not only lack moral legitimacy, they are wrong because they lead to a misallocation of resources. They lead to resources being employed in the 'maintenance of idleness' rather than in increasing the 'quantity of industry'.

Schumpeter evaluates Smith's treatment as follows:

having distinguished value in use and value in exchange, he dismisses the former by pointing to what has been called...the 'paradox of value' – which he evidently did believe to be a bar to progress on this line – thereby barring, for the next two or three generations, the door so auspiciously opened by his French and Italian predecessors. No talk about his 'recognizing the role of demand' can alter this fact. (Schumpeter, 1954, p. 309)

But Schumpeter is clearly wrong when he attributes Smith's change in direction to an inability to resolve the paradox of value. The 'bar to progress' does not arise from Smith's ineptitude. Smith does not dismiss the link between individual wants and effective demand in the theory of exchange, but he objects to the idea that 'exchange values' somehow reflect 'value in use' in the broader social context. Schumpeter observes that Smith proceeds to develop a theory of value in exchange based on costs of production in which 'wages, profit, and rent are the sources of revenue' and also 'of all exchangeable value'. This of course is quite similar to the neoclassical theory which demonstrates that in competitive markets a commodity's price is finally dictated not by demand but by the low point of the long-run average cost curve. This result, however, does not mean that in neoclassical theory the demand side is ignored.

Schumpeter acknowledges that 'the matter is complicated by the fact that a very large number of passages...seem to point to a labour theory of value or rather several' (ibid.). In the introduction I referred to Schumpeter's critique of Smith's labour theories of value, agreeing with him that Smith actually had no labour theory of value in the sense that labour could be shown to somehow 'create' values that are then expressed by market prices. Instead Smith would have us accept economic growth as a societal norm. Thus any input or output would be evaluated in terms of ability to enhance the productivity of labour.

Summary

Now let us summarize the interpretation given to Smith's treatment and place it in the context of his goals in writing *Wealth of Nations*. It is argued that Smith is in fact purposeful in his 'dismissal' of the links between individual utility and 'value in use' as a social norm. Thus he purposefully derails the progress towards a utilitarian theory until it is finally completed by Jevons, Menger and Walras. I disagree with the suggestion of Robertson and Taylor that Smith inadvertently downplays the role of value in use simply because he assumes his readers regard the argument as 'traditional, trite, and obvious'.

As outlined previously, my interpretation of Smith's value theory is couched in a broader interpretation of his overall theme which runs through *Wealth of Nations*. Indeed if this interpretation is accepted it sheds light on a number of other important analytical perspectives that Smith chooses to use and that annoy and perhaps confuse many of his interpreters.

Smith's norm, and what he argues should be society's norm, is economic growth. His concept of 'value in use' is directly tied to the question of what part an individual, raw material, machine, commodity or economic institution plays in the process of economic growth. Values assigned in exchange may or may not reflect an input's or output's real value in promoting economic growth. Thus Smith's explanation of 'value in exchange' is separate from his explanation of 'value in use'.

In his explanation of value in exchange, Smith does not dismiss the idea that it is consumers' subjective wants that are reflected in market demand. Instead what he dismisses is the normative implication that a summation of consumer wants can fully represent 'real' or 'true' social value. In other parts of *The Wealth of Nations* Smith develops his own interpretation of what constitutes true 'value in use'. Smith's labour standard of value is directly linked with the idea of labour's capacity to enhance economic growth. The labour-commanding attribute of a commodity's value may or may not be put to productive use; i.e. it may or may not be used to employ 'productive' labour, but its true value is the labour-commanding attribute. Similarly Smith goes on to evaluate the distribution of income and virtually all of the economic institutions of his day in terms of the part they play in promoting economic growth.

Ricardo's development of a fully-fledged labour-cost theory of value does not serve Smith's purpose to maintain the dichotomy between the two definitions. Whereas the utilitarian task is to explain value in use in terms of individual preferences and then explain value in exchange in the same way, Ricardo attempts to explain both value in use and value in exchange in terms of labour.

The particular paths taken by Malthus, Ricardo, Marx and other of Smith's followers are all nascent possibilities in Smith's arguments. However, were his followers less original and more true to Smith's purposes, his value theories would have been strengthened rather than obfuscated. Mill would have less support for his declaration that political economy is not concerned with the word 'use' in the sense that use is seen as opposed to the pleasure of individual consumers.

In one sense Smith's more recent critics are correct. Smith does set back the development in economic theory of the utilitarian idea that free markets allow for an allocation of resources which maximizes the subjective welfare of consumers. Smith wants to distinguish between (1) an allocation of resources which maximizes the satisfaction of individual subjective wants as expressed in effective demand, and (2) an allocation of resources that better reflects the social norm of an ideal path of economic growth. When we review the history of economic thought we must regret that when Jevons, Menger and Walras finally achieved what Smith is said to have delayed, there was the unfortunate consequence that the distinction Smith sought to make was again blurred. Although we cannot attribute the idea to all who follow in the utilitarian tradition, there remains embedded in the foundations of modern economic theory the idea that it is legitimate and sufficient to take individual subjective wants, as expressed in effective market demand, as the only thing to be maximized as resources are allocated. Smith resisted this idea but was ultimately unsuccessful. Upon reflection we may decide that the 'tragedy' of misdirected efforts and mislaid values does not belong to Smith but to many of his successors in both the classical and utilitarian tradition.

Notes

1. Matthew Stephenson (1972, pp. 127–39). According to Stephenson, Smith believes 'that the summation of the exchange values of individual goods equals the value of total wealth.' (p. 129). Our focus here is on Smith's treatment of the paradox of value and how his theory of value is consistent with his overall theme, the potential for increase in a nation's wealth. That Ricardo, Mill and others follow Smith in the distinction between individual and social estimates of 'value in use' is to be expected. But as I will argue here, while Smith's treatment is usually consistent with his overall theme, Ricardo and Mill depart from Smith's scheme in important ways.
2. Carmichael and Hutcheson attribute many of their ideas to Grotius and Pufendorf in such works as Hutcheson's *Introduction to Moral Philosophy* (1747) and Carmichael's notes to his edition of Pufendorf's *De Officio* (2nd edn, Edinburgh, 1724).
3. Smith illustrates further by a story of a merchant and a traveller meeting in 'the desarts of Arabia' where the price of water increased to '10 000 crowns for one cruise of water'. By contrast the famous Pits diamond which was of 'no real value' would not have been purchased for £250 000 had it not been for its scarcity and a 'prince so vain and proud, as well as rich, as Lewis 12 of France'.
4. 'It is most regrettable that the profession cannot be shaken from the opinion that Ricardo and Mill were unable to resolve the paradox of value; and that the utility contributions of the 1870s were required to break the deadlock' (Hollander, 1985, p. 935n.).
5. In fact, Ricardo begins his *Principles of Political Economy*, Chapter 1 'On Value' by quoting Smith: 'It has been observed by Adam Smith, that the word Value has two different meanings, and sometimes expresses the utility of some particular object, and sometimes the power of purchasing other goods which the possession of that object conveys. The one may be called *value in use*; the other *value in exchange*. The things, he continues, "which have the greatest value in exchange, have little or no value in use." Water and air are abundantly useful; they are indeed indispensable to existence, yet, under ordinary circumstances, nothing can be obtained in exchange for them. Gold, on the contrary, though of little use compared with air or water, will exchange for a great quantity of other goods.'
   Utility then is not the measure of exchangeable value...' (1951–73, p. 11).
6. Ricardo's *Principles* and Say's *Traité d'Economie Politique*.
7. Mill goes on to differentiate between Smith's concept of labour as standard 'Measure of Value' and Ricardo's theory of labour as a 'regulator' or 'determining principle' of value:
   'The idea of a Measure of Value must not be confounded with the idea of the regulator, or determining principle, of value. When it is said by Ricardo and others, that the value of a thing is regulated by quantity of labour, they do not mean the quantity of labour for which the thing will exchange, but the quantity required for producing it. This, they mean to affirm, determines its value; causes it to be of the value it is, and of no other. But when Adam Smith and Malthus say that labour is a measure of value, they do not mean the labour by which the thing was or can be made, but the quantity of labour which it will exchange for, or purchase; in other words the value of the thing, estimated in labour. And they do not mean that this *regulates* the general exchange value of the thing, or has any effect in determining what that value shall be, but only ascertains what it is, and whether and how much it varies from time to time and from place to place. To confound these two ideas, would be much the same thing as to overlook the distinction between the thermometer and the fire' (pp. 580–1).

References

Douglas, Paul (1928), 'Smith's Theory of Value and Distribution', in J.M. Clark et al., *Adam Smith 1776–1926; Lectures to Commemorate the Sesquicentennial of the Publication of 'Wealth of Nations'*, Chicago: University of Chicago Press, pp. 75–115.

Grotius, Hugo (1916), *De Jure Belli ac Pacis*, reproduction of the edition of 1646, Washington.

Hollander, Samuel (1973), *The Economics of Adam Smith*, Toronto: University of Toronto Press.

Hollander, Samuel (1979), *The Economics of David Ricardo*, Toronto: University of Toronto Press.

Hollander, Samuel (1985), *The Economics of John Stuart Mill*, Toronto: University of Toronto Press.

Hutcheson, Francis (1747), *Introduction to Moral Philosophy*, Glasgow.

Hutcheson, Francis (1755), *System of Moral Philosophy*, Glasgow.

Kauder, Emil (1953), 'Genesis of the Marginal Utility Theory', *Economic Journal*, **63**, pp. 638–50.

Kauder, Emil (1965), *A History of Marginal Utility Theory*, Princeton: Princeton University Press.

Mill, John Stuart (1965), *Principles of Political Economy*, in *Collected works of John Stuart Mill*, Toronto: University of Toronto Press.

Pufendorf, Samuel von (1724), *De Officio*, ed. Gersham Carmichael, Edinburgh.

Ricardo, David (1951–73), *The Works and Correspondence of David Ricardo*, 11 vols, ed. P. Sraffa, Cambridge: Cambridge University Press.

Robertson, H.M. and Taylor, W.L. (1957), 'Adam Smith's Approach to the Theory of Value', *Economic Journal*, XVII (June), pp. 181–98.

Say, Jean Baptiste (1803, 1814), *Traité d'Economie Politique*, 1st edn Paris 1803; 2nd edn 1814.

Schumpeter, Joseph A. (1954), *History of Economic Analysis*, London: Allen & Unwin.

Smith, Adam (1976), *An Inquiry into the Nature and Causes of the Wealth of Nations* [1776], ed. R.H. Campbell, A.S. Skinner and W.B. Todd, Oxford: Clarendon Press.

Smith, Adam (1978), *Lectures on Jurisprudence* [1751–2, 1762–3], ed. R.L. Meek, D.D. Raphael and P.G. Stein, Oxford: Clarendon Press.

Stephenson, Matthew (1972), 'The Paradox of Value: A Suggested Interpretation', *History of Political Economy*, Vol. 4, no. 1 (Spring), pp. 127–39.

11 Friedrich List and the political economy of protective tariffs

J.G. Backhaus

Introduction

The historian of thought has a task which is not dissimilar to that of an archivist. He is the archivist of his discipline. His purpose – and also his duty – is to correctly reconstruct the main ideas and to preserve with as little loss as possible the intellectual heritage of his discipline; his task is also to correct as far as possible misunderstandings that have occurred; and thirdly, he has to achieve this purpose with a view to the present, in order to prevent his contemporaries from entering into trains of analysis which have proven to be dead ends in the past.

Friedrich List is one of those classical contributors to our discipline who should not need our attention, since recognized scholars have taken care of his work. List himself ensured that his ideas became widely known and the most important lectures and correspondence have been available in an edition comprising ten volumes;[1] indeed, there are few economists who are the subject of an equally large secondary literature. Even in the textbooks of international trade, his name appears with regularity. Still I think that a key aspect is constantly overlooked; this aspect is the focus of the discussion which follows. My contribution is not intended as a substitute to the rich existing literature on List. It is intended to complement our understanding of Friedrich List's scholarly contribution to the economic analysis of the political and economic development of trading nations.

The central thesis of this essay is readily stated. List's developmental strategy was based on economic analysis and empirical observation; but it was not an economic theory; it was a doctrine for the administrative practice of a medium-sized tax state with a well established bureaucracy. List's doctrine met all the criteria which contemporary social science has developed for the evaluation of such a doctrine; but List's contribution was not an economic theory in the classical sense. Anyone who tries to read List with the eyes and the mindset of authors of economics textbooks will be puzzled and irritated by List's work.

This chapter consists of four substantive parts in addition to this introduction. Part I offers a selective overview of List's treatment in contemporary textbooks. Part II gives a short inventory of some of the major misunderstandings which recur in the academic literature about List. Part III offers a concise reconstruction of the political economy of protective tariffs as the key element of List's developmental strategy. Part IV explores some ramifications of List's approach in order to support the general line of interpretation followed.

I

One of the best textbook treatments of Friedrich List's economics can be found in the widely used text by Peter H. Lindert and Charles P. Kindleberger,[2] who give the following account:

> Of all the protectionist arguments, the one that has always enjoyed the most prestige among both economists and policy makers is the infant-industry argument, which asserts that in less developed countries a temporary tariff is justified because it cuts down on imports of modern manufacturers while the infant domestic industry learns how to produce at low enough costs to compete without the help of a tariff. . . . The infant industry argument differs from the optimal tariff argument in that it claims that in the long run the tariff protection will be good for the world as well as the nation. It differs from most other tariff arguments in being explicitly dynamic, arguing that the protection is needed only for a while. . . . To the extent that the infant industry argument is an argument for encouraging current domestic production, the above analysis applies. If the infant home industry will bring side benefits by causing the labor force and other industries to develop new skills, subsidizing production can achieve this more cheaply than can taxing imports. If the extra foreseen benefits take the form of future cost reductions for the same industry, through learning by doing, then there is another alternative more appropriate than either the tariff or the production subsidy. If an industry's current high costs are outweighed by the later cost cutting that experience will allow, then the industry can borrow against its own future profits and make it through the initial period in which costs are higher than the prices being charged on imports. . . . If the need for help is truly temporary, there is another argument against using the tariff to protect the infant. Tariffs are not easily removed once they are written into law, and there is the danger that an 'infant' that never becomes efficient will use part of its tariff-bred profits to sway policy makers to make a bad tariff immortal.

This exposition and critique cannot do justice to the economic analysis underlying List's developmental strategy. Although the authors are correct in pointing to the explicitly dynamic nature of List's argument, they fail to identify the source of the dynamics. List's political economy of development requires one central agent to whom the doctrine is also addressed. The entire strategy is tailored around the means and possibilities available to state economic policy at his time. The source of the dynamics, and the agent conducting economic policy, is the traditional tax state with its received sets of financial instruments. The three standard textbook arguments put forward against List and summarized again by Lindert and Kindleberger all overlook the institutional context in which List's doctrine needs to be placed. They simply ignore the state as the central economic agent in the historical context of List's work. From a welfare economic point of view it can be argued that subsidies are better than tariffs, provided the taxes necessary to finance the subsidies do not cause offsetting distortions. The argument, however, is irrelevant for an assessment of List's developmental strategy. The basic difference between the two instruments is readily identified. A protective tariff does not involve an additional burden on the state budget; in its initial phase it even yields a contribution; this is not true for subsidies. The medium-sized territorial states with their agriculture-based economies for which List developed his strategy would not have been able to finance the programme of subsidies modern textbook authors write about. In 1794 the Duchy of Württemberg needed 8 per cent of its total state revenues to provide for just one fairly small university, the 'Hohe-Karls-Schule'. Since the burden proved to be too heavy, the school had to be closed. It was, of course, the same Württemberg, by then somewhat enlarged and elevated to a kingdom, yet still underdeveloped, for which List designed his strategy of economic development just a few years later.

Credit financing the development of an entire industry presupposes the existence of a well developed capital market and the requisite banking institutions supporting such a capital market. This assumption, again, from the point of view of economic history is completely unrealistic. List at this time could not presuppose such a banking system with well developed capital markets, since such a system and such markets did not yet exist. In the German states it was above all the state, or rather the various German states, that tried to conceive banking institutions sufficiently large to foster economic development. The Prussian *Seehandlung* is a good example of this strategy.[3]

The third objection completely misses List's central point, which was the *reduction* of customs barriers. List's developmental strategy is convincing and cunning (*listig* in German), since the main economic instrument with which it works, the educational tariff, is used in such a way that it automatically renders itself ineffectual once it has served its (educational) purpose. His ruse (*List* in German) consisted in proposing educational tariffs in order to abolish fiscal tariffs.

One can not really dodge the question how it was possible that the leading scholarly activist working for the reduction of customs barriers and the creation of large common markets beyond national boundaries in the textbooks appears as the leading proponent of protectionist commercial policies. Our surprise about this discrepancy may become even bigger once we realize that the phenomenon of the two Lists is by no means recent and that there is no lack of attempts by leading scholars to expose the discrepancy between the true List and the List of the pamphleteers and textbook authors, to clear up misunderstandings and misrepresentations. A typical example is the well-known theoretician Heinrich Dietzel, who in 1912 devoted an entire book to his attempt to provide a corrected rendition of List's economics, not without mentioning, by the way, his many predecessors in the same endeavour. 'There have already been many objections against the attempt to "attribute protectionist tendencies" (Lotz) to precisely that man who wrote his only book in order to show the way which leads from protective tariffs to free trade.'[4]

Perhaps it should not really be surprising that an inveterate publicist and lobbyist such as Friedrich List himself became captured by the interests of powerful groups. He even lost his chair at the University of Tübingen when (and officially: because) he took up a consulting position with the Union of German Merchants in Frankfurt on the Main where the ambassadors to the German Confederation (Deutscher Bund) had their Federal Diet. Still, it is interesting to note that free trade was the explicit political objective for which List had drafted his petition on behalf of the Union of German Merchants and directed to the German Confederation. In this petition, he wrote:

> Strangulated by British, French, Dutch, *etc.* customs systems, Germany as a whole does nothing that could prod her neighbours to co-operate towards achieving freedom of trade; yet freedom of trade is the only means by which Europe can hope to attain the highest degree of civilization.[5]

Yet it is certainly surprising that List, who categorically rejected protective tariffs for agriculture in every and any circumstance, still is cited as an advocate of agricultural protective tariffs.[6]

List's analytical approach is readily illustrated as we more closely examine his reasoning on why agriculture can never be an industry deserving educational tariffs:

> From an economic point of view, nations have to go through the following stages: state of primitive nature – state of ranching and agriculture – state of agriculture and industry – state of agriculture, industry and trade.
>
> The industrial history of nations, and none better and more instructively than the history of England, shows that the transition from the primitive state to ranching, from ranching to agriculture and from agriculture to the first beginnings of industry and shipping can most expediently and most profitably be achieved by engaging in free trade with cities and countries that have already reached a later stage of development. On the other hand, a fully grown industrial power, an important navy and expansive foreign trade can best be achieved if the state intervenes with its powers. (1930, Vol. VI, p. 212; my translation)[7]

This quote, short as it is, still offers a glimpse of List's theoretical approach. We first note that List builds on quite a traditional stage theory of economic development, which he uses to derive the general postulate of free trade. This postulate has only one clearly circumscribed exception. On this exception he builds quite a specific set of commercial policies; and this policy programme becomes the focus of his book. An interesting and perceptive discussion of List's theory is offered by Gustav Schmoller. He stresses the fiscal and commercial policy focus of List's theory and writes:

Following quite a natural course of events, a generation after Adam Smith a new and equally important theory of international trade emerged which gave a justification for protective tariffs. This theory was based on Alexander Hamilton's *Report on Manufactures* (1791) and on Friedrich List's works (1827–1848), above all his *National System of Political Economy* (1841). *Alexander Hamilton* was Washington's collaborator, the co-author of the American constitution, the most able secretary of the treasury who solidified the public finances of the Union, and one of the greatest statesmen the United States had had. He wanted to save the Union which was almost disintegrating into its member states by centralizing the public debt, by instituting a central bank and a system of protective tariffs. . . . Friedrich List, although under the influence of Hamilton's thinking, put the theory of protective tariffs on a broader foundation. . . . His point of departure is a stage theory of economic development. . . . He defends the system of protective tariffs as a means to develop an industry in an agricultural state, but he recognizes the advantages of free trade for the period before and after this development. . . . He emphasizes that the temporary losses due to tariff induced price increases can be more than outweighed if they allow for the productive powers of the nation to be developed. The productive powers include intelligence and the ethics of the people, skills and technical as well as economic knowledge, and economic and social institutions. According to List's programme, these productive powers have to be strengthened, perfected and made effective.[8]

Schmoller's short characterization is essential for our understanding of List's theory. It is a theory of commercial policy, not of international trade. And it was developed from the point of view of a statesman concerned with commercial policies and public finance. To such a statesman the theory is addressed. Only if we read List's political economy in these terms are we able to reconstruct his theory without internal contradictions. The following section is devoted to such a reconstruction.

II

In the official register of the Kingdom of Württemberg published on Saturday, 3 January 1818,[9] 'Professor List' is described as the 'newly appointed full-time public teacher of public administration'. And, indeed, he was primarily concerned with the public administration of a medium-sized territorial state. The main task this state faces is the development of manufactures, i.e. commerce and industry. And the means the state can use to this end are the traditional instruments of public administration, as they were available during the first half of the nineteenth century. The problem is described as the active development and stimulation of the productive powers[10] with *every* instrument the public administrator can dispose of. Accordingly, his theory of productive powers lies at the heart of the entire work. With this 'theory' of productive powers, he did not try to describe and analyse the deployment of factors of production as we know the term in economic theory. His point was rather to go through the received set of tasks and functions of public administration, as they had been taught at German universities for more than a century by then, and to redefine these functions with a view towards the needs of the country's economic development. In this manner, the whole catalogue of public administrative functions received added significance. According to List's approach, economic policy is conducted as public administration with the traditional means and instruments of administration in both its regulatory and commercial parcemony in model construction; List's approach yields a greater variety of all the different policies needed for the development of the productive powers of a nation. By 'nation' List understands a coherent economic territory with a unified public administration (1930, p. 55):

> In all these respects, much depends on the state of society in which the individual has received his education and in which he operates; much depends on whether arts and sciences are prospering, on whether the public institutions and the law foster religion, ethical conduct and intelligence, on whether the state produces (!) personal security, the protection of property, liberty and the legal order, on whether a nation has developed all factors of material well-being, agriculture, industry and trade in harmonious proportions, on whether the nation is powerful enough in order to allow its citizens to pass wealth and education from one generation to the other in order to allow not only the fullest use and deployment of its own natural endowment, but also the natural resources of foreign countries by means of trade and the foundation of colonies.[11]

This large panorama of state functions, painted with the broad brush so typical of List's style, clearly reflects List's basic conviction that the state is a producer of a set of conditions, many bearing public good characteristics, which are essential for economic development or the development of the productive powers. Within this broad picture there is one set of very specific proposals which List has designed against the background of his own expertise and experience as a tax collector. I am referring to the theory of taxation which List had developed between 1817 and 1819 during his tenure as a professor of public administration in Tübingen. The term 'taxes' also comprises tariffs. Again, his theory of taxation is politically intended and hence combines analysis and prescription. The programme can be briefly summarized.[12] The basic idea is to substitute, as much as possible, indirect taxes by direct taxes. Trade was to be facilitated as much as possible by abolishing all taxes on transactions. And industry was to be supported by substituting the customary fixed taxes by a system of taxes on net income. Obviously List was aware of the enormous difficulties a fair and equitable determination of income presents to the public administrator. He therefore suggested the use of traditional forms of taxes the old free cities of the empire had developed in order to approximate income taxes. These cities, such as his own home town of Reutlingen, had lost their independence and had been integrated into the newly formed territorial states of the Napoleonic and post-Napoleonic era. Pausch summarizes List's contribution as follows: 'List is a classic of the southern German income tax systems, which had developed a separate tax for every different income component' (Pausch, 1989, p.23).

Tariffs presented List with a particular problem in designing a comprehensive tax system. On the one hand, they are in fact a tax on transactions, and as such according to his scheme they had to be abolished. On the other hand, List realized that for fiscal reasons the state could not readily do away with this important revenue source (List, 1930, p. 330). In his overall tax design, tariffs consequently formed a marring exception. What List did with this exception we can almost expect when we consider his two most remarkable character traits, as a consummate practitioner of public administration, and an equally determined system builder. The solution he found for the problem of tariffs reflects both of these qualities. Tariffs by their nature have two different functions, being a public revenue source (*Finanzzoll*) on the one hand and offering protection to local production on the other hand (*Schutzzoll*). This is a functional distinction, not a distinction in the manner of how tariffs are levied. It is important to note that the two functions are largely incompatible. The higher *ceteris paribus* the tariff, the lower the financial revenue from the tariff, but the larger the protective effect. The incompatibility of these two functions lies at the heart of his proposal. This proposal suggests that protective tariffs of 20–60 per cent (1930, p. 389) should be introduced for certain specific industries which are appropriate candidates for such a measure because the nation enjoys a natural advantage in the conduct of such industries (ibid., p. 57). The protective tariffs are in force for a limited time only. The lower boundary of the customs tariff is the traditional revenue maximizing rate, indicated by List as lying in the vicinity of 10 to 20 per cent. The upper boundary is determined by the protective functions and depends on the contestability of home markets. He argued: 'Protective tariffs which exclude foreign competition altogether are detrimental to a nation introducing them, since they reduce competition among industrial entrepreneurs and create a climate of indolence' (ibid., p. 56).

While the programme lasts, the tariff rates have to be continuously changed in order to ensure that the home-based industry can maintain its market volume (not market share), while the increase in market volume is not entirely captured by foreign industry. If this indeed happens, the rates of the protective tariffs have to be increased. On the other hand, the programme has to be discontinued if increasing tariff rates do not lead to improved prosperity for the home-based industry (ibid., p. 65).

The mechanics of List's programme become apparent when we look at its dynamics. The main players are the revenue-seeking tax authority which can vary the tariff rates, a home-based industry which has been targeted for tariff protection, and the respective foreign competition. Once a home industry receives tariff protection, tariff rates will gradually increase from the fiscally optimal base level of around 10–20 per cent to a maximum of about 60 per cent. The tariff rate is to be increased as long as the sales volume of the home-based industry stagnates or decreases. If the home-based industry keeps stagnating or shrinking despite increased tariff protection and the accompanying administrative measures to stimulate the 'productive powers', the tariff has to be brought back to the fiscally optimal base level once all iterations of successive rate increases have been exhausted, that is once the tariff rate has reached the level of around 60 per cent. If, however, the protective tariff leads to the desired result, this will lead to a decrease in the revenues from the tariff, but at the same time to an increase in business income tax revenues, the desired tax source in List's programme.

An active tax administration seeking to maximize long-term revenues essentially has two options, and it will choose that option which List desired. If the industry targeted for the programme proves to be internationally competitive, a reduction in tariff rates will result in an increase in revenues from customs duties, but a decrease in revenues from business income tax. The efficient tax administration will therefore only gradually decrease tariff rates, and thereby gradually expose the fledgling industry to international competition. If, on the other hand, the program of tariff protection has failed and the targeted industry has not become internationally competitive, the second effect (reduction in business income taxes) will have outweighed the first (reduction in revenues from customs). Therefore the efficient tax administration will drastically lower tariff rates and bring them back to the fiscally optimal base level.

The case of a passive, reactive tax administration does not yield very different results, although there will of course be delays. If the tax administration, after having gradually increased the protective tariff, lets it stay at the maximum rate, there are essentially two alternative outcomes. Either the targeted industry has become internationally competitive or it has not. In the second case, revenues from tariffs will gradually dry out due to more and more active smuggling in order to satisfy the needs the home-based industry cannot fulfil. The reduction in customs revenues will not be offset by business income tax revenues from the home-based industry. Alternatively, if the programme has been successful, revenues from customs will also dry up, but business income tax revenues will increase. As List discusses at length, in both cases the tax administration will ultimately have to take corrective action. Extensive smuggling will give rise to complaints by the home-based industry, however inefficient it may be, and – above all – from legitimate home-based commerce. In the case of the targeted industry remaining inefficient, the interest of the tax administration and home-based commerce will finally meet and bring tariff rates down. If the experiment has succeeded, consumer interests will ultimately voice complaints about the 'indolence' of the protected industry and insist that tariff rates be reduced in order to bring the prices of the home-based industry down. In neither case will the tariff protection last, being built, as List puts it, on political quicksand.

The ideal scenario of economic development repeatedly depicted by List takes the following course. The country's public administration will carry on its traditional tasks of establishing law and order and thereby creating a favourable business climate; of improving the needs of public transportation such as roads and riverways as well as, important in List's case, railroads; of establishing a simple tax administration and of carrying out a programme of regulatory reform in order to simplify the procedures faced by business; of supporting publications, improving public health services and increasing awareness of new technologies by organizing fairs, industrial and technological expositions and by setting up protoype sites of production. Still, there will be no bureaucratic expansion, since the central instrument, the protective tariff, is handled by an already existing administrative body and requires no additional resources whatsoever (1930, p. 330). As a consequence of all these complementary and secondary administrative measures, of the protective tariff and of occasional direct measures such as the attraction of particular entrepreneurs, competition on home markets eventually becomes intensified, prices decline and quality improves at the same time (ibid., p. 389). This will also have effects on agriculture, which is never subject to protective tariffs, by stimulating a general increase (shift) in the demand of agricultural goods and by leading to an increase in the value of land due to an increased demand for land for industrial purposes (ibid., pp. 330, 389) and housing, with the additional consequence (not mentioned by List) that yields from traditional property taxes will also increase. The revenues from customs will decline, since local price levels will decline and the demand for imported goods will consequently decline as well. Eventually this will lead to a drying up of revenues from customs, in the case of both high and low tariff rates. True to traditional administrative practice, the (by now) insignificant custom duty (*bagatelle* duty)[13] will be discontinued; and thereby the desired goal of free trade has been reached.

III

The interpretation of List offered in this paper, which sees him as an expert in public administration rather than as an economic theorist, is likely to raise eyebrows among economists, implying as it does that List stands in the tradition of the cameralists rather than following in Ricardo's footsteps. I should therefore like to complement my reconstruction by directly addressing a number of controversial points which tend to be raised in this context, but above all, because List himself had already addressed them.

The first paradox from the point of view of standard economics is the idea that due to protective tariffs, prices (costs?) in the protected domestic industry will fall more rapidly than in foreign industries. The point is important, since the protected domestic industry has to achieve substantial cost reductions in order to be competitive once protective tariffs are lifted. List is quite explicit on this point:

> And what have been the consequences of these protective tariffs? Do consumers pay 20–30 per cent more for German goods than they used to for the foreign imports, as mainstream economists tell us? Are these goods any worse than the imports? Not at all.... Internal competition and protection from foreign ruinous competition have achieved this miracle, of which mainstream economists know nothing and want to know nothing. It is, therefore, not true, as mainstream economists hold, that protective tariffs make domestic goods more expensive by the amount of the protective tariff. In the short run, increased prices may well result; but if a nation is in principle capable of industrialization, the protective tariff and internal competition will reduce prices more than free trade would have achieved.[14]

First we must take note of List's impressionistic style. He is offering us a possible scenario based on and in accord with his own experience. He is not offering an analysis in the context of a succintly defined model with a limited number of variables. As always, his analysis remains open, allowing him to emphasize different variables at different times, a procedure necessited by his focus on the multifaceted forces of production as his central analytical notion. Secondly, we notice that List correctly identifies a number of aspects which are likely to have a strong impact on the cost of production in the protected industry. Creating a climate of certainty and thereby lengthening the time horizon of the investment period clearly reduces the costs of investment, other things held equal. The intensification of competition ensures that reduced costs will also translate into reduced prices for consumers. The locational advantage pays off due to the protective tariff. All three factors can lead to the required higher (more rapid) reduction of domestic prices relative to the prices of the competing foreign industry. This scenario is conceivable even if learning and technological progress affect the domestic and foreign industry equally. But List explicitly underlines that this is a possible scenario, not a necessary one. If this scenario does not unfold and the targeted industry does not develop according to expectations, then the protective tariff has to be lifted, since 'this would be proof that the nation does not yet have the requisite means to plant its own industry' (List, 1930 p. 56). The long quote (from page 389) also shows clearly that List was not thinking of domestic price reductions due to monopolization exploiting economies of scale, since he is explicitly referring to the intensified domestic competition which translates cost reductions into price reductions.

It is also often asserted that List pushed for protective tariffs in order to promote a self-sufficient domestic economy. A defence of autarchical economic policies is not, however, what we can find in his writings. The goal of his customs policy is unequivocally the gradual lifting of customs duties, facilitated by his clever emphasis on the second function of levying tariffs, the educational or protective tariff, which leads to the tariffs' own abolition. List was interested in creating large common markets on the basis of free contractual agreements, a point he repeatedly emphasizes, perhaps most effectively in the following quote.

> The union of the three kingdoms (England, Scotland and Ireland) has offered the world the most impressive and irrefutable example of the manifold consequences of free trade between peoples. We only have to think of all nations on the earth united in like fashion, and the most vivid fantasy will not suffice to imagine the plenty of welfare and happiness which humans would reap from free trade in this union.[15]

Self-sufficiency is not what List has in mind, but 'the principle of *educating a nation to economic self-determination*' (List, 1930, p. 42), since economic dependence violates the principle of free trade.

List was well aware of the potential dangers of protective tariffs for free competition. Protective tariffs, as we have seen before, are admissible only for a limited period of time, for a specifically targeted industry and only if the economic territory (nation) enjoys a specific natural advantage, such as a locational advantage, which renders development of the targeted industry sensible. The protective tariff occupies such a central role in List's developmental programme because it is able to substitute for the fiscal tariff, which is a burden on commerce and industry. This is why the protective tariff fits so nicely into the tax reform package List had developed. But the strategy can only be chosen if the economic and political territory of the nation is sufficiently large to allow internal competition to emerge behind the protective walls of the tariff. If this is not the case and the territory is too small, common markets have to be formed. List explains:

> A sizeable population and a large territory with a variety of natural resources are essential conditions for normal nationhood; they are basic conditions for both human capital formation and material development as well as political might. If a nation is small in population and territory, in particular if it has a language of its own, it can only have a limited literature, and only inadequate institutions for the promotion of arts and sciences. Never can a small state fully deploy its various industries within its own territory. Here, every protection creates a private monopoly. Only by alliance with larger nations, by means of partially giving up the advantages of nationality and only with unusual sacrifices can such a nation maintain its independence with more or less success.[16]

Finally, it may again seem paradoxical that List, who went out of his way to criticize the practice of public administration, notably in his home country of Württemberg, should still assign such high priority to administrative measures in promoting economic development. Yet the paradox is readily explained. His own experience had taught List just how much damage a poorly organized and poorly performing public administration can do to economic development, and how beneficial a well organized and well performing public administration working under an enlightened administrative elite can be for the economic development of a country. Since he saw public administration as the key to economic development, he had to opt for a strategy based on public administrative measures. And likewise, since he considered tariffs an obsolete revenue source and an obstacle to economic development, he had to focus on tariffs and try to turn an obstacle into an engine of economic development. Not theoretical investigation, but practical experience were the soil on which List planted and built his ideas.[17] His practical experience lay almost exclusively in the field of practical administration, and fiscal administration in particular; it was this discipline of public administration, not economic theory, which List had learned, taught and mastered in all its respects.

IV

In this essay I have tried to show how Friedrich List, whose name tends to be associated with protectionism, tried to achieve large common markets and free trade as a result of economic development and how he used existing public administrative instruments, taxes and tariffs included, to this end. Central to the strategy is the dual function of tariffs as a public revenue source and as an instrument of economic protection, two functions that are largely mutually exclusive. List's strategy is shown to build on the conduct of three players: the government, domestic industry and foreign industry. His developmental strategy is designed in such a way that protective tariffs, once instituted, lead to their own abolition as a consequence of the politico-economic interplay of the three actors identified.

Notes

1. That edition, bound in twelve volumes, is referred to as List (1930). An earlier statement is his *Natural System of Political Economy* of 1937, originally written in French and translated by W.O. Henderson, referred to as List (1983). American readers will be interested in the American adaptation he wrote while in the States, entitled *Outlines of American Political Economy*, of 1827, reprinted in Margaret E. Hirst's *Life of Friedrich List* (1909), pp. 147–272 and in his *Collected Works* Vol. II (1931), pp. 97–155.
2. See Lindert and Kindleberger (1982, pp. 145–6). The same arguments can be found in other textbooks with few variations. A surprise can be found in Kenen (1985), who writes: 'List's views about the gains from trade are easily refuted. Countries such as Denmark, Australia, and New Zealand export agricultural products, but they have higher living standards than many other countries. Furthermore, List's argument contains a contradiction. If all countries tried to export manufactures, the terms of trade would turn against them; the prices of primary products would rise, and some countries would find it advantageous to export them. Nevertheless, List's argument won the day in Germany' (pp. 228–9). This 'refutation' misses the mark completely. First of all, List has no objections to the export of agricultural products. The exportation of refined agricultural products is completely in line with List's

approach. Secondly, pointing to the high standards of living in particular countries does not tell us anything about the relative merits of applying List's developmental strategy or not. Thirdly, List never suggested that every country exports the same products. He tried to select a limited number of particular industries on which his developmental strategy could be based.

3. See Backhaus (1989, pp. 210–5).
4. Dietzel (1912) with references to Lotz, Dix, Wätig and Harms.
5. See List (1989).
6. See the references in Dietzel (1912), footnote 1 and the long discussion by Gertrud Mayer, *Friedrich List als Agrarpolitiker* (1938).
7. See List (1930). 'In ökonomischer Beziehung haben die Nationen folgende Entwicklungsstadien zu durchlaufen: Zustand der ursprünglichen Wildheit – Hirtenstand-/Agrikulturstand – Agrikultur-/Manufakturstand – Agrikultur-/Manufaktur-/Handelsstand.

   Die Industriegeschichte der Nationen, und keine auf anschaulichere Weise als die von England, beweist, dass der Übergang aus dem rohen Zustand zu Viehzucht, von der Viehzucht zur Agrikultur und von der Agrikultur zu den ersten Anfängen in den Manufakturen und in der Schiffahrt am schnellsten und vorteilhaftesten durch den freien Handel mit weiter vorgerückten Städten und Ländern bewerkstelligt wird; dass aber eine vollständige Manufakturkraft, eine bedeutende Schiffahrt und ein grossartiger auswärtiger Handel nur vermittelst Einschreitung der Staatsgewalt zu erlangen sind.'
8. See von Schmoller (1923, p. 1280).

   'Es war daher ganz natürlich, dass ein Menschenalter nach A. Smith eine neue ebenbürtige handelspolitische Theorie, die den Schutzzoll verteidigt, entstand. Sie geht aus von Alexander Hamiltons *Report on Manufactures* 1791 und von Friedrich Lists Schriften 1827–1848, hauptsächlich von dessen nationalem System der politischen Ökonomie 1841. *Alexander Hamilton*, der Gehilfe Washingtons, der Mitbegründer der Verfassung der Vereinigten Staaten, der grösste Finanzminister der Union, der die Bundesfinanzen in Ordnung brachte, einer der grössten Staatsmänner, den die Vereinigten Staaten gehabt, wollte die fast auseinanderfallenden Einzelstaaten durch Zentralisierung des Schuldenwesens, durch eine Zentralbank und ein Schutzsystem zusammenhalten.... Friedrich List ist in seinen Gedanken von Hamilton beeinflusst, aber er hat die Theorie des Schutzsystems auf breitere Grundlagen gestellt.... Er geht aus von einer Theorie des Stufenganges der Volkswirtschaft... Er verteidigt das Schutzsystem als Mittel der Erziehung einer (!) Industrie in den Ackerbaustaaten, während er für die Zeit vorher und nachher die Vorteile des freien Handels einsieht.... Und er betont, dass zeitweilige Wertverluste durch Schutzzollverteuerung zurücktreten können, wenn dafür die produktiven Kräfte der Nation, die Intelligenz und Moralität der Menschen, die Geschicklichkeiten und technisch- wirtschaftlichen Kenntnisse, die ökonomisch-gesellschaftlichen Einrichtungen an Kraft, Vollkommenheit und Wirksamkeit wachsen.'
9. The document is reproduced in Wendler (1976).
10. On List's theory of productive forces, see Schmidt (1990).
11. List (1930, p. 176; my translation):

    'In allen diesen Beziehungen hängt jedoch das meiste von dem Zustand in der Gesellschaft ab, in welchen das Individuen sich gebildet hat und bewegt, davon, ob Wissenschaft und Künste blühen, ob die öffentlichen (!) Institutionen und Gesetze Religiosität, Moralität und Intelligenz, Sicherheit der Person und des Eigentums, Freiheit und Recht produzieren (!), ob in der Nation alle Faktoren des materiellen Wohlstandes, Agrikultur, Manufakturen und Handel, gleichmässig und harmonisch ausgebildet sind, ob die Macht der Nation gross genug ist, um den Individuen den Fortschritt in Wohlstand und Bildung von Generation zu Generation zu sichern und sie zu befähigen, nicht nur ihre innern Naturkräfte in ihrer ganzen Ausdehnung zu bemühen, sondern auch durch auswärtigen Handel und Kolonialbesitz die Naturkräfte fremder Länder sich dienstbar zu machen.'
12. See for details Pausch (1989).
13. As part of traditional administrative procedures in continental European tax administrations, there are regularly evaluations of tax yields and administrative costs. Bagatelle duties are duties resulting in insignificantly small net revenues, with sometimes very substantial gross revenues being consumed entirely by the costs of collection. Duties found to have fallen

into this category are routinely discontinued.

14. List (1930, p. 389; my translation). 'Wie aber haben diese Schutzzolle gewirkt? Zahlen die Konsumenten für ihre deutschen Manufaktorwaren 20–30% mehr als für die Fremden, wie sie doch der Theorie gemäss sollten? Oder sind diese Waren schlechter als die fremdem? Mitnichten.... Die innere Konkurrenz und die Sicherheit vor zerstörender Konkurrenz des Auslands hat jene Wunder bewirkt, von welchen die Schule nichts weiss und nicht wissen will. Es ist also nicht wahr, was die Schule behauptet, dass der Schutzzoll die inländischen Waren um den Betrag des Schutzzolls verteuert. Für kurze Zeit mag sie Verteuerung verursachen, aber in jeder zur Fabrikation berufenen Nation muss, infolge des Schutzes, die innere Konkurrenz bald die Preise tiefer drücken als sie bei freier Einfuhr sich gestellt hätten.'

15. List (1930, p. 164; my translation).
'In der Vereinigung der drei Königreiche (Grossbrittaniens und Irlands) besitzt die Welt ein grosses unwiderlegliches Beispiel von den unendlichen Wirkungen der Handelsfreiheit zwischen vereinigten Völkern. Man denke sich nun alle Nationen der Erde auf gleiche Weise vereinigt, und die lebhafteste Phantasie wird nicht imstande sein sich die Summe von Wohlfahrt und Glück vorzustellen, die daraus dem menschlichen Geschlecht erwachsen müsste.'

16. Again List (1930, pp. 210–11; my translation):
'Grosse Bevölkerung und ein weites, mit manigfaltigen Naturfonds ausgestattetes Territorium sind wesentliche Erfordernisse der normalen Nationalität, sie sind Grundbedingungen der geistigen Bildung wie der materiellen Entwicklung und politischen Macht. Eine an Volkszahl und Territorium beschränkte Nation, zumal wenn sie eine besondere Sprache hat, kann nur eine verkrüppelte Literatur, nur krüppelhafte Anstalten für Beförderung der Künste und Wissenschaften besitzen. Ein kleiner Staat kann innerhalb seines Territoriums nie verschiedene Produktionszweige zur vollständigen Ausbildung bringen. Bei ihm wird jeder Schutz zum Privatmonopol (!). Nur durch Allianzen mit mächtigeren Nationen, durch teilweise Aufopferung der Vorteile der Nationalität und durch übermässige Kraftanstrengung vermag er seine Selbständigkeit notdürftig zu behaupten.'

17. Gottfried Eisermann (1990) would even argue that only experience determined List's convictions, it even guided his (sometimes selective) reading of the classics in economic theory.

References

Backhaus, Jürgen G. (1989), 'Banking Institutions in Historical and Comparative Perspective: The Importance of the Entrepreneurial State', in *Journal of Institutional and Theoretical Economics*, **145** (1), pp. 210–15.

Dietzel, Heinrich (1912), *Lists nationales System und die 'nationale' Wirtschaftspolitik*, Tübingen: Mohr/Siebeck.

Eisermann, Gottfried (1990), 'Friedrich Lists Lebenswerk in historischer Perspektive', in Bertram Schefold (ed.), *Studien zur Entwicklung der ökonomischen Theorie*, Berlin: Duncker & Humblot.

Kenen, Peter B. (1985), *The International Economy*, Englewood Cliffs, NJ: Prentice-Hall.

Lindert, Peter H. and Kindleberger, Charles P. (1982), *International Economics*, Homewood: Irwin.

List, Friedrich (1930), *Schriften, Reden, Briefe*, edited on behalf of the Friedrich List Society by Erwin v. Beckerath, Karl Goeser, Friedrich Lenz, William Notz, Edgar Salin and Artur Sommer (1930). Vol. VI: *Das nationale System der politischen Ökonomie*, Berlin: Reimar Hobbing.

List, Friedrich (1983), *The Natural System of Political Economy* [1837], Trans. and ed. W.O. Henderson, London: Frank Cass.

List, Friedrich (1989), *Aller untertänigste Bittschrift der deutschen Kaufleute und Fabrikanten...* [1819], reprinted in A. Pausch, *Friedrich List als Steuerfachmann und Zollpolitiker*, Heidelberg: C.F. Müller.

Mayer, Gertrud (1938), *Friedrich List als Agrarpolitiker*, Stuttgart: Kohlhammer.

Pausch, Alfons (1989), *Friedrich List als Steuerfachmann und Zollpolitiker*, Heidelberg: C.F. Müller.

Schmidt, Karl-Heinz (1990), 'Lists Theorie der produktiven Kräfte', in Bertram Schefold (ed.), *Studien zur Entwicklung der ökonomischen Theorie*, Berlin: Duncker & Humblot.

von Schmoller, Gustav (1923), *Grundriss der allgemeinen Volkswirtschaftslehre*, Vol. II, Munich: Duncker & Humblot.

Wendler, Eugen (1976), *Friedrich List: Leben und Wirken in Dokumenten*, Reutlingen: Oerter & Spörer.

12 Popularizing classical economic ideas in nineteenth-century Britain: the education movement
W.D. Sockwell

Introduction

Current interest in rhetorical and sociological approaches to methodology has led some economists to suggest that the 'best' ideas may not always prevail and that equally important in determining which ideas become popular are the mode and success of the communication of the idea. A recent book, *The Spread of Economic Ideas*, edited by Colander and Coats, stresses this point by focusing on the process by which contemporary economic ideas have been communicated.[1] The book examines the role of funding in the spread of economic ideas, the spread of ideas from economist to economist, from economists to the lay public and from economists to policy-makers. Each of these components in the transmission of economic ideas has been insufficiently studied, but there has been a particular lack of serious study of the process by which economic ideas have been popularized.[2]

An examination of the methods of the popularizers and propagators is particularly helpful in analysing how economic theory affects policy in democratic societies in which public opinion has a major impact on policy. Nineteenth-century classical economists provide an excellent example of the methods used by economic popularizers. Gerschenkron asserts it was not the 'actual scholarly contents of classical doctrines', but a 'popular mythology' or 'ideology' that became 'the spirit of the age'. Furthermore, 'it was not the theories of the classical school, but convenient fragments thereof – at times words rather than concepts – that entered the laissez faire ideology'.[3] In this view, then, it was not the scientific economic theories themselves that had an impact on policy, but the translation of the theories into a 'popular mythology' that was critical. Gerschenkron (1969, p. 13) makes similar points about the economics of Karl Marx. He states, 'the total impact of Marx *as an economist* was very small, if not negligible. What was accepted was the implied ethical message of the doctrine rather than the doctrine itself.'

Gerschenkron maintains that complex economic ideas of the classical economists, in and of themselves, were unimportant; their importance was based on whether they could be translated into a doctrine that could be easily propagated. Noel Thompson agrees and suggests, 'while opinions of the classical economists were more sophisticated and more carefully qualified than those of their popularizers it was undoubtedly the ideas of the popularizers which had the greatest popular impact.'[4] If the thesis of Thompson and Gerschenkron is accepted, the popularizers of economic ideas may have played a more important role in the formulation and acceptance of policy than the original thinkers. Yet, as Scott Gordon noted in 1955, the propagaters as a group have been 'relatively neglected' by historians of economic thought.[5] This paper briefly surveys the methods used to popularize classical economic ideas, concentrating on describing the popularization of classical economics through education.

Methods of popularization

Economic ideas were popularized in many ways: popularizers directed their presentations to different audiences, varying the sophistication of the presentation according to the audience. Speeches, clubs, organizations, books, pamphlets, periodicals, newspapers and schools were all used to disseminate the ideas of political economy. The next part of this paper briefly examines the methods by which the popularizers spread their classical economic ideas.

Books and periodicals

The few previous studies of classical economic popularizers have most often focused on well-known scholars who wrote popular books on economics. In part, this is because books, figures on sales of books and reviews of books are readily accessible; evaluating the importance of a book is no doubt easier than determining the readership and assessing the influence of the various competing newspapers, or analysing the long-term effects of education in the schoolroom. For example, Jane Marcet, Harriet Martineau and Richard Whately, who wrote for the middle and lower classes,[6] and J.R. McCulloch and James Mill who wrote for a more sophisticated audience,[7] used books (in some cases in the form of monthly instalments) or textbooks as the primary vehicle for promoting economic ideas, and each owed his or her reputation to the popularity of the books.[8]

The first true popularizer of the nineteenth century was Jane Marcet, who in 1816 wrote her first economics book, *Conversations on Political Economy*. The book, which was aimed at the middle class, eventually went through 16 editions and was translated into Dutch, French, German and Spanish. Marcet initially did not think political economy should be taught to the labouring classes, but by the 1830s she had changed her mind. Her works of 1833 and 1851 consisted of economic stories and fairy tales aimed at the lower classes.[9]

The best known of the popularizers was Harriet Martineau, who published a series of stories in monthly instalments that were in reality lessons on political economy. Her series was immensely successful, reaching a circulation of

10 000 in England.[10] The potential political impact of her writings was immediately recognized. Lord Brougham, then Lord Chancellor, urged her to write a series on the Poor Laws to help popularize the recommendations of the Poor Law Commission, and Lord Althorp, Chancellor of the Exchequer, asked her to write on taxation to help pass his tax reforms (Routh, 1975, p. 189). It was the success of the books and stories of Marcet and Martineau that led Keynes to assert that 'the education stories of Miss Martineau and Mrs. Marcet...fixed laissez-faire in the popular mind as the practical conclusion of orthodox political economy' (Keynes, 1973, pp. 279–80).

Another popularizer deserving mention is Archbishop Whately, whose most popular book was *Easy Lessons on Money Matters, Commerce, Trade, Wages, etc. etc. for the Use of Young People, as well as Adults, of all Classes*. He felt his lessons on political economy could be adapted for all children aged eight and up. As one of the six Commissioners of National Education in Ireland, he had the opportunity in the 1830s to insert large sections of his *Easy Lessons* into the readers used in the schools of Ireland. These lessons were copied or adapted and used in English readers in the 1840s and 1850s. The lessons were so successful that 'virtually every advanced reader published by religious bodies from the late 1830s to 1880 had its quota of Whately or imitations or adaptations of his articles'. By 1859 nearly two million school readers were in use, most containing material by Whately. 'Whately, indeed, was in his time the most widely published of economists' (Goldstrom, 1966, pp. 133, 137–8).

Certain periodicals with widespread popular appeal were a good means of popularizing economic ideas. The *Edinburgh Review*, founded in 1802, pioneered the style of critical reviewing that became the standard in the nineteenth century.[11] Although the *Edinburgh Review* covered a wide range of topics, Fontana (1985, pp. 2, 111) notes that it 'was the first major vehicle for the popularization of the doctrines of political economy in nineteenth century Britain', and that it was 'the promotion of political economy in particular that remained the star achievement of the *Review*'.

All the original founders of the *Edinburgh Review* felt one of its major roles was as an educational tool (Clive, 1957, p. 36). Its long-time editor, Francis Jeffrey, thought the principal objective of the *Review* was 'doing good by educating readers...through explaining, in an abler way than they have been illustrated hitherto, the fundamental laws of criticisms, morals, and science...[and] demolishing popular errors and absurdities'.[12] Political economy was a major part of the educational material of the *Review*.

Soon other reviews arose to imitate the *Edinburgh Review*. The *Quarterly Review*, *Blackwood's Edinburgh Magazine* and the *Westminster Review* were founded as competitors and each offered coverage of economic topics. Before the advent of the *Edinburgh Review*, political economy was generally regarded as a subject only for the elite.[13] By introducing political economy to the middle class as well as many in the upper class, the *Edinburgh Review* and its progeny helped broaden the acceptance and influence of the ideas of the political economists.

Newspapers

Newspapers were arguably the most potent means of spreading the ideas of the political economist to a mass audience. In the early 1800s writers with working-class sympathies, who were particularly critical of the wages fund theory and interested in distributional issues, as well as the classical economists, became aware of the power of the newspapers. Writers with sympathies for the labouring class soon began to perceive that 'political economy in the hands of [classical economists] was an ideological buttress of the inequitable status quo; it was a theoretical rationalisation of the impoverishment of labour' (Thompson, 1984, p. 21). The year 1816 marked the beginning 'of a cheap, radical press with views to suit the predilictions and a price to suit the pockets of a working-class readership' (ibid., p. 3). From this point through to the mid-1830s, newspapers engaged in a great competition for the minds of the working class.

The labour movement sympathizers were at a disadvantage in the contest because they had no complete economic theory to combat the classical school on its own terms. In the mid-1820s, however, William Thompson, Thomas Hodgskin and John Gray provided a theoretical foundation for an anti-capitalist critique of the classical school. Each 'placed great emphasis on the need for the working classes to confront and defeat the political economists with the constructs, concepts, and analytical tools of political economy' (Thompson, 1984, p. 12).

Numerous working-class newspapers appeared, especially between 1830 and 1834, specifically to criticize the methods and concepts of the classical economists and to promote those of Hodgskin, Thompson or Gray. In the six years after 1830 'several hundred illegal anti-Establishment penny newspapers appeared on the streets of London' (Hollis, 1969, p. xii). The primary goal of the knowledge disseminated was to convince the working man of his right to vote and the right to the produce of his own labour. Popularization of the labour theory of value was common to all the radical newspapers. The *Poor Man's Guardian*, published by Henry Hetherington from 1831 to 1835, was perhaps the longest lived and most influential of these papers. It consistently asserted that capital was stolen labour, not stored up labour as the classical economists claimed (Hollis, 1969, pp. xxiv–xxxiii). Themes such as this were common in all the radical papers of the period: 'Radical papers mercilessly lampooned the dominant ideology of a divinely-ordained natural order as a fairy-tale invented by the rich to cheat the poor.'[14] Though important for a short time, after 1834 the working-class newspapers gradually died out or ceased to discuss the concepts of political economy.[15]

Although many writers contributed to the newspapers, most only wrote a few articles, were participants for a short time or simply did not want to reveal they were writing for newspapers. Boyce (1978, p. 20) claims that 'before 1840 the reputation of the press was low...journalists themselves were regarded as hacks or as demagogues, either in the pay of politicians...or worse, engaged in the nefarious business of arousing the people against their established rulers.' This attitude led many economists or other prominent individuals to distance themselves from the press, with the result that few economists appear to have made significant theoretical contributions solely through newspapers.

But two popularizers from the classical school are recognized for their strong and consistent influence over the economic ideas presented in their newspapers. From 1821 to 1843 John Black edited the *Morning Chronicle*, a leading Whig paper described by J.S. Mill as a vehicle for utilitarian radicals in the 1820s. According to Gilbert (1985), it gave its wholehearted support to the new science of political economy and was in fact 'the daily journalistic voice of Political Economy'. The second individual, James Wilson, founded and edited from 1843 to 1859 the weekly London *Economist*, which Scott Gordon (1955) calls 'the most important vehicle of laissez faire newspaper journalism'. Under Wilson's leadership, the *Economist* promoted doctrinaire individualist, *laissez-faire* economics; during the 1840s in particular, the *Economist* popularized theories supporting free trade (Gordon, 1955, pp. 461–8).

Speeches, clubs and organizations
Popularizers also used speeches and clubs or organizations to propagate their ideas. The most visible arena for making speeches was parliament, since parliamentary speeches were widely reported in newspapers of the day and were much discussed. Furthermore, a large number of British economists entered parliament and promoted classical economic ideas. Fetter considers 62 members of parliament to be economists during the period 1780 to 1868. He suggests that 'to get the full picture of the role of British economists...it is important to consider not only what they wrote but what they did as members of Parliament'.[16] Although not all the parliamentary economists promoted strictly classical economics, classical liberal ideas were a prominent feature of many parliamentary speeches. Among the economists in parliament who espoused these views were Francis Horner, Henry Brougham, David Ricardo, Robert Torrens and all of the Philosophical Radicals in parliament.[17]

In addition there were public lectures and speeches on economic subjects, such as J.R. McCulloch's series of 20 lectures in honour of Ricardo in 1824 (O'Brien, 1970, pp. 48–51). Several organizations that were dominated by classical economists sponsored lectures on political economy. The most successful organization of this type was the Mechanics' Institutes. William Ellis prepared a set of economic lectures, and Henry Brougham arranged for these to be read in Mechanics' Institutes throughout Britain in 1835.[18]

Clubs and organizations also served as meeting places for members to debate economic issues, published books and pamphlets on economic topics, helped promote economic legislation and served as repositories of information about economic subjects. One of the most well known economic organizations of the day was the Political Economy Club. Although Thomas Tooke was principally responsible for founding the club in 1821, James Mill wrote its rules. He stated: 'the Members of this Society will regard their mutual instruction, and diffusion amongst others of first principles of Political Economy, as a real and important obligation.'[19] Mill also indicated that

> it shall be the duty of the Society to study the means of obtaining access to the public mind through as many as possible of the periodic publications of the day and to influence as far as possible the tone of such publications in favour of just principles of Political Economy.[20]

As several authors have pointed out, however, the Political Economy Club did not turn out to be a club that promoted narrow economic interests. It was primarily a debating club that discussed a wide range of issues and heard many divergent views. Even so, it provided the leading economists, politicians, government officials and business leaders, 'who accepted as a general basis the kind of economics found in *The Wealth of Nations*', a forum to debate and promote these views.[21]

When the Political Economy Club turned into a discussion club rather than a propaganda organization, James Mill lost interest; in the late 1820s he devoted his energy to the founding of London University and organizations such as the Society for the Diffusion of Useful Knowledge (SDUK). In these activities Mill assisted Henry Brougham, who had earlier helped start the London Mechanics' Institutes.[22] Each of the activities helped further the promotion of classical economics. At London University J.R. McCulloch, a leading propagator of classical economics, was appointed to the first Chair of Political Economy. The SDUK provided the general public with reading materials on a wide assortment of subjects, including some material concerning economics. The Mechanics' Institutes, in addition to providing a forum for lectures on political economy, served as a forerunner to modern libraries by providing access for its members to books about their trade, as well as to books on classical political economy.[23]

Another organization that was generally associated with the ideas of the classical economists was the Anti-Corn Law League. The Anti-Corn Law League, formed to help lobby for the repeal of the Corn Laws, was a strong advocate of free trade. The League is not truly representative of the classical school because it focused on only one issue. O'Brien (1975, p. 272), in fact, suggests that it was the mistaken association of the Anti-Corn Law League and the Manchester School's advocacy of free trade with extreme *laissez-faire*, and the confusion of the activities of these groups with those of the classical economists, that led to the erroneous caricature of the classical economists 'as the die-hard defenders of laissez-faire'. In any event, the Anti-Corn Law League did help instil one idea of the classical economists in the mind of the general public.

Other organizations that, to a lesser degree, helped disseminate the ideas of classical economists included the (Royal) Statistical Society, the British Association and the Royal Society. Classical economists were members of each of these clubs and each group helped reinforce many of the ideas presented by other groups dominated by classical economists (O'Brien, 1975, pp. 12–14).

Classical economists and education

The role of the classical economists in the education movement has not been studied in depth, although as Mark Blaug notes, 'there is a small but growing literature' on the subject.[24] This literature provides a wide range of opinions concerning the impact of the classical economists on education policy. Statements range from those of E.G. West, who states that classical economists 'were of all people the most forceful advocates and pioneers of state education', to those of Blaug who writes, 'by paying close attention to dates ... we come to realize that the classical economists gradually adjusted their ideas on education in the wake of legislative changes; instead of having an influence on policy, policy had an influence on them.'[25] In addition to debating their influence on educational policy, previous works about classical economists and education considered whether or not these economists anticipated modern insights into investment in human capital. Again there is some disagreement, but the most common view is that while the classical economists briefly discussed education as an investment, they did not fully develop the concept.[26] Miller (1966, p. 295) contends that they failed to develop human capital theory because they felt individuals considered education to be a consumer outlay rather than an investment. He cites J.S. Mill, Cairnes and Senior as economists who emphasized that neither the child nor the parent had their eye fixed on ultimate returns. It would be more accurate to argue that the classical economists did not develop human capital theory because many of them were more interested in education as a social and political good rather than its microeconomic benefits to the individual consumer.[27] Political economists believed education, particularly education in economics, would prevent crime, promote good conduct, and lead to a more orderly society whose members could better assume a role in their own governance. Early nineteenth-century classical economists were quite excited by these possibilities. Blitz (1961, p. 3) recognizes this and argues: 'no school of thought in the history of mankind ever ascribed greater power to education for the future progress of the human species than the English Utilitarians. The Classical Economists shared these doctrines.'

Not only were classical economists effective advocates and pioneers in the field of education, but they were acutely aware of the possible benefits of education to society. Furthermore, in the nineteenth century they began to view the teaching of classical economic doctrine as the most effective tool for advancing the welfare of society. This promotion of economic ideas through education, largely because of its perceived social benefits, ultimately led to a more pervasive influence of classical economic ideas.

Early support for education among economists
As with many other subjects Adam Smith's *Wealth of Nations* was the foundation for the major thread that was to dominate the classical view of education. Smith only briefly mentioned that education could be an instrument for enhancing social welfare, but this important element of his thinking was passed on to later classical economists who were interested in education. According to Smith,

> the more [the lower classes] are instructed, the less liable they are to the delusions of enthusiasm and superstition, which among ignorant nations, frequently occasion the most dreadful disorders. An instructed and intelligent people besides, are always more decent and orderly than an ignorant and stupid one.... They are more disposed to examine, and more capable of seeing through, the interested complaints of faction and sedition, and...less apt to be misled into wanton or unnecessary opposition to the measures of government. (Smith, 1937, p. 740)

Smith (pp. 717, 721) also held that state provisions for education should be limited to school buildings, that teachers should be paid on a fee system to give them an incentive, and that school endowments had diminished the effectiveness of teachers. These latter thoughts were generally modified or ignored by later economists.

Though Smith is credited with endorsing education as an instrument for enhancing social welfare, his influence in this area was magnified by the stature of *The Wealth of Nations*; his ideas certainly were not original. The idea that education was a means to achieve happiness can be traced at least as far back as Plato and Socrates; in the nineteenth century the sentiment caught hold, leading to support for education of the masses. Among eighteenth-century economists E.G. West (1964, p. 162) cites Bentham as an early advocate of education as a means to reduce crime; West also notes the idea had been present in the writings of Smith's teacher, Francis Hutcheson, and in the works of the seventeenth-century economist, William Petty. In addition, 'the French Physiocrats wanted a national system of education because they could use it to propagate their new found knowledge of the "secrets" of the workings of the economy' (West, 1975, p. 122).

Education and the nineteenth-century economists

During the early nineteenth century, British classical economists not only promoted education of the masses, but began to believe that if the working class could comprehend basic economic principles, everyone would benefit. James Mill was among the first to recognize the need to spread 'the true principles of political economy'. As early as 1808 he lamented 'the great difficulty with which the salutary doctrines of political economy are propagated in this country' (Mill, 1808, p. 35). The 'great difficulty' of spreading economic ideas was mainly due to the lack of education in England. Early nineteenth-century British economists did not generally believe the existing school system could support the study of a difficult subject such as economics. It would be up to Mill and other later classical economists, such as Henry Brougham, to try to make economics and other secular subjects a viable part of the curriculum.[28]

T.R. Malthus was another classical economist who emphasized the notion that education was beneficial to the entire society. He noted that education fostered habits of sobriety, industry, independence, order, prudence and self-respect among the lower classes and, most importantly in his mind, contributed to the 'prudential check to population'. In addition, Malthus held that once educated the labouring classes 'would be on all occasions less disposed to insubordination and turbulence... would become more peaceable and orderly, less influenced by inflammatory and seditious publications', and less likely to be misled by 'ambitious demagogues'.[29]

Malthus's ideas on education were largely a product of his population doctrine and the possibility that education could serve as a 'prudential check' to population increases. Curiously, he did not believe, as had the Physiocrats before him, that economics could play a major role in inculcating proper habits into the lower classes; he thought that geometry, mechanics and economics could not be 'made sufficiently clear to be of considerable use'. He did assert, however, that 'if... a few of the simplest principles of Political Economy could be added to the instructions given in... schools, the benefits to Society would be almost incalculable.'[30] The latter notion was carried forward by later economic popularizers.

Henry Brougham was the first economist to consistently take actions designed to make the dreams of the early classical economists a reality.[31] Early in his career Brougham became interested in and gave assistance to the schools of Lancaster and Bell and was intrigued with the infant schools of Robert Owen.[32] Brougham's early writings on education denounced Mandeville's notions that a certain amount of ignorance and poverty were necessary for a happy society and that an hour of study by the poor was 'so much time lost to society'.[33] Ideas similar to Mandeville's, which were rampant among the British upper class, were one of the greatest hurdles to be overcome before education could be provided to all.

Brougham's later prominence as a politician allowed him to play a central role in efforts to implement a plan to provide a secular education, including economics, for the working class. Between 1817 and 1820 Brougham chaired several Parliamentary Select Committees on Education. His 1820 Royal Commission estimated (for the 1818 school year) that only one out of every fourteen or fifteen people in the population attended primary schools. This led Brougham to declare England 'the worst educated country in Europe',[34] and he attempted to rectify the problem with his Education Bill of 1820, which called for a universal and cheap educational system for children. Brougham's system was patterned after the Scottish system and was similar to the approach Adam Smith advocated.[35] Brougham's Bill, however, proved to be ahead of its time and failed to pass.

Brougham soon rebounded from this, and by the early 1820s his educational activities had attracted a group of followers who also believed that education of all classes was the best way to promote middle-class ideals. They felt the rudimentary education received by most of the population hindered the spread of middle-class utilitarian ideology; moreover, they believed that children, as well as adults, lacked the education necessary to participate in an increasingly industrialized society. This was so well understood by the Broughamites that J.A. Newman justly dubbed them 'the Knowledge School' for their efforts to spread education among all classes (Harrison, 1961, p. 42).

Brougham realized that there had been too much opposition to his parliamentary plans to educate children, so during the 1820s and 1830s he and his followers focused their attention on adult education. They believed it was necessary to teach parents about economics and other secular subjects before parents would allow their children to learn the subjects. Brougham (1824, p. 98) suggested that the major hindrances to spreading knowledge to the literate members of the working class were 'want of money and want of time'. His proposed solutions to the problems were the Mechanics' Institutes and the Society for the Diffusion of Useful Knowledge, institutions that have been described as the 'monuments of the Broughamites' (Harrison, 1961, p. 42). In addition, Brougham was instrumental in founding London University. Each of these organizations helped diffuse economic ideas and other secular topics among the general adult population and helped to facilitate the later introduction of these topics to children in the 1840s (Sockwell, 1991).

This intense interest in adult education is a vital and often overlooked phase in the British educational movement. The major innovation of the period was simply providing cheap and accessible material to the reading public. Brougham and other classical economists[36] were at the forefront of the movement and tried to propagate the classical economic ideology as general knowledge. They met with much resistance, primarily in the form of the unstamped press or popular novels, but they at least awakened great interest in secular subjects, such as economics, and helped create a demand for these subjects in schools.

Brougham and other early classical economists wanted political economy and other secular subjects to be taught in the schools, but they generally favoured a system of private education. Brougham, like Adam Smith, believed schools should be private except when government funds were necessary to finance school buildings. Later classical economists went much further in advocating that the government should do more than provide school buildings; they argued that government should be actively involved in financing at least some schools.[37] The first step in this process was when political economists began calling for education to be compulsory. John Roebuck, who became the leading spokesman for education in the House of Commons when Brougham became Lord Chancellor, forcefully demanded this in 1833. Nassau Senior agreed with Roebuck's position and noted, 'it is only the educated who are aware that education is necessary'.[38] J.S. Mill similarly justified the idea that education should be compulsory by maintaining that

> The uncultivated cannot be competent judges of cultivation . . . any well-intentioned and tolerably civilized government may think, without presumption, that it does or ought to possess a degree of cultivation above the average of the community which it rules, and that it should therefore be capable of offering better education and better instruction to the people, than the greater number of them would spontaneously demand.[39]

In addition to advocating compulsory education, many classical economists gradually began to advocate public provision of education. By the middle of the nineteenth century 'neither Senior nor Mill liked the type of school that the free market was providing' (West, 1964, p. 170). When J.S. Mill wrote in 1848 of the voluntary provision of education in England he complained, 'even in quantity it is and is likely to remain, altogether insufficient, while in quality, though with some slight tendency to improvement, it is never good except by some rare accident, and generally so bad as to be little more than nominal' (Mill, 1965, pp. 955–6). Even so, most political economists, including J.S. Mill, did not advocate that government should pre-empt the private schools. Mill (ibid., p. 956) noted,

> Though government teachers will probably be superior to the average private instructors. . . . It is not endurable that a government should . . . have a complete control over the education of the people. To possess such a control, and actually exert it, is to be despotic. A government which can mould the opinions and sentiments of the people from their youth upwards, can do with them whatever it pleases.

Mill felt, therefore, that governments should establish schools and colleges, but not compel people to attend them or prohibit rival schools from being established. He also extended the idea of subsidizing the poor further than any other classical economist when, in 1869, he proposed free secondary and university education for all members of the working class who exhibited ability.[40]

Blaug (1975, p. 592) suggests that the desire on the part of the political economists to de-emphasize private schools and their corresponding emphasis on public schools was because the economists did not believe private schools had the resources to compete effectively against religious schools. Richard Johnson concurs, adding that the lack of success of the political economists and other educational experts in implementing their educational programmes was due in part to the presence of the established church.[41] The economists had good reason to believe private schools could not compete with the church schools. The 1851 census showed that 90 per cent of elementary school places were filled by Church of England schools, with rural areas almost completely dominated by them. In addition, the census showed that the National Society raised £870 000, while the secular British and Foreign School Society, Wesleyans, Baptists and Congregationalists together managed to raise another £125 000. By this time the Treasury grant for schools had reached only £164 000, and even this was mainly administered by the church schools (Blaug, 1975, p. 584).

The major problem with church schools as far as the classical economists were concerned was that church schools tended to look with disfavour on almost all secular subjects, including political economy. The successful propagation of secular topics, through such organizations as the Mechanics' Institutes and the Society for the Diffusion of Useful Knowledge, gradually pressured the church schools to adopt some secular topics, particularly in their readers, but this was a slow process. The economists soon realized that promotion of their view of society would have to take place outside the established church system. With the strong competition and growing financial strength of the church schools, it is no wonder that most of these economists came to believe their best hope for promoting their ideas was through government-supported non-sectarian education.[42]

Though many classical economists began to focus on public schools as the best method of competing, most were still intent on making economics a part of the curriculum. They firmly believed that if all classes of society were aware of the basic principles of political economy, violent incidents could be avoided, a harmony of interests would prevail and society would prosper. Political economy was also viewed as a useful tool to indoctrinate the lower classes with good habits. If only the lower classes would practise abstinence, frugality, punctuality and similarly admirable traits, they could not fail to prosper. These were the important lessons the classical economists wished to impart through the rudimentary study of political economy. Senior, for example, defined education as the sum of the influences which one person intentionally exercises over another by precept of example....These influences are of two kinds: first, the imparting of knowledge, which may be called *teaching*; secondly, the creation of habits, which may be called *training*....As between teaching and training, there can be no doubt that training is by far the more important....Training, therefore, or the formation of habits, rather than teaching, or the imparting of knowledge, is the great business of society.[43]

The concept of education as primarily an instrument for training or the formation of good habits was typical of classical economists, particularly after the 1830s. Political economy was thought to be an especially useful tool in this regard. The political economy of Richard Whately that dominated the British and Foreign Society School and National Society readers after 1840 was a good example of this type of training. The best example, however, was the Birkbeck schools founded by William Ellis.

Ellis, who attended J.S. Mill's study groups in the mid-1820s and became a lifelong friend of the younger Mill, opened his first of seven Birkbeck schools in 1848.[44] Ellis was one of the last of the classical economists who attempted to implement a privately funded system of education for young children which was grounded in the principles of classical economics. He firmly believed that once children understood the laws of classical economics, which he referred to as social economy, as they grew older they would more willingly accept the existing system and would work diligently to improve their condition. In the prospectus for the first Birkbeck School Ellis wrote that, in addition to learning reading, writing, mathematics, mechanics and physical sciences, the children

are to be made acquainted with the laws of their own organisation in order that they may understand how much their health, general energy, physical happiness, and length of life are dependent on their own conduct, also with the laws of social economy, that they may properly understand their own position in society, and their duties toward it. (Blyth, 1892, p. 92)

Ellis originally anticipated that his Birkbeck Schools would have a relatively short life. He felt that when others saw the advantages of his schools they would be imitated throughout England, thus rendering his schools unnecessary. In fact numerous schools were patterned after the Birkbeck schools during the 1850s and 1860s, but they did not multiply as rapidly as he had hoped.

Ellis's popularizing of his method was not limited to his Birkbeck Schools. He also wrote numerous books on social economy as well as textbooks and guides for teachers. In addition, he helped train teachers at his own teacher training colleges and gave lectures that were attended by adults of all classes who were interested in teaching social economy. Noted educationists, such as George Combe and W.B. Hodgson, helped promote his ideas.

Despite all his efforts, Ellis never had as much success in popularizing his ideas as he had hoped. He faced obstacles similar to those Brougham had encountered twenty years earlier in his attempts to provide a secular education for adults. First, though acknowledging the importance of education, the lower classes strongly resisted efforts by those who were perceived to be of the middle or upper class to educate them. For example, W. Mattieu Williams, one of Ellis's disciples who taught at the Edinburgh Secular School, 'had been accused by the parents of his children, all skilled artisans, of being "a special pleader for the capitalists", and had been informed that the political economy lessons would be refuted at home'. Regardless of this resistance, Williams persisted, believing 'it was easier to convince children than parents of the truth of social science, for the parents would give such terms as "wealth", "capitalist", "labour", and "value" meanings derived from their experience of industrial life, which were not necessarily those of the political economists' (Stewart and McCann, 1967, p. 330).

The second barrier to Ellis's approach was that church schools still dominated education. Although they began to introduce some secular subjects into their curricula by the 1840s, they wanted any secular instruction to be tempered by a heavy dose of religious training. In 1848 when George Combe was about to start his secular school patterned on the Ellis model he wrote:

> In this city evangelical religion is strong, active, and penetrating; and it uses *all means* to command every class of the inhabitants. It will oppose our school, and vilify it and ourselves by every possible endeavour. Now it is so powerful that scarcely any person of the middle and none of the upper ranks here will lend his name or countenance to our school, through sheer fear of the theological outcry, although many wish us well. (E.E. Ellis, 1888, p. 60)

Ellis did have limited success in surmounting these problems. Ellis and William Lovett, a working-class leader and Chartist, collaborated to open a school based on Ellis's principles, and Lovett later published several books based on Ellis's teaching.[45] In addition, Ellis contributed financially and helped introduce his social economics into several church schools (E.E. Ellis, 1888, p. 115). He attempted to mollify critics from the church in several of his books. In *Religion in Common Life* (1857) he argued that when applied to everyday life the moral principles he taught using the laws of social economy were the same as those taught by religious teaching. The goal of both was to teach people to be thrifty, sober, honest and industrious in order to improve their well-being. In *Philo-Socrates* (1861–4, Vol. II, pp. 26–8) Ellis suggested that the Bible should not be taught until children were at an age when they could understand its implications. Ellis implored that he and his students be judged by their conduct rather than on whether they studied the Bible, for it was more Christian to work actively for Christian ideals than to stand back and talk of them without contributing.

Although a few church leaders and radical members of the working class were willing to endorse Ellis's social economy as the best method of teaching children, this was still a minority view among each group. Ellis received a great deal of intellectual support for what he was trying to accomplish, but few thought his schools could overcome the established order.

Most individuals simply chose to ignore Ellis's schools. This was particularly true after the publication of Charles Dickens's *Hard Times for These Times* (1854) in which Dickens savagely satirized schools of the Birkbeck variety, which he referred to as Gradgrind schools. Dickens apparently correctly tapped the popular perception that children drilled in the principles of political economy would grow up to be 'grovelling, selfish, and deceitful' rather than, as Ellis maintained, workers who were 'skillful, industrious, sober, honest, and punctual' (Gilmour, 1967, pp. 217–19). With this type of popular sentiment, it is little wonder that most members of the middle and upper class wanted to distance themselves from Dickens's savage portrayal. The *Westminster Review*, a publication for which Ellis had written numerous articles, declared in an 1854 article that no such schools as Gradgrind's existed: 'If there are Gradgrind schools, they are not sufficiently numerous to be known' (Gilmour, 1967, p. 212). Thus, despite all Ellis's efforts and successes, the existence of his schools was scarcely acknowledged outside his close circle of associates, and today they are almost completely forgotten.

By the mid-1850s most of the classical economists had acceded to the reality that the only way to have a universal non-secular education was through state-supported schools, even if these schools did not include political economy as one of their subjects. Ellis's crusade to include social economy as a major part of the curriculum effectively ended when the Newcastle Commission, which laid the foundation for the system of national education that passed parliament in 1870, refused to endorse his proposals.[46] His pleadings did apparently have some impact on the Commissioners. When they issued their final report it stated:

We feel bound to state that the omission of one subject from the syllabus and from the examination papers has left on our minds a painful impression. Next to religion, the knowledge most important to a labouring man is that of the causes which regulate the amount of his wages, the hours of his work, the regularity of his employment, and the prices of what he consumes. The want of such knowledge leads him constantly into error and violence, destructive to himself and to his family, oppressive to his fellow workman, ruinous to his employers, and mischievous to society. Of the elements of such knowledge we see no traces in the syllabus, except the words 'Savings Banks and the nature of interest', in the female syllabus. If some of the time now devoted to the geography of Palestine, the succession of the kings of Israel, the wars of the Roses, or the heresies in the Early Church, were given to political economy, much valuable instruction might be acquired, and little that is worth having would be lost.[47]

This comment, however, was lost in a report of several hundred pages; its effect was minimal. Social economy did not become a part of the curriculum.

Conclusion

Though the classical economists may not have completely realized their early educational goals, they appear to have been remarkably successful at presenting their economic ideas to a larger audience. They were particularly successful in helping to educate adults and in providing them with access to materials on classical economics and other secular subjects, thereby creating demand for secular subjects to be taught to children. They also successfully incorporated economics into primary school readers and started a number of private schools for young children that focused on economics. The classical economists were not ultimately successful in their attempt to make political economy a part of the curriculum, but their continued support of non-sectarian education played a role in the adoption of a state-supported school system. Their efforts significantly influenced educational policy in the nineteenth century and, at the same time, their early emphasis on political economy helped popularize their own ideas. Their success certainly contributed to the dominance of the classical doctrine by mid-century.

The effort on the part of the classical economists between the 1820s and the 1850s to educate the public, and particularly to popularize their economic ideas, has rarely been equalled. An understanding of this process may provide some interesting parallels with the methods used to spread economic ideas to the lay public in today's society.

Notes

1. Colander and Coats (1989). Goodwin (1972) also analyses the process by which economic ideas are spread.
2. This paper refers to economists who spread economic ideas to the lay public as popularizers or propagators. There is a tendency to think of popularizers as demagogues or those spreading half-truths for political or ideological reasons. This may sometimes be the case, but whenever one attempts to illustrate or simplify complex ideas there is a danger of misrepresentation. The term popularizer, as used here, is not intended to include everyone who tried to promote classical economics. It refers only to those economists who had an intimate knowledge of the subject, were vitally concerned with promoting the classical economic system, and made a significant contribution to the spread of classical economic ideas.
3. Gerschenkron (1969, pp. 6–8). Thomas (1979, p. 447) similarly argues: 'influential social and political philosophies make converts at different levels. There are those who are rationally persuaded by reading the works of the leading thinkers of a particular school. But they are probably outnumbered by those who, without grappling with the recondite literature, merely adopt the vocabulary as it is purveyed by a horde of less original publicists.'
4. Thompson (1984, p. 62). J.H. Hollander makes a similar point about the spread of Ricardian economics when he writes: 'favorable as may have been the time, and peculiarly endowed the man and his manner, economic science would never have felt the Ricardian influence to the extent that it did, but for the intellectual tenacity, the irrepressible enthusiasm and the propagandist activity of the group of friends, disciples, and expositors . . . who promptly espoused the new dispensation and gave it widespread currency' (Hollander quoted in Blaug, 1958, p. 1).

5. Gordon (1955) divides the study of economic thought into the 'three P's': The study of the *principal* figures, the *precursors*, and the *propagators*. Of these categories, he maintains that the first two have been carefully scrutinized while the last has been 'relatively neglected'.

6. Routh (1975, pp. 82–97) lists Jane Marcet, Harriet Martineau and Richard Whately as some of the most popular writers of their day. For other references to these relatively well-known popularizers see Chapters 1 and 2 on Marcet and Martineau in Lampen-Thompson (1973), and Goldstrom's article (1966) on Whately. For additional references to the role of Martineau see Blaug (1958), Chapter 7, and Webb (1960, pp. 99–133).

7. Checkland (1949) gave most of the credit for spreading Ricardian ideas to McCulloch and James Mill. Blaug (1958, p. 40) indicates that McCulloch 'was undoubtedly the most prominent of all contemporary economists', and suggests that his 'magisterial position was, perhaps, the major factor in the rapid propagation of Ricardian economics in the early years'. Schumpeter (1954, pp. 476–8), on the other hand, refers to McCulloch as one of the 'unconditional adherents and militant supporters of Ricardo's teaching' who added nothing substantial. He says McCulloch's textbook 'was the saleable stuff for the college course in general economics'. Blaug (1958, pp. 46–52, 62–3) asserts, however, that the charge that McCulloch (and James Mill) were merely 'faithful disciples' of Ricardo is 'unjustified'.

8. Lamm suggests that textbooks are still 'the natural market for most ideas in economics' and notes that sales of popular textbooks vastly exceed those of any other type of economics book. Donald S. Lamm, in Colander and Coats (1989, pp. 103–4).

9. See Routh (1975, pp. 182–4). Also based on Polkinghorn (1982, pp. 8–9).

10. Fletcher (1974, p. 370) compared Martineau's sales of 10 000 to J.S. Mill's *Principles* which sold 4 000 copies in its first four years. Blaug (1958, p. 129) makes a similar comparison to Mill's work and also notes that the *Edinburgh Review* had a peak circulation of 13 000, while many of Dickens's novels had sales of only 2 000 to 3 000.

11. For a description of the founding of the *Edinburgh Review*, see Clive (1957, pp. 186–97). Clive notes (pp. 133–4) the *Review* was an immediate success. The first edition of 750 copies immediately sold out and two further editions were printed. By 1814 nearly 13 000 copies were being printed and it was estimated that close to 50 000 read the *Review*.

12. *Constable and His Correspondents* (Letter from Alexander Murray to Archibald Constable, 15 January 1807, Vol. 1: pp. 258–9, quoted in Clive (1957, p. 54).

13. Fontana (1985, p. 108) suggests even Dugald Stewart, the political economy professor of most of the founders of the *Review*, believed economics was a subject for the elite.

14. Curren, in Boyce et al. (1978).

15. Noel Thompson asserts that the demise of the working-class press as a vehicle for anti-capitalist economics undercut the most effective means of promoting their thought. There remained very little discussion of anti-capitalist economic thought in Britain after this time until its revival in the late 1800s. Nevertheless, he felt that the classical economists were never able to win the minds of the working class; he maintains it was the radical work of William Thompson, Thomas Hodgskin and John Gray that won working-class minds.

16. Fetter's chief test for determining whether one should be considered an economist was whether the individual produced an organized body of writing about economic subjects. Fetter (1980, pp. 6–7).

17. For a discussion of the views of these economists see Smart (1910), Fetter (1980), Gordon (1976), Halévy (1955) and Thomas (1979).

18. For a discussion of the set of lectures prepared by William Ellis, see Sockwell (1989, pp. 154–70).

19. Quoted in Checkland (1949, p. 50).

20. James Mill, as quoted in Kanth (1986, p. 143).

21. O'Brien (1975, pp. 12–13). Also see Henderson (1983, pp. 149–52).

22. Thomas (1979, p. 133). See also Henderson (1983, p. 151), who notes, 'from 1826 until his resignation in 1835, James Mill attended only five meetings' of the Political Economy Club.

23. For a description of Brougham's role in each of these activities, see Sockwell (1991).

24. Blaug (1975, pp. 587–94) provides a good summary of many of the recent articles on classical economists and education. Also see O'Donnell (1985).

25. West (1970, p. 111) and Blaug (1975, p. 568). O'Donnell (1985, pp. 1–2) agrees with West

by emphasizing that classical economists were a part of the policy-making process. She notes: 'the political economists of the nineteenth century were often involved in the formulation of the educational policy which was being created. For the most part, they were teachers who wielded substantial influence in their respective universities; but, in addition, they were noted authors whose ideas commanded popular trust and whose works were liberally discussed throughout the intellectual community. Many of these economists were directly involved with policy making through their positions in government or as consultants to elected officials.'

26. See, for example, Blaug (1975, pp. 568–99), or Miller (1966).
27. Blaug (1975, p. 593) notes that classical economists rarely considered education as a tool for directly benefiting economic growth, but viewed it more as a sociological investment. O'Donnell (1985, p. 11) asserts that 'the macroeconomic and microeconomic examination of educational provision by the classical economists was quite thorough'. Her Chapters 3 and 4 examine the classical economists' perception of the macroeconomic and microeconomic benefits of education.
28. The kind of education most classical economists had in mind was not one that would lead to free and open inquiry. Rather, as James Mill wrote, it was 'the implanting in the mind, through custom or through pain and pleasure, an invariable sequence and association of ideas which would conduce in the end to the happiness of all'. The 'invariable sequence and association of ideas' Mill referred to were the doctrines of the classical economists he helped popularize (from the article on education by James Mill for the supplement to the 4th, 5th and 6th editions of the *Encyclopaedia Britannica*, quoted in Webb, 1955, p. 63). Brougham's role as a popularizer is discussed in Sockwell (1991).
29. T.R. Malthus, *An Essay on the Principles of Population*, 3rd edn, 2 vols (London: Printed for J. Johnson by T. Bensley, 1806), pp. 414–15, 420, 422, 498–9, quoted in Tu (1969, pp. 694–5).
30. Quoted ibid., p. 696.
31. O'Donnell (1985, p. 9) notes that the first legislation to deal with education was the Factory Act of 1802. This legislation limited the working day of apprentices in the cotton and woollen mills to 12 hours and specified that part of the apprentice's day be set aside for elementary instruction.
32. The major innovation of the Bell and Lancaster schools was the use of monitors by the headmasters to allow them to teach larger groups at lower cost.
33. Brougham (1810). The reference to Bernard Mandeville is to his 1714 poem, *The Fable of the Bees: or, Private Vices, Publick Benefits*.
34. Henry Brougham, as quoted in Vaughan and Archer (1971, p. 36).
35. For a brief description of the Scottish system and Smith's views of this system, see O'Donnell (1985, pp. 4, 93–4).
36. Several other classical economists were interested in education and pursued slightly different policies than Brougham. Silver (1975, p. 28) cites J.A. Roebuck and James Mill as two such economists.
37. Miller (1966, p. 302). The position of the classical economists on financing education was a major departure from their general principle of *laissez-faire*. It should be noted, however, that most economists did not advocate completely free education. They reasoned that students should be required to pay at least some fees to maintain competition between teachers and schools. West (1964, pp. 168–70). See also West (1970, p. 120), and West (1975, p. 209).
38. Nassau W. Senior, *Suggestions on Popular Education* (London, 1861), p. 74, quoted in O'Donnell (1985, p. 130). Senior also noted that even if the poor recognized the need for education, they might not be able to afford it. His 1841 'Report on the Hand-loom Weavers' took the compulsory system a step further by recommending subsidization of fees for the poor. Blaug (1975, pp. 581, 586).
39. J.S. Mill, (1965, p. 953). For further references to the recognition by classical economists that there was a lack of sufficient demand for education by the poor, see O'Donnell (1985, pp. 61–5). O'Donnell (p. 94) also notes that both J.S. Mill and Adam Smith would have preferred a system of examinations to test knowledge, rather than a compulsory attendance law.
40. Blaug (1975, pp. 585–6). Schooling became compulsory in England in 1881 and was essentially free by 1891.

41. Richard Johnson, 'Educating the Educators: "Experts" and the State 1833–1839', in Donajgrodzki (1977, p. 95). It should be noted that when Brougham introduced his Education Bill in 1820, it was the opposition of religious groups that doomed it to defeat. For further discussion of the early opposition of the church in the education movement, see Sockwell (1991).
42. As noted previously, the political economists were not completely unsuccessful in promoting their ideas through the church schools. Richard Whately was particularly successful in adding economic principles to the elementary school readers of all the church schools. By the 1850s, almost all readers throughout England contained lessons in political economy.
43. Nassau Senior, *Industrial Efficiency and Social Economy*, ed. S.L. Levy, (1928, pp. 329–31), quoted in Blaug (1975, pp. 578–9).
44. For more details on the life of William Ellis see Blyth (1892).
45. Blyth (1892, pp. 83–7) and Lovett (1920, pp. 390–1).
46. For more information on the Birkbeck Schools and Ellis's attempts to include economics as part of the curriculum, see Sockwell (1989, ch. 8).
47. As quoted in Blyth (1892, p. 208).

References

Blaug, Mark (1958), *Ricardian Economics*, New Haven, CT.: Yale University Press.
Blaug, Mark (1975), 'The Economics of Education in English Classical Political Economy: A Re-Examination', in A.S. Skinner and T. Wilson (eds), *Essays on Adam Smith*, Oxford: Clarendon Press.
Blitz, Rudolph (1961), 'Some Classical Economists and their Views on Education' (unpublished translation: Vanderbilt, pp. 1–44), originally printed in *Economia*, **72–3**, pp. 34–60.
Blyth, E.K. (1892), *Life of William Ellis*, 2nd edn, London: Kegan Paul.
Boyce, George, Curren, James and Wingate, Pauline (eds) (1978), *Newspaper History: From the 17th Century to the Present Day*, London: Sage Publications.
[Brougham, Henry] (1810), 'Education of the Poor', *Edinburgh Review*, **33** (November), pp. 60–1.
[Brougham, Henry] (1824), 'Education and the People: Mechanics Institutes', *Edinburgh Review*, **81** (October), pp. 96–122.
Checkland, S.G. (1949), 'The Propagation of Ricardian Economics in England', *Economica*, N.S. **16** (February), pp. 40–52.
Clive, John (1957), *Scotch Reviewers*, London: Faber & Faber.
Coats, A.W. (1971), *The Classical Economists and Economic Policy*, London: Methuen.
Colander, David and Coats, A.W. (eds) (1989), *The Spread of Economic Ideas*, Cambridge: Cambridge University Press.
Donajgrodzki, A.P. (ed.) (1977), *Social Control in Nineteenth Century Britain*, London: Roman & Littlefield.
Ellis, E.E. (1888), *Memoir of William Ellis*, London: Longman.
Ellis, William (1857), *A Layman's Contribution to the Knowledge and Practice of Religion in Common Life*, London: Smith, Elder, & Co.
Ellis, William (1861–4), *Philo-Socrates*, 4 vols, London: Smith, Elder, & Co.
Fetter, Frank W. (1980), *The Economists in Parliament, 1780–1868*, Durham, NC: Duke University Press.
Fletcher, Max E. (1974). 'Harriet Martineau and Ayn Rand: Economics in the Guise of Fiction', *American Journal of Economics and Sociology*, **33** (4) (October), pp. 367–79.
Fontana, Biancamaria (1985), *Rethinking the Politics of Commercial Society: the Edinburgh Review 1802–1832*, Cambridge: Cambridge University Press.
Gerschenkron, A. (1969), 'History of Economic Doctrines and Economic Theory', *American Economic Review*, **59** (2) (May), pp. 1–17.
Gilbert, G. (1985), 'The *Morning Chronicle*, Poor Laws, and Political Economy', *History of Political Economy*, **17**, 4 (Winter), pp. 507–21.
Gilmour, Robin (1967), 'The Gradgrind School: Political Economy and the Classroom', *Victorian Studies*, December, pp. 207–24.

Goldstrom, J.M. (1966), 'Richard Whately and Political Economy in School Books', *Irish Historical Studies*, **15**, pp. 131–46.

Goodwin, C.D.W. (1972), 'Economic Theory and Society: A Plea for Process Analysis', *American Economic Review*, **62** (May), pp. 409–15.

Gordon, Barry (1976), *Political Economy in Parliament: 1819–1823*, London: Macmillan.

Gordon, Scott (1955), 'The London Economist and the High Tide of Laissez Faire', *Journal of Political Economy*, **63** (6) (December), pp. 461–88.

Halévy, E. (1955), *The Growth of Philosophic Radicalism*, Boston: Beacon Press.

Harrison, J.F.C. (1961), *Learning and Living, 1790–1960*, London: Routledge & Kegan Paul.

Henderson, J.P. (1983), 'The Oral Tradition in British Economics: Influential Economists in the Political Economy Club of London', *History of Political Economy*, **15** (2), pp. 149–79.

Hollis, Patricia (1969), Introduction to *The Poor Man's Guardian 1831–1835*, London: Merlin Press.

Kanth, R.K. (1986), *Political Economy and Laissez-Faire*, Totowa, NJ: Rowman & Littlefield.

Keynes, J.M. (1973), *The Collected Writings of John Maynard Keynes*, ed. D. Moggridge and E. Johnson, Vol. IX, London: Macmillan.

Lampen-Thompson, Dorothy (1973), *Adam Smith's Daughters*, New York: Exposition Press.

Lovett, William (1920), *Life and Struggles of William Lovett*, with an introduction by R.H. Tawney, New York: Alfred A. Knopf.

[Mill, James] (1808), 'Thomas Smith on Money and Exchange', *Edinburgh Review*, **13** (October), pp. 35–68.

Mill, J.S. (1965), *Principles of Political Economy*, New York: Augustus M. Kelley.

Miller, William L. (1966), 'The Economics of Education in English Classical Economics', *Southern Economic Journal*, **32**, (3) (January) pp. 294–309.

O'Brien, D.P. (1970), *J.R. McCulloch*, New York: Barnes & Noble.

O'Brien, D.P. (1975), *The Classical Economists*, Oxford: Clarendon Press.

O'Donnell, Margaret G. (1985), *The Educational Thought of the Classical Political Economists*, Lanham, MD: University Press of America.

Polkinghorn, Bette (1982), 'The Popularizers of Political Economy: Social Control or Education?', paper presented at the History of Economics Society conference, May.

Routh, Guy (1975), *The Origins of Economic Ideas*, White Plains, NY: International Arts & Sciences Press.

Schumpeter, Joseph A. (1954), *History of Economic Analysis*, New York: Oxford University Press.

Silver, Harold (1975), *English Education and the Radicals*, London: Routledge & Kegan Paul.

Skinner, A.S. and Wilson, T. (eds) (1975), *Essays on Adam Smith*, Oxford: Clarendon Press.

Smart, William (1910), *Economic Annals of the Nineteenth Century, 1801–1820*, London: Macmillan.

Smith, Adam (1937), *The Wealth of Nations*, New York: Modern Library.

Sockwell, W.D. (1989), 'Contributions of Henry Brougham and William Ellis to Classical Political Economy', Ph.D. dissertation, Vanderbilt University.

Sockwell, W.D. (1991), 'Contributions of Henry Brougham to Classical Political Economy', *History of Political Economy*, **23** (4), (Winter) pp. 645–73.

Stewart, W.A.C., and McCann, W.P. (eds) (1967), *The Educational Innovators: 1750–1880*, New York: St Martin's Press.

Thomas, William (1979), *The Philosophic Radicals*, Oxford: Clarendon Press.

Thompson, Noel (1984), *The People's Science: The Popular Political Economy of Exploitation and Crisis, 1816–1834*, Cambridge: Cambridge University Press.

Tu, Pierre N.V. (1969), 'The Classical Economists and Education', *Kyklos*, **12** (4), pp. 691–718.

Vaughan, Michalina and Archer, Margaret Scotford (1971), *Social Conflict and Educational Change in England and France, 1789–1848*, Cambridge: Cambridge University Press.

Webb, R.K. (1955), *The British Working Class Reader: 1790–1848*, London: Allen & Unwin.

Webb, R.K. (1960), *Harriet Martineau: A Radical Victorian*, New York: Columbia University Press.

West, E.G. (1964), 'The Role of Education in Nineteenth-Century Doctrines of Political Economy', *British Journal of Economic Studies*, **12** (2) (May), pp. 161–72.

West, E.G. (1970), *Education and the State*, 2nd edn, London: Institute of Economic Affairs.

West, E.G. (1975), *Education and the Industrial Revolution*, London: Batsford.

13 The 1923–4 national accounts of the Soviet Union

Zoltan Kenessey[1]

Introduction

The Balance of the USSR National Economy of 1923–4 (*Balans Narodnogo Choziaistva Soyuza SSR 1923–24 Goda*, hereafter referred to as *Balans*) was published in Moscow in 1926 by the Central Statistical Office (CSO) and was edited and co-authored by the chief of the CSO (See Popov et al., 1926). This book is among the more unusual and interesting works in the history of quantitative economics. The *Balans*'s pioneering into national economic accounting was unique in the 1920s and its preparation and results were highly relevant to the heated and crucial Soviet debates in that decade. Our review focuses on four related points.

The first is the place of this work in the twentieth-century development of economic statistics. The large volume of the *Balans* consists of two parts: the first, of 350 pages, deals with issues of methodology and with the analysis of the data, while the second (275 pages) presents statistical materials. The *Balans* was probably the first extensive system of national accounts produced by an official statistical body in the twentieth century. The introduction by Popov relates both the burdens and the stimulation involved in the new endeavour: 'Owing to the absence of similar works in Western Europe, America and in our republic, as the work went along it was necessary to resolve both the methodological problems and to overcome the technical difficulties in connection with the inadequacy of statistical material' (Popov et al., 1926, pp. v–vi). Certainly this little-known work should be accorded a noteworthy place in the history of national economic accounting.

The second point is that the *Balans* is of considerable historical interest owing to its relevance to the current debates in the former Soviet Union about the role of the markets and planning, the role of the private and public sectors, and many other issues. It sheds light on important concepts discussed at the time. A notion of economic equilibrium, for example, was widely entertained in the USSR (and in the book) in the 1920s. However, this concept was related to Bukharin's thinking and fell into oblivion after 1929 in the drive for forced collectivization, industrialization and total domination by Stalin.

The third point is a sombre one. The fate of the first national economic accounts of the Soviet Union and that of its preparers in the 1930s was a sign of the subordinated role assigned to statistics in the evolving command economy. The symptoms of the time included changes by Stalin in statistical organization and statistical programmes as well as demotions, or worse, for key statisticians. Therefore this essay, among others, intends preserving the memory of some of the economists and statisticians who pursued their profession in a tragic era.

The fourth and last point is the place of the *Balans* in the long chain of intellectual efforts culminating in the Nobel prize-winning work of Wassily Leontief. An economic history of the USSR refers to this in the following way:

> Using data from 1923–24, a group of gifted men led by Popov and Groman created the 'grandfather' of the input–output tables of later years. They invented a new idea, without which planning could hardly begin. It was necessary to trace the interconnections of the sectors composing the economy.... The attempt was in many ways inadequate.... But it was the first such attempt, if one excepts Quesnay's *Tableau Economique*. (Nove, 1989, p. 124)

I The *Balans* and the history of national accounts

Estimating the income of nations can be traced back at least 300 years. In the seventeenth century Gregory King's *Two Tracts* included his famous 'Natural and Political Observations and Conclusions upon the State and Condition of England', which compared estimates for England with those for Holland and France in respect of the years 1688 to 1695. In the eighteenth century François Quesnay's even better known *Tableau Economique* dates from 1758. In the nineteenth century estimates for the income of nations were extended to more countries, and by the beginning of the twentieth century the availability of national income estimates (typically furnished by private scholars) was the rule and not the exception.

At the same time a turn in economic thinking to predominantly micro-economic (and marginalist) analysis in the latter part of the nineteenth century made the embracing of national income calculations less likely by official statistical systems. The re-emergence of macroeconomic interest (in the wake of the Great Depression) in general, and the impact of Keynesian economics in particular, finally provided the impetus for the introduction of more detailed national economic accounts at the governmental levels in the late 1930s and the early 1940s. The needs of the war economy for systematic economic data ultimately eliminated the remaining hesitations about the usefulness of such systems.

As late as 1926, in the German Verein für Sozialpolitik, Karl Diehl argued that estimates of national income and wealth deserve no attention – and was largely supported by the members of his committee in the Verein. Indeed, he expected that after his critique of these concepts the last respect for 'attempts to call a simple sum national income and national wealth will disappear' (Diehl, 1926, p. 156).

In the United States in the early 1930s at the request of Congress the US Department of Commerce, with the involvement of Simon Kuznets, prepared detailed estimates of national income. However, these sets of data were not quite yet the national economic accounts of later years.

The national accounts of our time are, without doubt, the descendants of the earlier works on national income estimates, especially those undertaken by Simon Kuznets, Colin Clark and others. Nevertheless, in the 1930s qualitatively new developments took place. These were related to the work of Ragnar Frisch (1942); also to several other papers by Frisch in the early 1930s and studies with his collaborators, for example Aukrust, Bjerve and Frisch (1948); and to studies by Lindahl and others (1937). Among Dutch authors the work of Tinbergen (1939), which was in part connected with thoughts of Frisch, and the efforts by Derksen (1946) for 1938 were part of the innovative new strand of research. The pioneering inter-industry explorations for the US economy (see Leontief, 1936) also belong to the prehistory of contemporary national accounting. The most influential new effort in national income accounting emerged in England during the early 1940s. This development occurred under the intellectual tutelage and personal influence of Keynes. Specifically, Keynes's *How to Pay for the War* (1940) contained an appendix with national income estimates in line with his macroeconomic precepts. Subsequent UK statistical work was undertaken first by Meade and Stone (1941). Later this was greatly elaborated by Stone (1947) and set the example for most other efforts, including the international recommendations accepted by the United Nations.

The systems of national accounting, to which we have grown accustomed after the Second World War, have at least two features not characteristic of earlier national income statistics. One is the introduction of double-entry bookkeeping techniques (especially the application of interrelated sets of two-sided accounts) into national income systems. The other is the increased reliance on more tightly knit sets of explicit macroeconomic definitions (mostly of Keynesian origin).

The *Balans* of 1923–4 is among the early intellectual strands of the prehistory of modern national accounting. But can we consider the *Balans* as an effort in 'national accounting' as such? Judging by the preceding two distinguishing characteristics of national accounting, the answer to this question seems to be a somewhat qualified 'yes'.

Regarding the first distinctive characteristic a circumspect answer is required. Clearly, the *Balans* did not apply the technique of double-entry bookkeeping as it emerged in western national accounting a couple of decades later. Yet it did apply certain tables that were the precursors of the modern input–output tables. Modern input–output tables were originally separate from national accounting proper, but later were incorporated into the revised UN System of National Accounts by Sir Richard Stone. Thus, in effect, the presentation system of the *Balans* contained the early version of one sophisticated element of the present-day national accounting system, albeit not the two-sided accounts it utilizes.

In respect of the second characteristic, the *Balans* extensively relied on explicit macroeconomic categories and relationships. Often the concepts used were Marxian constructs or were labelled as such, especially in the chapters written by Popov. But there were many references to Quesnay, and we know that most of the authors of the book were non-Marxists (for example Litoshenko), perhaps with some Mensheviks and Social Revolutionaries among them. At any rate, extensive macroeconomic grounding can be seen in most chapters of the volume.

Accepting the *Balans* as part of the intellectual heritage of national accounting seems to be justified. At the same time, there is little direct influence we can accord to the *Balans* for shaping today's system. The Stalinist repression was very effective in severely curtailing its impact. Moreover, the emphasis on the limited (material) concept of production made this framework less than suitable for modern economies characterized by ever-growing service production activities.

II   The *Balans* and its times

The *Balans* was the result of the collective effort of many statisticians working at the CSO. The two leading roles were played by L.N. Litoshenko and P.I. Popov. Apparently Litoshenko was in charge of the overall methodological effort, and supervised work done in the different divisions of the CSO. Last but not least he played an important role in the summary of the results and in their analysis. Presumably Popov, as editor, set the general tone of the volume. The significance of Popov's work is clear from his sole authorship of the first and second chapters of the book, which dealt with the overall conceptual matters and the general analysis of the data, respectively. Finally, he was also the author of the concluding summary chapter of the text. In turn, Litoshenko's leading technical-statistical role is affirmed by his sole authorship of the key third chapter, 'Methodology of the Construction of the Balance of the National Economy'.

Interestingly, Litoshenko was not the author of the relatively short chapter on the estimation of national income, which was written by F.G. Dubovikov. In fact Dubovikov offered some criticism of Litoshenko's views on national income, which were reflected in his first estimates mentioned for Soviet Russia. This criticism contained no reference to the 'non-Marxian' broader concept of production favoured by Litoshenko in his work, even though Dubovikov and the *Balans* adhered to a narrower definition of production, with reference to Marx as intellectual antecedent. Rather, Dubovikov questioned Litoshenko's preference for estimating national income from the 'income side' and his doubts about procedures to estimate it from the 'product side'. At any rate, the tone of Dubovikov's comments was measured, even polite, in addressing them to 'Prof. Litoshenko'. Nonetheless, the criticism by one of the less prominent authors of one of the two senior authors in the volume itself (even on technical grounds) seems to suggest a degree of precariousness in Litoshenko's standing. More importantly, the adherence in the *Balans* to the narrower concept of production; the placing of the work in a Marxian frame; and the fact that the national income chapter was not written by Litoshenko attest to the limits of his influence. However, 1926 was not 1929 or 1930, and Dubovikov's admiration for national income work done by the National Bureau of Economic Research in the US indicates this difference. Dubovikov's chapter even includes a table showing US data estimated by the National Bureau of Economic Research for 1909 through to 1919. This table, which shows only fairly small discrepancies between estimates from the 'income' and from the 'product' sides, was cited as disproving Litoshenko's views on the relative merits of these two procedures.

At any rate, references to Marx and Lenin, while prominently displayed by Popov (and Dubovikov), were kept in proportion by references of nearly similar length to François Quesnay's *Tableau Economique*. The approach taken by Popov to Bukharin was the most immediate and consequential: references were numerous, lengthy and substantive in nature. The link with Bukharin's thinking manifested itself, in particular, in the embracement of his concept of economic equilibrium. The argument can be made that the construction of the *Balans* in itself testifies to the belief in such a concept. After all, an interdependent statistical picture of all sectors and processes in the economy is a quantification of the existent equilibrium. Knowledge of the existent equilibrium, of course, permitted the quantitative analysis of proposed radical interventions into the economy.

Popov was quite explicit in emphasizing this concept, and paid particular attention to the relationship between production and consumption.

> The equilibrium between production and consumption – this is the basic precondition of reproduction of the social economy.... Therefore, the question regarding equilibrium is the most important problem of economics. N. Bukharin is right, when he says: 'To find the [theoretically explanatory] law of this equilibrium is the fundamental problem of theoretical economics'. (Popov et al., 1926, pp. 14–15)

The concept of economic economic equilibrium was relevant to the debate between the proponents of 'teleological' and 'geneticist' planning in the 1920s. The adherents of the former claimed that the victory of the revolution in October 1917 circumvented the old laws of economics which had evolved in capitalism.

In their view, this setting radically accelerated economic targets and social transformations (such as collectivization of agriculture). In contrast, 'jumps ahead' were not deemed feasible or prudent by the 'geneticists', who emphasized the need for gradual growth and accepted the existing economic and social circumstances of the New Economic Policy (NEP). Both schools believed in the need for industrialization and in the construction of a 'fully socialist' economy, but they sharply differed regarding the time horizon in which this goal could be reached. Equally sharp were their disputes about methods, such as forced collectivization of agriculture, which were considered permissible by some 'teleological' planners but remained unthinkable to the 'geneticist'.[2]

In the early 1920s the methodology and the form of economic planning were far from clear in the Soviet Union. Interestingly, the experiences of war economic planning (especially as applied in Germany) seemed to exercise an influence on Russian economists. Also, a non-Marxist planning work entitled *The State of the Future*, which first appeared in 1898 in Germany, was published in Moscow after the revolution (see Ballod, 1920). Popov extensively criticized Ballod in the *Balans*.

By the end of the 1980s and the beginning of the 1990s the collapse of 'teleologically' furthered economic machineries in East Central Europe and in the Soviet Union were history's verdict on voluntarist planning.[3] In itself, this collapse has not proven the validity of 'geneticist' planning, which has not been given a historical trial. Strict adherents of 'free markets' would argue that even a clearly 'geneticist' approach in constructing a socialist economy would have failed over time. They may be right, especially under the political conditions of one-party control, which was after all the framework even in the era of the NEP. Conceivably, the more gradual 'geneticist' approach could have achieved economic success in a multi-party political system relying on a mixed economy. Whether such success would be ascribed to 'socialism' is another question: after all the most successful 'capitalist' economies of Europe, North America or Asia seem to have just such a concatenation of economic-political conditions.

However, at the time of the publication of the *Balans* in 1926 these questions were perceived as still widely open in Russia. The 'geneticist' approach, implied by the NEP, was supported not only by theoretical arguments but also by the political power of key leaders. In those years

Rykov was the the most illustrative representative of the moderate strain in Russian Bolshevism. On becoming premier in 1924, at the age of forty-three, he carried an unbroken identification with the party's right wing, beginning his opposition to Lenin's April Theses in 1917 and his advocacy of a coalition socialist government in October... [Rykov was] a perennial foe of grandiose economic projects and teleological planning schemes, he shared Bukharin's abhorrence of Preobrazhenskii's 'law' as a 'scandalous theory' [concerning Russia's industrialization through a 'tribute' imposed on the peasantry] which, if implemented, would 'mortally compromise socialism'.... No other Bolshevik, including Bukharin, personified so unambiguously the political and economic philosophy of NEP. (Cohen, 1975, p. 229)

The construction of the *Balans*, in the field of statistics, testified to the ability and expertise of a government agency – which at the time was under the administrative influence of Rykov – in dealing with the pressing economic and social issues of the time in a conscientious and factual manner, that is in a way preferred by Rykov.

Bukharin, unlike Rykov, was a so-called 'left Communist' in the early period of the October revolution and its aftermath. Thereafter he embraced the policies and the philosophy of NEP and became its most significant ideological expositor and supporter. After Trotsky, Zinoviev and Kamenev (who in some important ways were senior to him) were removed from the centre of power, Bukharin and Stalin were the dominant leaders of Russia between 1925 and 1927. The cooperation of these two leaders (Cohen calls it a 'duumvirate') was based mainly on the struggles carried out by both of them against Trotsky, Zinoviev and Kamenev. In this period Bukharin, in the ideological-political rivalry with his opponents, benefited from the organizational skill and power of Stalin. Stalin, in turn, was unable to challenge such astute politicians on a conceptual-political level by himself. In the final analysis, Bukharin's help made the consolidation of Stalin's power possible. Of course, after the fall of Trotsky and the others, who were the key countervailing powers against Stalin, Bukharin alone was no match for Stalin's organizational strength and brutality, and he was removed from the centre of power as well. However in 1926, when the *Balans* was published, Bukharin was at the height of his power and influence.

From the viewpoint of the NEP, and of the *Balans*, the fact that Felix Dzerzhinskii, Chief of the Secret Police (*Cheka*) was appointed chairman of the Supreme Economic Council was of considerable importance. This change was related to Rykov's appointment to premiership in February 1924. In this context it should be mentioned that the government decree instructing the CSO to compile the balance of the national economy for 1923–4 (and in preliminary form for 1924–5) was dated 21 July 1924. Dzerzhinskii's chairmanship of the Supreme Economic Council gave the Right an organizational toughness it was lacking.

The Politburo's right, according to Cohen's analysis, was strengthened both by the help of Dzerzhinskii and by the widespread staff support it enjoyed in government agencies. The reasons why so many non-party specialists supported the Right included the following: (a) most of them preferred evolutionary, gradualist approaches to economic growth; (b) they generally considered the Right's economic policies more desirable; and (c) non-party specialists usually were fearful of both Stalin and Trotsky, who appeared to be bent on resuming the intolerance and strife of the era of War Communism. Non-party specialists felt, and this fear was fully justified later, that in such a case 'Their considerable service and influence in the Soviet government would terminate' (Cohen, 1975, p. 233).

At the time the *Balans* was published in 1926, changes in the economy prompted consideration of important issues about the future. A key one was that existing industrial capacities were operating nearly fully, and market forces were deemed unwilling and/or incapable of allocating capital to the desired expansion of heavy industries. The development of heavy industry was considered paramount for industrialization and for military preparations (there was a growing fear of war in 1927). Bukharin hoped that with prudent policies industrialization would be feasible without creating havoc in the economy of the country. Hence in 1927 he agreed to the creation of the first five-year plan for the economy.

Yet, as Stalin imposed radically accelerated targets for industrial growth, and moved to finance his scheme through the expropriation of and from the peasants, in 1928 Bukharin made his famous attack on the Stalinist version of the five-year plan. His 'Notes of an Economist' appeared in *Pravda* on 30 September 1928, while he was still the editor of the paper (a position he assumed at the end of 1917). Bukharin's strong attack harked back to his study, *The Economics of the Transition Period* (Ekonomika perekhodnogo perioda), which was published in May 1920. As mentioned, a notion of economic equilibrium was important in Bukharin's economics. The concept of economic equilibrium was viewed by Bukharin not in the context of a static, but of a 'moving' or dynamic, economy. In 1920 Bukharin suggested (and in later debates reasserted) the following thoughts about economic equilibrium:

> In a society with a social division of labour... there must be a certain equilibrium of the whole system. The necessary quantities of coal, iron, machines, cotton, linen, bread, sugar, boots, etc., etc., are produced. Living human labour is expended in accordance with all of this in the necessary quantities in relation to production. There may be all sorts of deviations and fluctuations, the whole system may be enlarged, complicated and developed; it is in constant motion and fluctuation, but, in general and in its entirety, it is in a state of equilibrium. (Bukharin, 1920, pp. 127–8)

Bukharin appeared to have a grasp of what we call today the technologically determined interrelationships of production. These connections involve physical quantities of materials and goods and the 'necessary quantities' of labour. Bukharin found a significance for such input–output relationships in the framework of economic equilibrium. His respect for these unavoidable linkages of production was apparently one of the intellectual bases for his opposition to planning schemes which disregarded technological realities and the actual conditions of the economy. At the same time Bukharin's view of economic equilibrium postulated purely economic preconditions as well: 'One thing is clear: if any branch of production systematically does not receive back the costs of production plus a certain additional increment corresponding to a part of the surplus labour and adequate to serve as a source of expanded reproduction, then it either stagnates or regresses' (Bukharin, 1928, p. 2).

Bukharin's views on planning reflected, among others, the following beliefs: (a) targets have to be calculated on the basis of actual statistics and in a realistic manner, not on the basis of voluntary wishes and preconceptions; (b) targets ought to be regarded as flexible guidelines (in today's terminology he preached 'indicative planning'); (c) targets have to be set with strict regard to the prevailing proportions in the economy between agriculture and industry, between light and heavy industry, between output and the demand from consumers and producers; and (d) in order to avoid crippling disproportions both monetary reserves and reserves of physical resources need to be maintained. As history has shown, Stalin's scheme disregarded every one of these sensible precautions. Stalin's actions indeed resulted in the great economic and social calamities that were feared by Bukharin. However, probably even Bukharin could not have imagined that Russia's economy in the 1990s would still suffer the dire consequences of the end of the 1920s.

Returning to the issues of the *Balans*, the hostility of Stalin to such broad statistical works was 'logical': the results of statistical balances could not support his economic schemes. Stalin's plans, in fact, flagrantly disregarded the existing proportions of the Russian economy and the existing conditions of economic growth in the Soviet Union. Only an embracing of the tenets of 'teleological' planning and increasing terror and coercion in governance could provide the means of implementing Stalin's fateful designs.

Stalin of course knew that the non-party specialists were supporting Rykov and Bukharin. The Shakhty affair in 1928 clearly signalled his intent to break this support for the Right, when 55 engineers and technicians were arrested and charged with 'counterrevolutionary' activities. Their trial foreshadowed the terror that soon engulfed Russia and its intellectuals. And after the removal of Bukharin, Rykov and Tomskii from the centres of power, Stalin did not long delay his further purges.

Owing to its relevance to our topic, only the 1931 trial of the Mensheviks is mentioned here. The principal defendant of this trial was Vladimir Gustavovich Groman, who, according to Alec Nove, was instrumental, with Popov, in the creation of the *Balans* (Nove, 1989, p. 124). The trial involved two officials from the Supreme Economic Council, two from the People Commissariat of Trade, two from the State Bank, one from the Central Union of Consumer Cooperatives, and one from Gosplan (the State Planning Office). Service to the Soviet Union, such as Groman's extensive high-level work on economic affairs, was not accepted as an excuse for the defendants. For example, on 10 October 1917 it was in one of the defendants' (Sukhanov's) apartments on the Karpovka, in Petrograd, that the Bolshevik Central Committee met and adopted its decision to launch the armed uprising. Our review of the *Balans* is not the place to describe the accusations and the way they were concocted against the ex-Mensheviks; a detailed account of the trial is accessible in Solzhenitsyn's *Gulag*. Yet the discussion of the *Balans* would be incomplete without mentioning this tragic moment in the lives and careers of people who only a few years earlier had attempted to put economic policies on a quantitative basis.

Bukharin and Rykov themselves were arrested on 27 February 1937, put to trial in 1938, and shot on 14 March 1938. Their names thus joined the list of names of other Russian economists and planners who were persecuted before them as 'saboteurs', 'plotters' and 'enemies of the people' – notwithstanding their past efforts for the USSR.

III Statistical organization after 1917
In statistical organization Tsarist Russia usually was not considered among the advanced countries of Europe. No large agency comparable to the later CSO in Moscow was maintained by the government in St Petersburg, no modern population censuses were carried out on a periodic basis (though there was the census of 1897), and national data series on important economic, demographic and social phenomena were often lacking. Yet the regional statistical collections by Zemstvo statisticians were illuminating regarding agriculture, the conditions of the peasants and other economic and social concerns. Zemstvo statistics also provided a training ground for Russian statisticians and economists. Despite their value, the Zemstvo statistics – collected by and for local administrative bodies – were often not comparable and made national aggregation of the data difficult or impossible. A high Soviet statistical official in 1967 expressed this view of the Russian past in statistics: 'The Soviets inherited from tsarist Russia a statistics set-up in a very sorry state, divided among various ministries and departments, with no central body to co-ordinate statistical research on a nation-wide scale' (Yezhov, 1967, p. 11). A definitive evaluation of the overall Russian statistical effort before 1917 will probably yield a more positive statement. There were many statistical initiatives in Russia before 1917 which resulted in interesting statistical analyses and publications. At any rate, after 1917 there was a great deal to be done in order to provide a comprehensive statistical picture of Russian economy and society.

Indeed the need for serious statistical effort was accepted immediately after the revolutions in 1917 when industrial and agricultural statistics were centralized in the Census Department of the newly created Supreme Economic

Council (Bukharin was closely involved in the creation of the Council). A national congress of statisticians was held in June 1918. A draft statute on government statistics worked out by the congress was submitted for government approval. After final editing by a special commission, on 25 June 1918 (only eight months after the October revolution), the statute was signed and the CSO (by its Russian initials: TsSU), was established.

This is not the place to review the considerable efforts made by statisticians between 1918 and 1929 to furnish a statistical map of the country. The general atmosphere of this era is described by Alec Nove:

> The twenties were an intellectually exciting period. Not only were there debates among Bolshevik leaders and intellectuals, among whom were men of great eloquence and wit, but quite independent ideas were put forward by men who were not Bolsheviks at all. Gosplan [State Planning Office] and VSNKh [Supreme Economic Council] experts included many former Mensheviks, later to be accused of being plotters and saboteurs. Men like Groman, Bazarov and Ginzburg contributed significantly to policy debates. Ex-populist [*narodniks*], ex-SRs [social revolutionaries], were active too, for example the famous economist Kondratiev, the agricultural experts Chayanov and Chelintsev. Even non-socialists, like Litoshenko and Kutler, could raise their voices. There was a one-party state, there were no legal means of organizing an opposition, but conditions were far from resembling the monolithic thirties. The communists were very weakly represented at this time among the planners, Thus in 1924, out of 527 employees of Gosplan, only forty-nine were party members, and twenty-three of these were drivers, watchmen, typists, etc. (Nove, 1989, pp. 124–5)

P.I. Popov, who was the head of the CSO when the *Balans* was prepared, seems to have been a member of the party at the time. However, Popov's presentations to the government were probably influenced by his non-party collaborators. This assumption is particularly important in connection with Litoshenko. In Popov's introduction to the *Balans*, under 13 headings there is a long listing of the participants in the work. On page v the list is preceded by Popov's statement that 'The work on the compilation of the balance, in accordance with the plan, was distributed among the divisions of the CSO and was carried out under the leadership of the following persons:

I. Methodology	Litoshenko, L.N., Popov, P.I.
IV. Consumption	Dubenetsky, N.I., Litoshenko, L.N.,
	Lositsky, A., Polliak, G.S.
XI. Summary	Litoshenko, L.N., Morozova, I.A.,
(*and the integration of the*	Popov, P.I.
components of the Balans)	

While the listing is alphabetical, the prominent showing of Litoshenko's name (before that of Popov's) for two key elements of the actual organization of the work methodology, and the summary integration of the parts of the balance), may be attributable not only to Popov's politeness and to the placing of the first letter of Litoshenko's family name in the alphabet. A more substantive reasoning is supported by the fact that among the 11 authors of the 21 chapters of text only Popov and Litoshenko wrote three chapters each. Also, Litoshenko has been recognized as the pioneer of national income estimating (for the years 1922–3 and 1923–4) in Soviet Russia (see Vainshtein, 1969, p. 81). Vainshtein also identified Litoshenko as 'one of the leaders and theoreticians of this collective work' (ibid., p. 89).

From Vainshtein it is also known that Litoshenko's national income estimates mentioned above (but not the *Balans*),

> uniquely in the USSR, took as their basis *not the Marxian*, but the *bourgeois* concepts of this economic category. Namely, the author views and calculates national income as the sum of personal incomes of all members of the given country, and considers such a perception more realistic and practically more interesting. (ibid., p. 81; italics in original)

More importantly, Vainshtein states that: 'At the end of the twenties, as testified by Sorokin [in the 1 December 1963 issue of *Pravda*, in connection with the work of N. Voznesensky] Stalin issued instructions concerning the discontinuation of all statistical work for the construction of the balance of the national economy' (ibid., p. 79). Stalin's claim at the time, that there was a 'playing with numbers', reflected his distaste for what the numbers were showing and the ways his opponents could (and probably did) use them as arguments against his shift in policies and methods. By discontinuing the construction (and certainly the publication) of such balances he would ensure that statistical support should not be available for future challenges to his policies. Vainshtein believes that for internal purposes simplified estimates were made for 1935, 1937 and 1938. Of course, by that time the opposition to Stalin's policy was already crushed, and critics could not have accessed these materials anyway. Referring to reports published in 1960 Vainshtein states that 'in the thirties, work on the balances was limited to methodological explorations' (1969, p. 80). As a result, the systematic statistical evidence presented in the *Balans* about the economy in the 1920s was not available by the 1930s to anyone, not even to Stalin.

Statistical work in the 1930s did not only suffer the effects of Stalin's influence on statistical presentations. 1929 was a watershed year in overall Soviet development. As one sign of the times, the earlier independence of the CSO was abolished: 'On January 23, 1930, the Council of People's Commissars decided to reorganize the Central Statistical Office into a department of economic accounting under the State Planning Commission' (Yezhov, 1967, p. 20). And in May 1931 'the government considered it necessary to strengthen the centralized supervision over the methods and organization of all statistical operations' (ibid., p. 21). The new situation was entirely different from the one in 1926 when the head of the CSO 'was granted a vote in the Council of People's Commissars [Council of Ministers]' (ibid., p. 20).

The dangers of subordinating statistics to planning in the command economy of Stalin were much more serious than carrying out statistical activities in substantive departments of the government before the revolution. An organizational change of this sort would have mattered much less even in the years of the NEP in the 1920s. During the NEP economic plans provided only 'control numbers', which were tentative targets of no great administrative consequence. In Stalin's command economy the obligation to 'fulfil the plan' was a very different demand – it was often a matter of life and death. As it was the statistician's role to measure the 'fulfilment of the plan' it was in the interest of all powers of 'substantive' responsibility (including, of course, the planners) to place statistics in a role subordinate to themselves.

Notwithstanding the pervasive control of statistics by planners, or precisely because of the profoundly unhealthy circumstances, the huge operation of the population census of 1937 was pronounced a failure and in 1939 an entirely new census was taken. Nove's account of and comments on this matter are as follows:

A census was taken in 1937. Its preliminary results displeased the authorities for reasons unknown, so it was scrapped and its authors arrested. A new census was taken in 1939. One may be pardoned for concluding that these and other similar experiences affected the work of the surviving statisticans, and therefore the quality and reliability of statistics. (Nove, 1989, p. 229)

By 1948 the lack of adequate statistics became a serious concern for the Soviet leaders. Despite the unprecedented centralization of power, even Stalin and the limited circle of insiders in the party and government lacked sufficient economic and social information. Lower-level officials, and the public, were kept entirely in the dark about the results of most statistical investigations. During the war and the postwar years, until after Stalin's death, statistical yearbooks, etc. were no longer in the public domain. Yet, owing to the submerging of statistical activities to planning and other factors, the scope and quality of these secretive 'hard data' was questionable. By 1948 the restoration of the statistical service to its independent status that existed before 1930 could no longer be avoided. Nevertheless, until Stalin died, public dissemination of data was not reintroduced. Even after his death, for years the resumption of statistical publication was selective and halting.

Available sources do not offer a complete and balanced review of Russian statistical developments of the time. It merely indicates that, like other things and persons, statistics suffered terribly under Stalin's rule. The termination of statistical work on broad national economic accounts such as the *Balans* at the end of the 1920s was apparently only the first, albeit significant and symbolic, denigration suffered by the statistical system under his dictatorial rule. Some of the organizational harm done in the 1930s was remedied after the 1948 re-establishment of the CSO. But the recognition of the pioneering work of Popov, Litoshenko and others was delayed. In Eastern Europe the earliest postwar article about the *Balans* was probably the one written by the author of this review, published in the Hungarian journal *Statisztikai Szemle* in 1958 in Budapest (Kenessey, 1958, pp. 315–22). In Russia, Academician Nemchinov called attention to the early work of Popov and others in 1959; see Nemchinov (1964). And the short history of national economic accounts in Russia and in the Soviet Union filled in some further gaps (see Vainshtein, 1969).

IV   The input–output connection

As mentioned, Popov traced the intellectual basis of the *Balans* to Quesnay and Marx and the exposition of the Marxian reproduction schemes by Bukharin. In contrast, no explicit linkages were shown to the intellectual efforts of prewar Russian thinkers. Yet prewar Russian inter-industry concepts were relevant to the exegesis of this sophisticated work, and it is unlikely that Popov or Bukharin were unaware of the prewar concepts. Indeed it must be assumed that they had at least a general familiarity with the work of the writers to be mentioned below. Yet it is possible that the Russian intellectual antecedents regarding inter-industry matters appeared unimportant to Popov as they pertained to a seeming technicality. Such an interpretation is strengthened by the circumstance that in the *Balans* similar inter-industry concepts were treated in a matter of fact way and without claiming much significance for them. Conceivably the creators of the *Balans* did not realize the conceptual significance of the technical advancement made in their own work towards what was later fully developed in the input–output system of Wassily Leontief. On the other hand, recognizing the links between their concepts and prewar Russian thinking involved political peril. In particular, it would have linked the *Balans* (and, perhaps more importantly, the concepts of economic equilibrium of Bukharin) to the so-called Legal Marxists of prewar Russia, and even to marginalist economics.

The names of Tugan-Baranovsky and Struve, the leaders of the so-called Legal Marxists, were well known to the Bolsheviks, at least from Lenin's disputes with them. Important intellectual links with Struve or the others, therefore, were probably problematic even in the relatively free atmosphere of the NEP. At any rate, and perhaps conveniently, the intellectual linkage to them was via certain explorations of Dmitriev, whose work was much less well known. Struve, on his part, attempted to merge Ricardian precepts with those of the marginalist ideas of Böhm-Bawerk. Kaser provides an illuminating description of the situation:

> Struve thought to place a 'realistic theory of economic phenomena within the wide and grandiose frame of Marx's sociological system', and eventually found the intellectual link in Dmitriev, whom he called a 'Ricardo elaborated and verified in logic and mathematics.' Dmitriev died young, but his brilliance was demonstrated in his sole published work, *Economic Essays*, which appeared in Moscow in 1902. Like Marx and Tugan-Baranovsky, he built conceptually upon Quesnay's *Tableau Economique*, but he went on from them to set out the formulae of inter-product flows in terms of cumulative labour inputs; such a set of simultaneous equations could be used (although Dmitriev did not push his argument this far) to determine the direct and indirect outlay for each identified good with the technology implicit in the reported relationship. (Kaser, 1970, p. 30)

Kaser also reports that Dmitriev's

> ideas retained some currency after the Revolution: there are, for example, more references to him than to Marx in Yurovsky's *Essays on Price Theory*, published in Saratov in 1919. From then until 1959 he had no Soviet recognition: the veteran Academician Nemchinov rescued him from that official oblivion, partly to rehabilitate marginalism and partly to claim Russian priority for a genesis of the input output table. (Ibid., p. 31)

Neither Dmitriev nor the inter-industry statistical tables of the 1923–4 balance of the Soviet Union made use of technical coefficients the way Leontief did in the context of his inter-industry matrices. According to Kaser, in 1928 the Soviet planner Barengolts demonstrated the need for the coefficients, yet without the matrix framework for calculating them. And when decades later, after Stalin's death, serious interest evolved in inter-industry economics the planners turned to Leontief's system as it evolved in the US.

Leontief was familiar with the inter-industry work that was manifested in the *Balans*. Indeed, he published a short review regarding this effort in *Planovoe Khoziastvo* issue 12, in 1925, and a more substantial one in Germany in the same year, entitled 'The Balance of the Russian National Economy – A Methodological Study' ('Die Bilanz der Russischen Volkswirtschaft – Eine methodologische Untersuchung' in *Weltwirtschaftliches Archiv*).[4]

Wassily Leontief, the father of modern inter-industry research,

> was born on August 5, 1906 in St. Petersburg, Russia (now Leningrad). His father was an economist; his grandfather had amassed a fortune in textiles. The young Leontief was a brilliant student of philosophy, mathematics and economics at the University of Leningrad. But he was also an outspoken Menshevik and by 1925, when he won the degree of 'Learned Economist' at the age of 19, he had repeatedly gotten into trouble for his political views. He thus embraced an opportunity to leave Russia [for Germany] soon after obtaining his degree. (Carter and Petri, 1989, p. 8)

Oftentimes achievements of foreign-born American scholars elicit certain nationalistic claims from circles in their country of birth. It is not surprising, therefore, that there were Russian claims of priority in inter-industry work. Yet the facts speak for themselves: modern input–output work in its theoretical-economic elaboration, in its sophisticated matrix design, in its computer applications, and in its spread throughout the world (including in the USSR) is the result of the endless toils of Wassily Leontief. The significance of his pioneering work is not reduced by the recognition of early works, including those of Dmitriev and Popov, which exhibited conceptual brilliance and statistical sophistication respectively. However, for reasons discussed earlier, the early initiatives were not permitted to flower in their home country and could exercise but little influence in Russia or elsewhere until the late 1950s.

Summary
The national economic accounts of the Soviet Union for 1923–4, which included the first known attempts at national input–output statistics, indicate wide interest and considerable sophistication on behalf of the Russian statisticians involved in this work. The publication of the *Balans* was undoubtedly a remarkable event for its time.

The political debates and the economic issues of the NEP provide the indispensable background for this early statistical initiative. Indeed the aims, results and ultimate fate of this major statistical undertaking cannot be understood without reference to such matters. In particular, the role and policies of Bukharin provided an important context for the construction of the 1923–4 *Balans*. The concept of economic equilibrium he embraced influenced, technically as well as analytically, the structural exploration of the Russian economy in the 1923–4 national economic accounts.

The development of statistical organization in Russia in the 1920s and the 1930s and the course of broadly based national accounting in the Soviet Union were intimately linked. The statistical reorganizations, just as the creation and the abandonment of the early national accounts, were symptoms of the broader politico-economic tendencies and the fateful turbulences of those years.

In 1926 3 000 copies of the *Balans* were printed, only few of which are extant today. The time that has elapsed is one of the reasons, the unfortunate fate of the book under Stalin is the other. Indeed, *Habent sua fata libelli....* My first access to this book occurred in 1958 in Moscow, where at my request Lev Markovich Tsirlin, Senior Economist of the CSO, gracefully provided me with an original copy. However, on my transfer to the UN Statistical Office in New York and subsequent immigration to the US this copy was lost. Three decades later, in 1989, V.N. Kirichenko – the head of Goskomstat (State Committee for Statistics, the successor agency to the CSO) – at my request kindly furnished a photocopy of the full publication to me.[5] One can only hope that one day, perhaps in less strained economic times, a full or partial reprint of the *Balans* will appear in Moscow, facilitating further research and commemorating this classic volume. It is probably no exaggeration to claim that neither before nor after the publication of the *Balans* did the CSO of Moscow issue a volume of similar sophistication or of comparable economic and political significance.

Notes

1. The author is Director of the International Statistical Institute, Voorburg, The Netherlands; formerly Senior Economist, Board of Governors of the Federal Reserve System, Washington, DC.
2. Among the Russian economists and statisticians of the 1920s, Bazarov, Groman and Kondratiev are usually mentioned as favouring 'geneticist' planning and Krizhanovskii, Strumilin and Mendelson as advocates of 'teleological' planning. Regarding the debates on this topic see Carr (1958), Carr and Davies (1969), Dobb (1960) and Ehrlich (1960).
3. Recently Charemza and Kiraly (1990) reported econometric test results based on Soviet and Eastern European data relevant to this matter. They found that 'For the USSR both NMP [Net Material Product] and consumption, the hypothesis about teleologically created plans can be maintained. The predominantly teleological nature of Soviet planning seems to confirm the persistent influence of the early Strumilin theories on post-war planning in the Soviet Union' (p. 571).
4. The Russian review was an unauthorized version based on Leontief's German study. (Communication of Professor Leontief to the author.)
5. The author wishes to acknowledge with sincere thanks the photocopy of the entire *Balans* received from V.N. Kirichenko, President of Goskomstat.

References

Aukrust, O., Bjerve, P.J. and Frisch, R. (1948), *A System of Concepts Describing the Economic Circulation and Production Process*, Oslo: University of Oslo.

Ballod, K. (1920), *Gosudarstvo budushego* (The State of the Future), Moscow: Izdatelstvo Nauka.

Bukharin, N. (1920), *Ekonomika perekhodnogo perioda* (The Economy of the Transition Period), Moscow.

Bukharin, N. (1928), 'Zapiski ekonomista' (Notes of an Economist), *Pravda*, 30 September, p. 6.

Carr, E.H. (1958), *Socialism in One Country, 1924–1926*, Vol. I, London: Macmillan.

Carr, E.H. and Davies, R.W. (1969), *Foundations of a Planned Economy, 1926–1929*, Vol. I, Part II, London: Macmillan.

Carter, A.P. and Petri, P.A. (1989), 'Leontief's Contribution to Economics', *Journal of Policy Modeling* II, (1) (Spring), special issue in honour of Wassily Leontief, pp. 1–30.

Charemza, W.W. and Kiraly, J. (1990), 'Plans and Exogeneity: The Genetic-Teleological Dispute Revisited', *Oxford Economic Papers*, 42, pp. 562–73.

Cohen, S.F. (1975), *Bukharin and the Bolshevik Revolution: A Political Biography, 1888–1938*, New York: Vintage Books.

Derksen, J.B.D. (1946), 'A System of National Book-keeping', Occasional Paper X, London: National Institute of Economic and Social Research.

Diehl, K. (1926), *Volkseinkommen und Volksvermögen. Begriffskritische Untersuchungen*, Munich, Leipzig and Stuttgart: Kuhlman.

Dobb, M. (1960), *Soviet Economic Development since 1917*, London: Routledge & Kegan Paul.

Ehrlich, A. (1960), *The Soviet Industrialization Debate, 1924–1928*, Cambridge, MA: Harvard University Press.

Frisch, R. (1942), *Noen innledningsmerknader til Okosirksystemet (det okonomiske sirkulasjons-system)*, Oslo: University of Oslo.

Kaser, M. (1970), *Soviet Economics*, New York: McGraw Hill.

Kenessey, Z. (1958), 'A szovjet nèpgazdasàg 1923–24 èvi mèrlege', *Statisztikai Szemle*, **4**, pp. 315–22.

Keynes, J.M. (1940), *How to Pay for the War*, London: Macmillan & Co.

Leontief, W.W. (1936), 'Quantitative Input and Output Relations in the Economic System of the United States', *The Review of Economic Statistics*, **18** (3), pp. 105–25.

Lindahl, E., Dahlgren, E. and Kock, K. (1937), *National Income of Sweden, 1861–1930*, Vols I and II, London: P.S. King & Son for the Institute of Social Science, Stockholm University.

Meade, J.R. and Stone, J.R.N. (1941), 'The Construction of Tables of National Income, Expenditure, Savings and Investment', *Economic Journal*, **51**, pp. 216–33.

Nemchinov, V.S. (ed.) (1964). *The Use of Mathematics in Economics*, London and Edinburgh: Oliver & Boyd.

Nove, A. (1989), *An Economic History of the USSR*, London: Penguin.

Ohlsson, I. (1953), *On National Accounting*, Stockholm: Konjunkturinstitutet.

Popov, P.I. et al. (1926), *Balans narodnogo khoziaistva Soyuza SSR 1923–24 goda*, Moscow: SSSR, Trudi Tsentralnogo Statisticheskogo Upravlenia, Vol. XXIX, 14–15.

Solzhenitsyn, Aleksander I. (1974–8), *The Gulag Archipelago 1918–1956: An Experiment in Literary Investigations*, trans. from Russian by Thomas P. Whitney [1st edn], New York: Harper and Row.

Stone, R. (1947), 'Definition and Measurement of the National Income and Related Totals', in *Measurement of National Income and the Construction of Social Accounts*, Geneva: United Nations, pp. 21–113.

Tinbergen, J. (1939), *Statistical Testing of Business-Cycle Theories*, Vols I and II, Geneva: League of Nations.

Vainshtein, A. (1969), *Narodnii dokhod Rossii i SSSR, Istoria, metodologia ischislenia, dinamika*, Moscow: Izdatelstvo Nauka.

Yezhov, A. (1967), *Organization of Statistics in the USSR*, Moscow: Progress Publishers.

14 The Gorbachev reforms and the Left Opposition of the 1920s

M.H.I. Dore

It is an elementary logical proposition established by Lucretius that if one does not care about the past, then one cannot care about the future. This is indeed a fundamental justification for the study of history and for seeking lessons from history through a search for historical parallels as well as patterns that display some coherent regularity. This paper attempts to search for the historical roots of some of the changes occurring in Eastern Europe and especially the former Soviet Union.

Two most widely accepted accounts of the changes in the USSR are (1) the 'inevitable' failure of socialism, formalized in the von Mises-von Hayek thesis; and (2) the elevation to power of Gorbachev, a chance element or a historical accident ('Cleopatra's Nose' and all that). Neither of these accounts is plausible: a detailed refutation of these explanations is outside the scope of this paper. Instead it will be argued that the events in the Soviet Union at least are a vindication of the position of the anti-Stalinist opposition of the 1920s, particularly the Left Opposition in the CPSU, which Stalin ruthlessly and brutally eliminated within the USSR. Next the paper attempts to show that, as a result of these changes, there remains a real possibility of the emergence of socialist democracy and the fulfilment of the programme of the Left Opposition,[1] which was once led by Trotsky, and the 'Rightist' ideas of Bukharin[2] and his supporters on the role of the market in an economy in transition to socialism.

Section I is confined to an analysis of what was happening in the USSR between 1980 and 1985 in the light of the debates in the 1920s and early 1930s. In Section II the early history of Soviet economic policy and the role of the market is retraced from a historical perspective, in order to understand the proposed reforms in the Soviet Union. The concluding section draws the strands together and ends by considering the implications of the analysis for the future role of the working class as well as its vanguard the Communist Party both in the Soviet Union and in the advanced capitalist countries.

I

Soon after Stalin consolidated his power, Trotsky, the leader of the Left Opposition, was exiled in 1929 to Turkey. By 1930 he formed the International

Left Opposition, which after 1933 functioned as the Fourth International. The latter was officially set up in Paris in 1938.

This opposition in exile criticized Stalin for (a) bureaucratization and regimentation of social life in the Soviet Union; (b) political intolerance and the abandonment of socialist democracy; (c) failure to support the extension of the socialist revolution in the advanced industrial countries such as Germany; and (d) the foolhardy attempt to build socialism in one country. Trotsky summed up the Stalinist betrayal of the revolution as the 'Soviet Thermidor'. But lacking popular support in the countryside, and blaming the capitalist encirclement, Stalin adopted rather harsh and repressive measures, long after Trotsky had led and won the civil war in the USSR. Although before 1929 the Left Opposition advocated collectivization of agriculture, it opposed the way it was carried out by Stalin, who imposed forced collectivization with Nazi-like brutality, the facts of which are too well known in the West.

Three important planks in the programme of the Left Opposition were: (1) the right to form factions and tendencies within the CPSU, with the eventual future legalization of a multi-party system; (2) the (eventual) decentralization of power, which was to be in the hands of workers' councils or soviets – summed up in the slogan, 'all power to the soviets'; (3) the right of recall of deputies, which meant no professional class of politicos, no emergence of a permanent bureaucratic elite, and where the right of recall meant regular elections. Thus deputies would face regular elections and be answerable to the general population.

In his 1917 *April Theses* Lenin set out, *inter alia*, the following. There was to be worker and peasant control over all forms of production and distribution. In agriculture, large estates were to become model farms and were to be under the control of the Soviets of Poor Peasants. In industry there was to be worker or state control (see Carr, 1952, for further details).[3] Later, after Lenin's death, the Left Opposition often invoked Lenin as an ally, as someone who would have sided with them.

What we saw in the Soviet Union during 1980–85 was

1. the acceptance of regular elections;
2. genuine debate within the CPSU and its Politburo;
3. the steady erosion of the privileges of the bureaucratic elite;
4. the decentralization of power to the republics and to the soviets;
5. the separation of the state and the Party;
6. the acceptance of the right to organize politically in the form of a multi-party system, and the abandonment of the monopoly role of the CPSU;
7. the acceptance of private property, especially in agriculture;
8. the abandonment of centralized planning and procurement, and the rehabilitation of a price mechanism for all goods with the possible exception of military hardware.

The last-mentioned goal was to be fully implemented in the Thirteenth Five Year Plan in 1991, when the accent was to shift from administrative control of production to price-based incentives, with the state using indirect *economic* levers such as interest rates, taxation and other financial incentives to influence the economy; the role of the central allocation and supply was to be drastically reduced.[4]

The resurgence of nationalism was in part a direct result of decades of rigid central control and lack of democracy, and it is nationalism that has now become the single most important challenge to central control. Isaac Deutscher,[5] a Polish communist and a supporter of the Left Opposition, has analysed the inherent dangers of centralized control; he calls it substitutionism. First the Party becomes the substitute for the working class, and then the Party Central Committee substitutes for the Party. The Central Committee in turn is substituted by the Politburo. It was the Politburo which then allowed Stalin to assume absolute power. Thus Stalin alone made decisions, which were then approved by the Politburo, and each successive body in the chain of command simply rubber-stamped the decision taken by its immediate superior in the hierarchy.

In the economic sphere, the political structure dominated decision-making. In the early industrialization debates the Left Opposition supported the so-called 'teleologists', whose policy was to attempt to break the output constraints of both agriculture and industry, a proposition formalized in the Marx–Feldman model of growth. In contrast the 'geneticists' favoured a more balanced growth, with adequate regard for the needs of the peasantry, which would ensure adequate food supply for the nation as a whole. Stalin at first vacillated between the two approaches, but after annihilating the Left Opposition he suddenly adopted its programme, changed course and ordered the march towards forced industrialization and collectivization of agriculture. In the mean time no political preparation was carried out; the very people who could have helped secure political acceptance of both policies had in the main been hounded out or killed, or imprisoned on trumped-up charges.

The disastrous consequences for agriculture are well known; it is this legacy of forced collectivization from which Soviet agriculture never recovered: although output has increased, the goal of food security for the entire population has not been achieved over the last 70 years. The Soviet Union has had to continue to rely on the import of meat and grain on a massive scale in most years.

In industry, for years gross output targets (in quantity terms such as total tonnage of steel or other physical units) have been met without regard to quality, technical efficiency or cost. In consumer goods, production has largely imitated western goods, but without much regard for what consumers would like to buy. In industry, with the exception of defence and armaments, technological innovation has been either non-existent or very slow (see Gomulka, 1986). Thus Soviet industry as a whole has been grossly inefficient.

It was the crisis in the economy that forced the leadership to try out a long series of 'reforms', starting with the Liberman reforms in the 1960s. None of these reforms restored any vitality or technological spur to industry. The facts are too well known to need detailed justification.

The set of Gorbachev reforms evolved as a historical necessity. It is indeed remarkable that the most important political reforms came close to the programme of the Left Opposition. A recent proposal of Gorbachev would see either the elimination of the Politburo or its decline in importance as a decision-making body. The Politburo was to be replaced by representatives from the fifteen republics.

II

Before turning to the Soviet Union once again, consider the reasons for the technological superiority of the capitalist mode of production. Why has it been able to innovate and grow so much? Is it simply the motive of accumulation? The answer lies in the fact that capitalist production has faced fairly strong and organized unions, who on behalf of the working class claimed higher and higher real wages. In times of prosperity capital has had no choice but to give in to the wage demands. The response of capital has been to invest in labour-saving capital equipment. Consequently the dominant trend in technological change has been the substitution of capital equipment for live labour. In the labour theory of value, capital equipment is nothing but congealed labour, and it is capital equipment that began in these times of prosperity to compete increasingly with live labour. The higher wage demands were nothing but an expression of the class struggle (although orthodox Marxists might call the unions 'reformist', or even reactionary). The unions therefore forced capitalist firms to innovate.

If we accept the hypothesis that capitalist innovation has been designed mainly to cut labour costs, and that the labour unions' main fight has been to secure a larger share of the growing national output, then it is clear that it is the class struggle that has ironically given capitalist production technological superiority through the need to innovate.

In twentieth-century capitalism, price competition between large capitalist firms has played a role of secondary importance. Indeed competition has played a role mainly through international trade – North American capitalism versus Japanese capitalism, and European capitalism versus Japanese capitalism.[6] But this competition is not the main spur for the technological prowess of western capitalism. For North America and Europe it has in fact been the need to defend and increase profit margins. An important way of defending profit margins is through labour-saving innovations.

In the advanced capitalist countries, the very success of technological innovation has inevitably led to the decline in the numerical strength of productive workers. In Marxist terms, as congealed labour competes with live labour, the socially necessary labour (i.e. live labour) declines. So the classical working class, defined as workers who produce surplus value, has declined in numbers. Industries that produce surplus value are: all agriculture, all manufacturing, forestry, transportation and construction. In all these industries the replacement of labour by machines has been evident. With the advent of the silicon chip, and the development of the use of computer technology and robotics, this trend has accelerated particularly over the last ten years. Already completely automated integrated steel plants exist; hydroelectric or nuclear power plants that need very little labour also exist. The day is not far off when we shall see fully automated factories: congealed labour will replace live labour more and more.

According to classical Marxism, the moral justification for the working class taking power was its numerical superiority.[7] Indeed, taking power, through its vanguard the Communist Party, was its historic duty. Those material conditions no longer exist. Employment growth is more and more concentrated in the unproductive sector: accountants, lawyers, marketing professionals, advertising agents, teachers, administrators, doctors, nurses, artists, entertainers, health care specialists, researchers, engineers, laboratory technicians and so on. These are unproductive in the technical sense, in that they do not produce surplus value, but they are by no means unnecessary. Thus working-class power has lost its moral force.

In the Soviet Union this technological spur for innovation, which, as we saw, originates in the actions of the working class, was entirely missing in the early 20th century; instead, industrial management was completely bureaucratized; detailed orders were received from above, and there was little room for initiative – except to fulfil (and overfulfil!) the plan.

But from the above analysis it does not follow that private ownership of the means of production is a necessary condition for technological innovation. It does, however, suggest the need to decentralize and deregulate production decisions, some investment decisions, and for workers (both productive and unproductive) to be given the right to determine their own incomes, and the right to strike. It also suggests that as part of decentralization, enterprises and individuals be given the right to hold foreign exchange, and the right to import when it happens to be in the interest of the enterprise to do so. It also suggests that enterprises should go bankrupt if they have made the 'wrong' choices (McIntyre, 1989, p. 11).

While private ownership is not a necessary condition, the reintroduction of the role of a controlled market mechanism is now necessary. The market mechanism was abolished prematurely by Stalin, as argued below. But here again we turn to the Left Opposition for their view of the role of the market mechanism in a society in transition to socialism.[8] Consider the following quotation from Trotsky (1932, pp. 29–30):

> If there existed the universal mind that projected itself into the scientific fancy of Laplace, a mind that would register simultaneously all the processes of nature and of society, that could measure the dynamics of their motion, that could forecast the results of their interaction, such a mind could, of course, draw up *a priori* a faultless and an exhaustive economic plan, beginning with the number of hectares of wheat and down to the last button for a vest. In truth, the bureaucracy often conceives that just such a mind is at its disposal; that is why it so easily frees itself from the control of the market and of Soviet democracy. But in reality the bureaucracy errs frightfully in its appraisal of the mind's spiritual resources. . . .
>
> The innumerable living participants of the economy, state as well as the private, collective as well as individual, must give notice of their needs and of their relative strength not only through the statistical determinations of plan commissions but by the direct pressure of supply and demand. The plan is checked and to a considerable measure realized through the market. The regulation of the market itself must depend upon the tendencies that are brought out through its medium. The blueprints brought out by the offices must demonstrate their economic expediency through commercial calculation. . . . Without a firm monetary unit, commercial accounting can only increase the chaos.

This passage makes it quite clear that to the Left Opposition the transition to socialism required a harnessed market mechanism, i.e. planning would determine the fundamental direction of the economy, including the rate of investment, but that efficiency and innovative activity requires decentralized decision-making through financial autonomy of firms – the so-called *khozraschet* principle.[9]

Soviet economic history ever since 1917 has been plagued with the vexed question of the role of the market. War Communism (1918–21) was a response to the civil war, the British naval blockade, the more or less complete collapse of the economy, and hyperinflation resulting from the printing of money to finance the civil war. Under War Communism the market was abolished; all industry was centrally directed, and all payments were in kind, i.e. money had been abolished. Industry acquired a military character, and no goods were sold to the peasantry except on the receipt of grain deliveries. Under this policy the peasantry was at a great financial disadvantage. The policy threatened the worker–peasant alliance which was the backbone of the Soviet regime. After strong recommendations by Trotsky, War Communism was ended in March 1921, and the regime adopted the NEP (New Economic Policy), formulated by Lenin. The NEP was designed to consolidate the support of the peasantry for the Soviet regime. The worker–peasant alliance was called the *smytchka*.

Under NEP, the market was largely rehabilitated: small-scale light industry was denationalized, charges for services reintroduced, and in agriculture a progressive tax in kind was imposed, with the peasantry being free to sell its grain surplus on the market. But under NEP problems continued: the state sector (heavy industry) could not be revived, and only a small segment of the peasantry benefited from the NEP. A succession of crises connected with the NEP meant that market-determined development would have meant giving up socialist goals, and the preservation of market equilibrium would have meant that the necessary structural transformation of the economy would not have been possible. However, this structural transformation required exportable grain surpluses, which were not forthcoming even after years of NEP.

The Platform of the Left (September 1927) set out this faction's agricultural policy in greater detail. It envisaged a much larger commitment of resources to expand the base of *kolkhozes* and *sovkhozes* which were to be the main form of socialist construction of the countryside in the future. Its steady expansion was to render individualistic forms of production disadvantageous to the peasant; the Left had no plans for forced collectivization; fiscal measures and a rational prices policy, organization and propaganda among the peasantry were the only instruments that the Left was then ready to use.

Lenin's two conditions for the survival of the Soviet regime in a peasant economy were (1) a successful workers' revolution in the West coming to the aid of the USSR, and (2) alliance with the countryside (the *smytchka*). The end of War Communism and the adoption of NEP was necessitated by the failure of a socialist revolution in the West, as the *smytchka* became the only guarantee for survival of the Soviet regime. The failure of Soviet agriculture to attain food security without queues has eluded the Soviet leadership. Private plots of land in the USSR accounted for 3 per cent of the land, but produced 40 per cent of the marketable surplus. The survival of the socialist state requires some revolutionary change in agricultural policy; historical parallels suggest the necessity of a new *smytchka*, with the granting of land tenure to the peasantry on a massive scale: perhaps 50 per cent or more land should be handed back to those who work the land. A dramatic – market-based – increase in food is required as a precondition for the further development of a food processing industry and manufactured consumer goods. A significant reversal in the rural–urban terms of trade in favour of the former would also have to be a necessary concomitant. Here again there is a historical parallel.

In 1922 the agricultural policy of NEP had produced an increase in the prices of agricultural goods over industrial goods. But the formation of marketing syndicates in state-controlled industry secured, after 1922, a movement of prices in its own favour. The cause of the price increase was the monopoly position of state industry. Trotsky demonstrated the worsening terms of trade at the 12th Party Congress in March 1923, which threatened the *smytchka*. His report on the 'price-scissors' was part of a plea for greater planning and rationalization of industry together with rapid industrialization.

The queues and shortages of food products in the former USSR were completely misunderstood by the western press. First of all, the shortages and rationing were regional in character. Second, there was *no* shortage on the free market, where one could buy all sorts of goods, even US dollars. But the free market prices were considerably higher than the prices in the state shops. Third, Aganbegyan (1988, p. 91) noted that a number of foods were heavily subsidized; in 1986, 14 per cent of the total state budget was spent on food subsidies. For example, the ratio of the cost of production to price is a staggering 266 per cent for meat; for milk the ratio is 207 per cent. That is, the goods were being sold *for less than half the cost of production!* No wonder there was excess demand, and no wonder that there were queues at the state shops, but none at the free markets. With such subsidies, it is not at all surprising that goods had to be rationed. No doubt output will have to be raised but prices too will have to be raised steadily to reduce the subsidies.[10]

To raise output, the entire Eastern Europe could learn from the agricultural policies of the governments of capitalist North America and Europe, where there are huge surpluses of grain, meat, butter and wine. These surpluses are made possible through a variety of price supports, guaranteed prices, marketing boards and other programmes. Planning agriculture requires favourable terms of trade, but also long-term incentives to raise the productive potential of the land. Security of land tenure is perhaps a necessary condition.

Agriculture was not the only sector encountering problems in the USSR; industrial output too had failed to grow, especially in the 1980s. The administrative and bureaucratic structure of industrial management, with central allocation of resources, came into effect under Stalin, after he eliminated all opposition in 1929. For the next 30 years there was remarkable growth in the industrial power of the USSR, and steady improvement in the standard of living of the Soviet citizen. However, in the 1970s growth began to slow down, and in the 1980s it ceased altogether. According to Aganbegyan (1989), Gorbachev's main economic adviser and the architect of the economic dimension of perestroika, in the 1980s per capita growth of real GNP in the USSR was virtually zero. The 1980s saw a growing realization in the ruling circles of the vulnerability and technological weaknesses of the USSR. Historians will have to explain what objective conditions led to the policy of glasnost, championed by Gorbachev, which seems indispensable for perestroika to succeed. But with the openness there had been in the 1980s an increasing recognition of the paralysis and parasitic nature of the Soviet bureaucratic management elite of the industrial sector.

Perestroika and glasnost tried to change that. A veritable revolution that began as a new tolerance in the arts and culture had been extended to political life. A series of articles by Boris Kagarlitsky (e.g. Kagarlitsky, 1988, 1989) show that the ideas of the Left Opposition of the 1920s re-emerged, with refinements, in the Marxist debates of discussion groups of a new Left, who could not be dismissed by the establishment as 'dissidents'. Kagarlitsky (1988) also reports that in many factories workers had begun to demand changes in the organization of labour; there are demands for glasnost at the workplace, dismissal of incompetent and corrupt managers, a shortening of the work week and an end to overtime. There were spontaneous strikes and meetings. Kagarlitsky argued that the reform leadership had also understood the political dimension of the reform, after two years of defeats; they had understood that since the reform attacked a privileged stratum, it could not succeed without the support of specific social interest groups, i.e. without a mass base. To this end, demonstrations in support of the reform in every city were cautiously welcomed.

The economic programme of the reform had three main elements (see Aganbegyan, 1988, 1989). The first was the reorientation of production *towards social needs*; in the past the entire production structure was geared towards investment, or 'self-reproduction'. This in turn had three priorities: the rapid expansion of housing construction, an increase in food supply through higher food prices which would undoubtedly emerge from the operation of the market, and increased expenditure on public health and education. The second element was reform of management, in which administrative methods would give way to the use of market-based controls, such as interest rates, taxes and pricing policies. The reform of management was to be accompanied by the introduction of workers' self-management at the enterprise level. The third element was a planned increase in technical efficiency: cost reduction and an increase in labour productivity, which should follow if the second were successful.

The economic reform was spearheaded by Aganbegyan, Zaslavskaya, and other social scientists at the Novosibirsk Institute. They also seemed to have carried out a thorough Marxian analysis of the situation in the USSR today. They issued a memorandum which defined the state of affairs as a growing split between the relations of production established in the 1930s and the forces of production of the 1980s. This suggested that the scholars in the USSR were aware of the gravity of the crisis in the Soviet economy: such an analysis was also a clear signal that a revolutionary situation existed in the USSR in the late 1980s.

On the basis of what was happening in the USSR, Teodor Shanin (1988) had stated that: 'The Soviet Union is going through its most radical transformation since the 1930s, or arguably... since the 1917 revolution. The mood suggests the Europe of 1968, from Paris to Prague.'

Conclusion

This paper has attempted to trace the internal coherence and the dynamics of change within the Soviet Union and the CPSU. The reform movement is a historical vindication of the political programme of the Left Opposition, as it evolved within the Soviet Union in the 1920s and was further refined outside the Soviet Union after Stalin banished or killed the opposition. It is indeed remarkable how each and every main element of the Left Opposition had become part of the official reform movement.

The failure of a socialist revolution in the advanced capitalist countries meant that the Soviet Union had to maintain an alliance with the countryside; but Stalin violated the alliance and ensured the continuation of the Soviet regime by a reign of terror. It also seemed clear that the regime did not now have the support of the countryside. It is extremely doubtful whether a socialist revolution can now occur in the advanced capitalist countries, particularly as the development of technology (i.e. the productive forces) has led to a decline in numerical strength of the classical working class. Ironically, it is the class struggle that has led to the development of the productive forces in the capitalist countries, which has led in turn to the secular decline in the requirements of live labour power, as capital equipment is substituted for labour. In confirmation of the decline of the working class, the Communist Parties of both France and Great Britain were contemplating their own demise,[11] more or less in line with what had occurred in Hungary, East Germany, Poland, Czechoslovakia and Bulgaria. The same may occur in Yugoslavia.

Only the Soviet Union stood apart, with its distinct heritage of a revolutionary past. A democratic and civil society seemed likely to emerge, if the Gorbachev reforms had succeeded. Such a society would harness both the plan and the market, with conscious control through planning of key investments. But with a multi-party system, there is a real possibility of the CPSU losing power. Indeed the CPSU might even reconstitute itself as a social democratic party, as has occurred in Eastern Europe. Even the very nature of a centralized Soviet Union may change drastically: a new union treaty between the republics is likely to produce a looser confederation, possibly with a different name.

As Isaac Deutscher (1967) argued in his *Unfinished Revolution*, the urban working class in 1917 was a small minority of the nation – about three million. After three years of war, the little industry that Russia possessed had collapsed, and the capital stock in industry had been used up.[12] The workers in 1917 had become dispersed, and the working class was bodily not there. So the Bolsheviks substituted for it and, as argued above, the substitution did not end there. Like the Decembrists, Populists and Narodnovoltsky, the Bolsheviks were a revolutionary elite without a revolutionary class, but they came to power. The single party system was against the ideas and inclinations of Lenin, Trotsky, Bukharin, Kamenev and the other Bolsheviks, but the logic of the situation took over. Successive oppositions sought to bring the Party back to its revolutionary democratic traditions and socialist ideals, but each schism was suppressed, until the late 1980s.

The crisis in the economy has revived the ideals of the Left Opposition. While the classical working class grew – as the bourgeois and proletarian revolutions were telescoped into one – the further development of the productive forces in the USSR would have had to lead to decline in socially necessary labour, and a decline in the numerical strength of the working class. If the CPSU is the vanguard of that working class (which, we have seen, historically it never was), it must now necessarily transform itself over the years to come. As the working class declines, no elite will be able to claim or cling to power on its behalf. The social and political legitimacy of a Communist Party will now be in question, both in the West and in the USSR.

The evolution towards the programme of the Left Opposition may not be linear: there may indeed be some setbacks and possible compromises. Further developments are likely to be dogged by and dictated by the imperatives of the national question, a problem that has been neglected for far too long. Partly for the success of the domestic reform, the new leaderhip of the Soviet Union has refused to let the US set the agenda in foreign policy (reductions in destructive power and the arms race); instead Gorbachev has taken unilateral decisions on disarmaments which increasingly make both the Warsaw Pact and NATO look obsolete.

It is an irony of history that a class that first grew in numbers in the aftermath of the industrial revolution, and engaged in a class struggle against capital, was itself to wither away both in the capitalist West and in the Soviet Union. In the light of this, Marxism as a critical social theory is also undergoing change; the change, which, like class growth, began in the 1920s, has transformed Marxism with the intellectual efforts of Karl Korsch, Lucien Goldmann, Max Horkheimer and Theodor Adorno. Critical theory (of the 'Frankfurt School' as it is called) is the logical development of Marxism, in which proletarian hegemony and the infallibility of the Communist Party are both denied:[13] the liberation of the proletariat is still supported but now becomes a special case of human liberation. With the coming demise of the Communist Party as a world system, social democracy in its classical sense will acquire new responsibilities, but this is outside the scope of this paper.

Postscript

The above paragraphs, written in March 1990, have been overtaken by events. The CPSU and even the USSR no longer exist; Gorbachev's *perestroika* succeeded in dismantling state terror. But the growing political freedom was accompanied by an accelerated decline of the command economy, with rampant shortages of virtually everything in the 'organized' state sector. Judging from recent reports, the 'free' market, which ranges from private shops to impromptu curbside sale of wine or milk from tankers, will likely lead to the complete collapse of the state sector in Russia. Just as there was no theory of a transition to socialism, there are no guiding principles for the transition from state control back to capitalism. A variety of commodity exchanges are being set up, and there appears to be a flurry of advertising activity in the Anglo-American style; but the goods are hardly available. One commentator (Jamey Gambrell) has described the new Russia of 1992 as a postindustrial society of hunters and gatherers, as market booths and kiosks spring up in unexpected places and quickly vanish. The search for daily necessities will continue to be time-consuming, until markets for consumer goods become better organized.

Culturally and perhaps even politically, the new Russia is harking back to the pre-Bolshevik days. It is not clear what influence this tendency will have in the building of legal and political institutions that the country will need in the near future. Will it lead to the complete abrogation of all the vestiges of socialist ideology? Will nothing remain as a heritage of the seventy years of revolutionary ideals? Was this a failure of Bolshevism, or of all socialism? If the roots of the Party were thoroughly corrupt with no popular support, then socialist ideals will be forgotten. If, on the other hand, the ideals had taken hold in the culture of the people, then after the initial chaos, the Russian Federation (whatever its final form) could see a rebirth of the ideals of the 1920s. We may then see democratic socialism emerge gradually over a period of years, without much fanfare. But it is equally possible that there may be a dramatic swing to the right. The Soviet experience suggests that collective action and the building of a Jerusalem is an impossible task, that *social agency* is doomed to failure. But the social experiment is far from over; the only clear lesson is that it cannot be founded on terror. Both the right and the left opposition of the 1920s in the USSR had come to that conclusion, but they came to it too late. For both were guilty of some degree of complicity in the terror.

Notes

I am grateful to William J. Barber, Robert Dimand, Zoltan Kenessey and Todd Lowry for comments on an earlier version of this paper. I alone am responsible for any remaining deficiencies.

1. The Left Opposition (also called Moscow Opposition, Opposition of 1923, and 'Trotskyists') coalesced around Trotsky in 1923 after expressing disagreements with the ruling group of the Party (Stalin, Zinoviev and Bukharin). In a letter to the Central Committee, the 'Declaration of the 46', prominent Communists sided with Trotsky on a whole range of issues dealing with the nature and role of planning as well as bureaucratic control. Among the signatories were Piatakov and Preobrazhensky. In 1926 the group was joined by the so-called Leningrad Opposition, led by Zinoviev, Kamenev, Krupskaya, Slutsky, and others. The resultant fusion created the Opposition Bloc of Bolshevik-Leninists. In December 1927 the whole Left Opposition was expelled from the Communist Party. For details, see Carr (1952), Erlich (1960), Spulber (1964), and especially Trotsky (1957, pp. 314–15).

2. In the early 1920s Bukharin was also a member of the Left Opposition, but in the period 1923–6 he was Stalin's ally in the struggle against Trotsky and the Left Opposition. By July 1928 there were signs of a rift between Stalin and Bukharin, who was identified by Stalin as being part of the 'Right danger'. At the joint plenary session of the Central Committee and of the Central Control Commission in April 1929, Stalin openly broke with Bukharin and his supporters Rykov and Tomski, who were called the 'rightist deviation' by Stalin. Bukharin was then removed as head of the Communist International and as editor of *Pravda*. Tomski was dismissed as head of the trade unions. A few days later (23–9 April 1929) the Sixteenth Communist Party Congress was held, at which the Bukharin group was formally denounced. For sources, see note 1, on the Left Opposition.

3. Later, in his *State and the Revolution*, Lenin changed his mind by stating that 'all citizens were to be transformed into hired servants of the state . . .'.

   However, state capitalism was an ally in the march towards socialism, because state capitalism was an enemy of the enemy, private capitalism.

4. The acceptance of the 'Shatalin Plan' in the Russian Republic envisages the complete rehabilitation of the market mechanism within two years.

5. See Volume II of his brilliant trilogy on Trotsky (Deutscher, 1959).

6. Much has been written on the nature of competition in the present phase of capitalism; however this is not the place to develop the relevant hypotheses and the corresponding evidence.

7. Isaac Deutscher (1971, p. 29) too took this proposition for granted: '[the] peasantry is vanishing! The proletariat is growing in numbers. Proletarianization, that horror of the bourgeoisie, is progressing with every year of our welfare state.' This text is part of a lecture Deutscher gave at the London School of Economics. The welfare state refers to Britain in 1965.

8. This topic is vast, and again much has been written on it. It centres around the 'law of value' in a society in transition to socialism, and the nature of the price system. See for example, Bettelheim and Sweezy (1971), Dobb (1967, p. 229), Brody (1970), and Sererka, Hejl and Kyn (1970).

9. The above passage also remarkably anticipates the 'Millions of Equations' debate on the feasibility of a socialist economy. See Dore and Kaser (1984).

10. According to Aganbegyan (1988, p. 91), price reforms, which will include price increases for many foods, are planned for 1990; however, there will be public debate 'for at least four months in advance' of the price increases. It is likely that public pressure will delay the changes for a long time.

11. In Britain there are two communist parties: the (older) Communist Party of Great Britain, led by Nina Temple, with some 50 000 members, and the newer and smaller Communist Party of Britain, with 2 000 members. It is the older party that is contemplating its own demise.

12. Deutscher claims that in terms of accumulated capital the economy had been thrown back by more than half a century.

13. Wallerstein (1989, p. 437–8) also denies the 'leading role' of the industrial proletariat. He also claims that the proletariat was a minority even in 1850, and that it will also be a minority in 2050. But his analysis is not rooted in the development of the productive forces, as has been argued in this paper.

References

Aganbegyan, A. (1988), 'New Directions in Soviet Economics', *New Left Review*, **169** (May–June), pp. 89–95.

Aganbegyan, A. (1989), *The Challenge: Economics of Perestroika*, London: Hutchinson.

Auerbach, P., Desai, M. and Shamsavari, A. (1988), 'The Transition from Actually Existing Capitalism', *New Left Review*, **170** (July–August), pp. 61–78.

Bettelheim, C. and Sweezy, P. (1971), *On the Transition to Socialism*, New York: Monthly Review Press.

Brody, A. (1970), *Proportions, Prices and Planning*, Amsterdam: North-Holland.

Carr, E.H. (1952), *The Bolshevik Revolution, 1917–1923*, Vols I and II, London: Macmillan.

Deutscher, I. (1959), *The Prophet Unarmed. Trotsky: 1921–1929*, Oxford: Oxford University Press.

Deutscher, I. (1967), *The Unfinished Revolution: Russia 1917–1967*, Oxford: Oxford University Press.

Deutscher, I. (1971), *Marxism in Our Time*, ed. Tamara Deutscher, Berkeley, CA: Ramparts Press.

Dobb, M. (1960), *An Essay on Economic Growth and Planning*, London: Routledge & Kegan Paul.

Dobb, M. (1967), *Papers on Capitalism, Development and Planning*, London: Routledge & Kegan Paul.

Dobb, M. (1969), *Welfare Economics and the Economics of Socialism*, Cambridge: Cambridge University Press.

Dore, M.H.I. and Kaser, M.C. (1984), 'The Millions of Equations Debate: Seventy Years after Barone', *Atlantic Economic Journal*, **12** (3) (September), pp. 30–44.

Erlich, A. (1960), *The Soviet Industrialization Debate*, Cambridge, MA: Harvard University Press.

Gomulka, S. (1986), *Growth, Innovation and Reform in Eastern Europe*, Brighton: Wheatsheaf Books.

Kagarlitsky, B. (1988), 'Perestroika: the Dialectic of Change', *New Left Review*, **169** (May–June), pp. 63–83.

Kagarlitsky, B. (1989), 'The Importance of Being Marxist', *New Left Review*, **178** (November–December), pp. 29–36.

Luxemburg, R. (1954), *What is Economics?*, New York: Pioneer Publishers.

McIntyre, R.J. (1989), 'Economic Change in Eastern Europe: Other Paths to Socialist Construction', *Science and Society*, **53** (1) (Spring), pp. 5–28.

Preobrazhensky, E. (1965), *The New Economics*, Oxford: Oxford University Press. (English translation first published in Moscow, 1926).

Sererka, B., Hejl and Kyn, O. (1970), 'Price Systems Computable from Input–Output Coefficients', in A. Carter and A. Brody (eds), *Contributions to Input–Output Analysis*, Vol. I. Amsterdam: North-Holland.

Shanin, T. (1988), 'Introduction to Aganbegyan', *New Left Review*, **169** (May–June), pp. 85–8.

Spulber, N. (1964), *Soviet Strategy for Economic Growth*, Bloomington: Indiana University Press.

Trotsky, L. (1932), *Soviet Economy in Danger*, New York: Pioneer Publishers.

Trotsky, L. (1957), *The Third International After Lenin*, trans. John Wright, New York: Pioneer Publishers.

Wallerstein, I. (1989), '1968, Revolution in the World-System', *Theory and Society*, **18**, pp. 431–49.

15 Benjamin Graham and the ever-normal granary

Mary Ann Dimand and Robert W. Dimand

Benjamin Graham's analysis of the ever-normal granary is a landmark in the development of the economics of storage and of commodity price stabilization, yet Graham's contribution has been largely forgotten. Even Albert G. Hart (1987) merely mentions Graham as an originator of commodity reserve currency, without indicating the subtlety of Graham's storage and backing scheme. Graham's proposal embodies interesting work on the theory of a monetary economy. Like social credit and other programmes discussed with it in the pages of the *Economic Forum* (Dimand, forthcoming), the ever-normal granary is an attempt at policy which could alleviate the Depression. As macroecononics before and contemporary with the *General Theory*, Graham's work is of interest. As an acknowledged precursor of Keynes's international buffer stock scheme (Dimand and Dimand, 1990), Graham's ever-normal granary has a distinct place in the history of microeconomics.

In spite of his renown as a theorist on securities analysis, much of Benjamin Graham's professional life was devoted to promoting the institution of an ever-normal granary for American basic commodities, and to a commodity reserve currency based on such stocks. Graham was a professor of finance first at Columbia, then at UCLA, who is probably best known as the co-author, with David L. Dodd, of *Security Analysis* (1934). Markowitz (1959, p. 305) calls this 'the classic book on security analysis' and, 'Adam Smith' (1968, pp. 15–16) states that it leads the field of books on security analysis. In a recent article in the *New York Times Magazine*, L. J. Davis (1990, p. 17) indicates that billionaire investor Warren E. Buffett is even now 'renowned as a follower of Benjamin Graham, widely regarded as the father of modern securities analysis'.

In 1933, writing in the short-lived journal *Economic Forum*, created as a liaison between academic economists, businessmen and government planners, Benjamin Graham stated that 'A three-word dilemma confronts America: – "Inflation or what?" ' (Graham, 1933, p. 186). His answer to the problem of depression was an ever-normal granary which would stabilize the prices of commodity bundles stored, while bundles back a new type of currency, the Federal Note, at a rate of 60 per cent, with gold backing the remaining 40 per cent. To Graham, as to many Depression-era policy theorists, unstable and declining prices seemed a cause of the Depression, rather than a symptom. To stabilize prices then was to cure, moderate or prevent Depression. Unlike Franklin D. Roosevelt and his advisers in setting up the National Recovery Act, however, Graham did not feel that restriction of output and exercise of monopoly power was the route to follow in stimulating recovery. One virtue of the government storage programme he proposes is that

> The ability to turn basic goods into money at a respectable price will increase the rate of production of many basic commodities above the present subnormal level, and increase employment in these fields. The beneficial effect of this increased purchasing power will communicate itself rapidly and give a tremendous impetus to the fields of manufacture, distribution, transportation and finance. (Graham, 1933, pp. 190–1).

In this passage, Graham recognized that an increase in income for producers of the stored commodities will increase incomes in other sectors. This is not a recognition of the finite multiplier, although by 1933 J. M. Clark, L. F. Giblin, R. G. Hawtrey, R. F. Kahn and J. Warming had published papers deriving such a multiplier (Dimand, 1988, forthcoming). Graham simply displays awareness of the circular flow of income in the economy.

Despite his concern with price increase and stabilization, Graham was even more concerned with the storage-backed currency as a monetary tool than with the price-stabilizing aspects of storage. He stated that

> It has been properly asserted that we do not need more currency as such. We need more purchasing power, whether it consist of cash or bank deposits. The prime virtue of this plan is not that it provides more currency but that it raises the price level by taking basic commodities off the market and by placing the purchasing power directly in the hands of the producers.... Even if the additional currency should tend to accumulate in the banks, it would stimulate a more liberal credit policy. The dangers of the *excessive* expansion of business, speculation in commodities, and an undue rise in prices, are all avoided by the present proposal, because speculative advances will be promptly checked by the sale on all the exchanges of commodities obtainable in unit form by the *redemption of Federal Notes* at their Standard Level. (Graham, 1933, pp. 190–1)

Graham was sure that it was necessary to increase the real purchasing power of consumers, but feared that an increase in unbacked or partially backed paper issue would result in pure inflation. An issue of commodity-backed Federal Notes, on the other hand, would increase the purchasing power of commodity producers and hence others, but the purchase of commodity bundles at a given price and their sale at a given higher price would forestall inflation due to the new issue. 'By converting oversupply directly into purchasing power, the forces of deflation will be checked and our economic pendulum will be started on the wide upswing into prosperity' (1933, p. 186). An additional benefit of the plan, in Graham's eyes, was that it supports and stabilizes national income but need not be financed by means of taxation or borrowing, as the seignorage spread between buying and selling prices for commodity bundles could cover the costs of storage. He proclaimed that 'a measure is here proposed which represents a sound and practicable compromise between the extremes of orthodox do-nothingness and unqualified currency expansion. It levies no taxes, and requires no government expenditures, borrowing, or guarantees' (ibid., p. 186).

In *Storage and Stability: A Modern Ever-Normal Granary* (1937) Graham discussed and justified his scheme in more detail. He stated in his preface that

> Most attacks upon the problem of depression may be ranged under two distinct headings: those related to so-called overproduction and those related to defects of our monetary and credit system. The concept of storage is unique in that it lies at the intersection of these two lines of difficulty, offering at once a synthesis and a solution of both. (Graham, 1937, p. v)

The structure of his book shows his consciousness of the two traditions he united in the idea of an ever-normal granary whose contents back currency. Repeatedly Graham cited the Chinese ever-normal granary and the storehouses of the Incan civilization as evidence that commodity storage has been found valuable. He was well aware of the connection between his price-stabilized commodity bundle and the index theory of Jevons and Fisher (ibid., p. ix), and displayed considerable acumen in setting up his commodity bundle and tracing the effect of the change in the price of one good within it. He noted that Thomas Edison had proposed a commodity-reserve currency scheme, and spent an entire chapter comparing the monetary system he proposed to others such as Fisher's compensated dollar. Graham evidently felt that such previous instances of storage and commodity-backed currency supported his synthetic scheme, as he triumphantly wound up his preface by saying that 'In this synthesis the diverse precedents will have made their several contributions. Confucius will stand beside Edison: Irving Fisher will improve upon the Incas of Peru' (Graham, 1937, p. x).

As he indicated in 'Stabilized Reflation', the goods which form the stored commodity bundle should have the characteristics of storability at reasonable cost, well-defined grades on a public exchange, and importance in US production or consumption. The first two requirements restrict goods in Graham's ever-normal granary to those whose storage cost can be fairly readily financed, and which have well-defined prices depending on their characteristics. The third requirement is necessary for more than convenience, however: Graham implicitly assumed that if the commodities stored are 'important', then the stabilization of their prices stabilizes prices in general. Graham also suggested that a good which satisfies his conditions might be included in the bundle if this is desired by the exchange in the market for that good, and the exchange must be willing to do the storage (1937, p. 51). He felt that 'It is obvious that all the component commodities, i.e., their producers, will be benefited by inclusion in the plan' (ibid., p. 68), and that therefore these industries might be willing to finance part of the storage scheme if necessary. 'The producers of the component commodities, together with the exchanges dealing therein, shall to the extent necessary assume the burden of storing their share of the units and maintaining same in good condition (ibid., p. 49).

The proportions of each good in the commodity bundle would be determined by their 'importance' in the US economy. The larger of relative consumption and production in the decade from 1921 to 1930 would be the weight for each commodity, following the method of Moody's Price Index of Basic Commodities (ibid.). Similarly the base price for the granary would be determined by the average price over the base period, from 1921 to 1930 (ibid., p. 55). Curiously Graham supposed that

> The weighting is solely a matter of the relative quantities produced or consumed over the base period. Hence price fluctuations during this period have no effect whatever upon the weightings: they make themselves felt only in the ultimate determination of how large a composite unit shall be made equivalent to a dollar. (1937, p. 55)

Either Graham has momentarily forgotten that price affects supply of and demand for a commodity, or he is implicitly assuming that the slopes of these curves are close enough to linear so that the average demand (supply) is nearly equal to demand (supply) at the average price.

Graham was quite light-hearted about the financing of the ever-normal granary. In *Storage and Stability*, as in 'Stabilized Reflation', he suggests a seignorage spread between buying and selling prices for the bundle of commodities, which would finance at least part of the storage (1937, pp. 111–12). Given that the base price for the granary was the 'right price' as determined from the data of the 1920s, Graham was sure that selling stocks would be no problem. One merely waits until 'effective demand develops', as witnessed by a willingness to pay the granary's selling price (ibid., p. 42). Not only did Graham think that the benefits to a commodity's exchange were sufficient to make them willing to share storage costs, he felt that storage costs must be low in any case, as private stocks existed, and he advocated rotation of stocks (ibid., pp. 42–3). In the second chapter he noted that the Brazilian and Canadian governments had made profits from the storage of 'surplus commodities', so that doing so must be possible (ibid., pp. 31–3). This argument may well be spurious. Dimand (1977) details the débâcle in which Brazilian coffee restriction led to a loss of market share for Brazil, as well as heavy expenditures on kerosene to burn the excess beans. Boyle (1937) discusses Canadian wheat storage as an expensive failure. Graham finished up his discussion of financing the granary with the ringing but somewhat mysterious announcement that '*The State can always afford to finance what its citizens can soundly produce*' (ibid., p. 43). Later, he noted intelligently that 'Since the commodities will be stored at many separate points, the fire hazard and other risks will be spread, permitting the project to carry its own insurance' (ibid., p. 111).

Graham recommended pegging the price of a bundle of commodities rather than the price of each good in the bundle, and felt that the government might rely on arbitragers springing up to assemble appropriate bundles of warehouse receipts, to buy and sell them as shifts in price require, '[keeping] track of the current quotations on all the different exchanges' (ibid., p. 59). The government's research, then, could initially be limited to calculating the weightings for goods in the bundle, the base price of the bundle based on the 1921–30 data and the seignorage spread to be used by the granary in buying and selling warehouse receipts. No mandarin need watch the exchanges from day to day, as it would profit arbitragers to do so.

Graham was aware that real supply and demand changes can affect the relative price of a good in the short or long run, saying:

> Let us now point out that the whole idea of permanently fixed prices, or price relationships, for a number of individual products is economically unsound because it fails to take into account variations in costs of production and other supply-and-demand factors that may develop over a period of time. (1937, p. 194)

He suggested that whenever futures prices were lower than spot prices for a good (a contango), signifying current shortage, futures contracts for the good be substituted for warehouse receipts in the commodity bundle (ibid., p. 70). Thus the problem of severe shortage in the short run would be avoided. Clearly, such futures contracts would be bought only when the current price of one bundle, including the cost of the futures contract, was less than the price the government was willing to pay in commodity-backed currency for the bundle. Graham further suggested that it would be possible to suspend a 'runaway' commodity from the bundle (ibid., p. 72), and indicated that a decennial revision of the composition of the bundle 'will serve to prevent the creation of any anachronisms in the unit' (ibid., p. 76).

It is interesting that Graham felt no concern about whether stabilizing the price of a bundle of basic commodities would stabilize the general price level, particularly in view of his analysis of the effects of a change in the price of one commodity, X, in the bundle. He was aware that when the bundle's price had been stabilized at the target level, a rise in the price of X would cause a rise in the price of the commodity bundle and thus sales of the bundle. Such sales drive down the price of the bundle, driving down the prices of the goods other than X below their previous levels, while the price of X remains above its previous level. Graham argued, however, that a rise in the price of one good would cause quite a small percentage decrease in the prices of other goods in the bundle (ibid., pp. 68–9). He seemed to be principally concerned with the justice aspect of this question – why should the price of cotton fall just because the price of corn rises? He believed that the respective commodity exchanges would feel that their losses, when their price was driven down by a rise in the price of another good, would be compensated by a smaller fall in their price when it went down due to the spreading effect of the bundle's price stabilization (ibid., p. 72). Later Graham noted that

> If the farm component in the dollar should fall, say, 10 per cent, from 70 to 63 cents, this must produce an advance in the nonfarm component from 30 to 37 cents, or fully 23 per cent. It follows that a relatively small decline in the farm price level will create a sufficient rise in other prices to stimulate production and reestablish a balance in the supply of both components. (1937, p. 191)

Graham nonetheless never considered the possibility that stabilization of the price of a commodity could be destabilizing to the price level as a whole.

To Graham, the second virtue of the ever-normal granary was that it not only stabilized the price of a commodity bundle, but, as backing for money, stabilized the value of the dollar in another way. He had little doubt that a stable-valued dollar was desirable, quoting Franklin D. Roosevelt in the headnote to his Chapter 6 as saying 'We shall seek to establish and maintain a dollar which will not change its purchasing and debt paying power in the succeeding generations' (ibid., p. 77).

Similarly, in his foreword to *Storage and Stability*, Alvin Johnson stated that

> We are all fairly agreed as to the qualities we wish to see realized in our standard money. We want it to be as nearly as possible stable in value. A dollar should buy about as much of the necessities of life in 1977 as in 1937. (ibid., p. xvi)

Graham's only real doubt about the desirability of a stable-valued dollar was whether it was desirable in the face of technical progress. He noted that, with technical progress and increased productivity, the result might be a lower price level and an unchanged wage or an unchanged price level and a higher wage. He argued that the unchanged price level he believed his commodity dollar would provide, combined with a higher wage, would be more desirable than the alternative. A fixed price level, creating transfers to neither debtor nor creditor, would make debts more likely to be repaid than a price level decline with fixed wages (ibid., pp. 82–3).

Graham also considered briefly the question of whether the business cycles he hoped to damp were undesirable:

It is by no means certain that business cycles are bad things, in the sense that we should be better off if all such fluctuations could be eliminated. We *are* certain, however, that a downward business cycle of the intensity experienced between 1930 and 1933 is a very bad thing indeed. (ibid., p. 86)

As in the case of his examination of technical progress, his view is sound and admirably pragmatic.

Graham suggested that commodity reserve currency could enter financial markets as simply a different sort of money. In order to show that this was possible, in Chapter 11 he enumerated the types of currency which coexisted at the time of publication. Like many monetary theorists of this and earlier periods, Graham felt that an unbacked dollar was almost by definition inflationary. It was his belief, stated at some length in Chapter 10, that the decline in gold backing of the dollar causes a decline in public confidence in the dollar, which is likely to cause a rise in the price level. A fully backed commodity dollar, on the other hand, always redeemable for warehouse receipts, would not be susceptible to this weakness. Despite the commodity reserve dollar's status as 'good money', though, Graham stated in Chapter 12 that he did not believe that Gresham's Law would operate on the superior commodity reserve dollar, driving it from circulation. Where there are so many types of currency already in circulation, and so little interest in the distinctions between them, he argued, the public would not hoard commodity reserve dollars.

The ever-normal granary, then, where stocks are paid for by the creation of commodity reserve money, would have a number of benefits (1937, p. 50). It would absorb the commodity surpluses which '[overhang] the markets, [break] the price level and [demoralize] the entire business fabric' (ibid., p. 87). It would thus equilibrate business conditions, also providing insurance against war, drought and other disasters. It would stabilize the price of the commodity bundle, thus stabilizing the dollar, and also create a stable, convertible currency.

Graham found other benefits in his scheme as well. It would form 'the concrete means of developing a steadily higher living standard for all' (ibid., p. 50), a statement which is only partially explained. He thought it likely that stocks of the commodity bundles would tend to increase over time (ibid., p. 79), although he was well aware of the stock-out problem. In this case, Graham suggested that such stores might buttress the nation against war or drought emergency (ibid., pp. 96–7), or that 'measures [might] be adopted to bring the excess into consumption, thus raising the national standard of living' (ibid., pp. 49–50). On the other hand, if reserves continued to burgeon and thus cause the money supply to increase, it must be the case that the purchase dollars are going to wealthy people who hoard them, preventing the price of the commodity bundle from rising due to increased consumption. In this case, legislation to alter the income distribution would solve the problem (ibid., pp. 104–5).

In addition, Graham suggested that the ever-normal granary might be 'the most rational investment of our national Social Security reserve funds' (ibid., p. 50). He later justified this statement with the argument that *'the social security fund cannot properly be expected to earn interest'* (ibid., p. 102), since if it is invested in government debt, the government is merely shifting funds from one pocket to another!

An interesting benefit Graham perceived in his granary plan shows him approaching fairly closely to Keynes's 1936 analysis of the problem of underemployment equilibrium:

> The problem of unemployment and the problem of surplus seem to be dual aspects of the same underlying paradox. In a practical sense, we cannot find room for idle workers because those at work already produce too much. Widespread unemployment operates as a crude mechanism for correcting the unbalance of demand and supply. An unemployed person produces nothing and consumes something. (1937, p. 90).

And, as Graham suggested in his preface, 'a sound plan for monetizing basic commodities held in storage would "put teeth" in Say's law: for a crucial sector of production would then actually create the monetary wherewithal for its purchase' (ibid., p. vii). There is no evidence that Graham had read *The General Theory* by 1937. He does cite *The Revision of the Treaty*, though no doubt due to a typo it is attributed to one L.M. Keynes.

Alvin Johnson, writing a laudatory foreword for *Storage and Stability*, nonetheless stated that

> One who reads Mr. Graham's book with a critical attention to detail will note that there are minor problems which the author has deliberately skimmed over for the sake of concentrating attention on the major issue. How would such a form of money work in international trade? What would happen if a great war drew out all the commodity reserves, after a nation had become habituated to this form of money? Mr. Graham has reflected much on most of these problems, but he has wisely and considerately left it to the reader to do some thinking for himself. (Graham, 1937, p. xviii).

The problem of the effect of such money in international trade is a genuine one, unconsidered by the domestic-minded Graham. As Hart (1987) implies, to make a commodity reserve currency acceptable, the basic bundle must be decided by some international body.

The possibility of a stock-out problem caused by war or another disaster, however, is one that Graham does address:

> It should be evident, therefore, that our proposal will actually stabilize the value of our commodity unit *as long as any units remain in monetary storage* .... Were

any such complete withdrawal to take place after our Reservoir system had been in operation, we should be back to where we were before we started. We should have had the benefit of both the reservoir and the price stabilization as long as they lasted. Equally important, perhaps, the existence of the commodity units later drawn out would have been most beneficial in meeting the demand that manifested itself in their withdrawal. (Graham, 1937, pp. 78–9)

This recognition that once the stock runs out, one cannot buffer, but is not necessarily worse off than if without buffering from the outset, remains the most that can be said about this situation.

More fundamentally, Milton Friedman (1953) noted that stabilizing the price of metals would historically have destabilized other prices rather than stabilizing them, and the variance of other prices around the price of metals is greater than their variance around the price of gold, the traditional currency backing. As Friedman noted, there is no reason to believe that a stable price for a bundle of commodities would be stabilizing in general: it is surprising that Graham, who noted destabilizing price effects within the bundle, did not consider this.

Friedman's objection to commodity reserve currencies on the grounds that producing them uses up real resources seems less justified in a case where the currency's backing is commodities which are, as a bundle at any rate, in surplus at a reasonably determined price. Where a farmer who was not income constrained might choose to hold his produce off the market until its price rose, surely storage of the commodity by the government does not unduly extract real value. Instead, it merely frees the producer from income constraint.

In his 1962 essay in Leland Yeager's *In Search of a Monetary Constitution* Graham published a letter he received from Lord Keynes in 1943. As Friedman did, Keynes had found that 'a currency stable in terms of a composite commodity, whilst serving certain objects, either did not achieve stable national prices or postulated stable efficiency-wages without having the power to impose them'. Moreover, Keynes noted that he is 'not clear about the advantages . . . of stabilizing a composite commodity as compared with those of stabilizing individual commodities. For the latter is a better means of stabilizing the national income of individual raw-material producing countries' (Graham, 1962, p. 216).

In fact, Graham's work in 1933 and 1937 anticipated proposals by Keynes (1938, 1974) for international buffer stocks (see Dimand and Dimand, 1990), in which he referred to Graham. Keynes's work does not suggest commodities as backing for paper money and does not display the theoretical errors of Graham's work. Many of the methods Keynes suggests for working the buffer stocks and allowing for periodic price revision, however, are due to Graham.

In the 1930s respectable academic publications in the infant study of macroeconomics could appear in startling places. Writing in the *Saturday Evening Post*, J.E. Boyle, Professor of Rural Economy at Cornell, doubted whether a storage scheme might simply justify a totalitarian regime in the United States, and whether it would simply serve to divert the US's potential exports from the ships to the cellars (Boyle, 1937). The fear of totalitarianism associated with a comprehensive programme such as the ever-normal granary is one which Henry A. Wallace expressed with regard to any domestic system of dealing with agricultural surplus (Wallace, 1934). Wallace, an empirical agricultural economist who became Roosevelt's secretary of agriculture, was later strongly associated with the proposal of an ever-normal granary which would act as an insurance fund for farmers, to which they could pay premiums and receive indemnities in the form of crops (Graham, 1937, pp. 179–80).

Boyle's contention that foreign countries stood ready to buy the US's so-called surpluses if not prevented by the existence of an ever-normal granary is an interesting one. In his article he seems to have forgotten that the Depression of the 1930s was felt worldwide, so that demand for normal goods from every source declined. There is nonetheless some merit in his criticism. Graham suggested setting the price of the commodity bundle based on the weights and average prices of 1921–30. To the extent that 'basic commodities' are imports, and to the extent that tariffs were placed on them in the base period, their contribution to the price of the bundle will bias it upwards relative to world prices. On the other hand, the tendency of such tariffs to decrease the domestic price of exports and to decrease trade with the rest of the world would tend to offset this effect.

Graham himself claimed in his 1962 paper that his concern with the ever-normal granary was always principally on the price stabilization side. Friedman (1953) also held this view. Graham's emphasis on the need to increase domestic purchasing power in the 1933 *Economic Forum* paper and the five chapters he devotes to the US monetary system in *Storage and Stability* belie this statement. In fact, Graham was intent on developing a monetary tool which could be used in a period when unbacked money was generally feared, despite its existence. His commodity reserve currency plan would automatically increase the domestic money supply when depression caused surpluses of commodities, thus stimulating the economy through countercyclical income policy and countercyclical money supply at once.

One of the greatest weaknesses of his plan has gone unremarked heretofore: surpluses of basic commodities and declines in national income need not have a correlation all that close to 1. When the two do not coincide, the ever-normal granary would automatically produce inappropriate monetary policy. If all fluctuations in commodity prices were caused by aggregate demand shocks, not only would commodity-backed currency be a built-in stabilizer, but producers would welcome price stability. The trouble with Benjamin Graham's scheme, like that with the idea behind the NRA, is that it gets the cart before the horse. Graham, unlike President Roosevelt's advisers, did not quite believe that if the price level were lifted everything would work out. He did, however, feel that the Depression was 'caused, or in any event measurably aggravated, by the world-wide stocks of basic commodities' (Graham, 1937, pp. 86–7). In his certainty that this was the case, Graham implicitly assumed a correlation of 1 between depression and surplus commodities. As Friedman somewhat unfairly said, 'his primary interest was in [his plan's] contribution to the "problem of raw materials" and of "burdensome surpluses", whatever they may be' (Friedman, 1953, p. 205, fn.).

Despite its fundamental flaws, Graham's book on the ever-normal granary and commodity reserve currency plan is well worth reading. As a pioneering work in the theory of storage and price stabilization and as an early work in macroeconomics it is of great interest. Graham anticipated both Keynes's work on buffer stocks and Holbrook Working's analysis of the economics of storage, as well as the subsequent literature on commodity reserve currency.

Note

We gratefully acknowledge the help of Catherine W. Martinsek, social science librarian at Morris Library, Southern Illinois University at Carbondale.

References

Boyle, J.E. (1937), 'That Ever-normal Granary', *Saturday Evening Post*, 8 May, pp. 14–15, 67–71.
Davis, L.J. (1990), 'Buffett Takes Stock', *New York Times Magazine*, 1 April, pp. 16–17, 61–3.
Dimand, R.W. (1977), 'Government Intervention in Agriculture: "Valorization" of Brazilian Coffee Prices', *McGill Journal of Political Economy*, **1** (1) (February), pp. 1–18.
Dimand, R.W. (1988), *The Origins of the Keynesian Revolution*, Aldershot, UK: Edward Elgar; Stanford, CA: Stanford University Press.
Dimand, R.W. (forthcoming), *The Rise and Development of Macroeconomics*, Aldershot, UK: Edward Elgar.
Dimand, R.W. and Dimand, M.A. (1990), 'J.M. Keynes on Buffer Stocks and Commodity Price Stabilization', *History of Political Economy*, **22** (1) (Spring), pp. 113–23.
Friedman, M. (1953), 'Commodity-Reserve Currency', reprinted in *Essays in Positive Economics*, Chicago and London: University of Chicago Press.
Graham, B. (1933), 'Stabilized Reflation', *Economic Forum*, **1** (2) (Spring), pp. 186–93.
Graham, B. (1937), *Storage and Stability: A Modern Ever-Normal Granary*, with a foreword by A. Johnson, New York and London: McGraw-Hill.
Graham, B. (1962), 'The Commodity-Reserve Currency Proposal Reconsidered', in L.B. Yeager (ed.), *In Search of a Monetary Constitution*, Cambridge, MA: Harvard University Press.
Graham, B. and Dodd, D.L. (1934), *Security Analysis*, New York and London: McGraw-Hill.
Hart, A.G. (1987), 'Commodity Reserve Currency', in John Eatwell, Murray Milgate and Peter Newman (eds), *The New Palgrave Dictionary of Economics*, London and New York: The Stockton Press.
Keynes, J.M. (1938), 'The Policy of Government Storage of Foodstuffs and Raw Materials', *Economic Journal*, **48**, pp. 449–60.
Keynes, J.M. (1974), 'The International Control of Raw Materials', *Journal of International Economics*, **4** (3), pp. 299–315.
Markowitz, H.M. (1959), *Portfolio Selection: Efficient Diversification of Investment*, New Haven and London: Yale University Press.
'Adam Smith' (1968), *The Money Game*, New York: Random House.
Wallace, H.A. (1934), *America Must Choose*, New York and Boston: Foreign Policy Association and World Peace Foundation.

Name index

Abu Yusuf, 45
Adorno, Theodor, 205
Aganbegyan, A., 202, 203
Ali, Basharat, 49
Althorp, Lord, 159
Aquinas, Thomas, 45, 57, 58
Aristotle, 41, 95
Augustus, 33–4
Aukrust, O., 179

Ballod, K., 182
Baudeau, Abbé, 106
Beer, Max, 107
Bentham, Jeremy, 164
Bjerve, P.J., 179
Black, John, 161
Blaug, Mark, 163, 168
Blitz, Rudolph, 163–4
Blyth, E.K., 169
Boulakia, J. David, 46
Boyce, George, 161
Boyle, J.E., 212–13, 217–18
Brewer, Anthony, 64
Brougham, Henry (Baron), 159, 161,
    162, 165–7
Bryson, 41, 42, 44
Buffett, Warren E., 209
Bukharin, Nikolai, 177, 181, 183–6,
    187, 190

Caesar, Julius, 36
Cantillon, Richard, 64–75
Caracalla, 34
Carmichael, Gersham, 131–2
Carr, E.H., 196
Carter, A.P., 191
Cassius Dio, 34
Cicero, 32, 33, 36
Clark, Colin, 179
Clark, J.M., 210
Clive, John, 159
Coats, A.W., 157
Cohen, S.F., 183, 184

Colander, David, 157
Combe, George, 169, 170
Confucius, 102, 108

Davis, L.J., 209
Dawwâni, al-, 41
de Martino, F., 35
De Neeve, P.W., 34
De Quincey, Thomas, 135
Dempsey, Bernard W., 57
Derksen, J.B.D., 179
Deutscher, Isaac, 197, 204
Dickens, Charles, 171
Diehl, Karl, 178
Dietzel, Heinrich, 144–5
Dimand, R.W., 209, 210, 212, 217
Dimashqî, Abûl-Fadl Ja'far bin 'Ali
    al-, 41–4
Diocletian, 34, 35
Dmitriev, 190, 191
Dodd, David, 209
Douglas, Paul, 137
Duboeuf, F., 117, 119
Dubovikov, F.G., 180–81
Dupont de Nemours, Pierre Samuel, 95
Dzerzhinski, Felix, 183

Edison, Thomas, 211
Ellis, E.E., 170
Ellis, William, 161, 169–71

Farabi, Abu Nasr al-, 41, 45, 48
Farrukh, Omar A., 50
Fetter, Frank W., 161
Fisher, Irving, 211
Fontana, Biancamaria, 159
Foster, Benjamin, 55, 56
Frank, T., 35
Friedman, Milton, 217, 218, 219
Frisch, Ragnar, 179

Gabba, E., 31, 32, 36
Gambrell, Jamey, 206

Subject index

agriculture
  in ancient China, 6
  in Mameluke Islam, 48
  productivity of, 68–9
  in Soviet Union, 197, 201–2
  in Tamil society, 16, 22
  tariffs on, 145
  in Turgot's model of social progress, 77–80
Anti-Corn Law League, 162–3
Arab world see Islam
autarchy, Quesnay on, 106–8

bagatelle duty, 150
balance of trade, 65–6, 67
banking, 123, 144
Birkbeck Schools, 169–71
books and periodicals, economic, 158–60
British Association, 163

capital markets, 144
capitalist system, 198–9
  Smith on, 121–2
  in Turgot's model of social progress, 86–90
China, ancient
  agriculture in, 6
  countercyclical policies in, 5–6
  government in, 1, 4–9
  'light-heavy' doctrine in, 2–3
  monetary policy in, 1, 7–8
  price control in, 1, 5, 6–7, 8
  public expenditure in, 5–6
  state monopolies in, 1, 4–5
  statistics in, 8–9
  taxation in, 1, 4, 8
  trade in, 7
church schools, 168, 170
class see social differentiation
classical economics, popularizing of, 157, 158–63
  education movement and, 163–72

clubs and organizations, economics in, 161–3
commodity price stabilization, 209–19
commodity reserve currency, 209, 210–11, 214–15, 217
common markets, 152
communism
  primitive, in Tamil society, 28
  see also Soviet Union
community of property, 106
competition
  in Islamic economic thought, 50
  and protective tariffs, 151, 152
cost, Quesnay on, 96
countercyclical policies: in ancient China, 5–6
credit markets
  in Islamic economic thought, 52, 53
  in Tamil society, 27

defence expenditure: in ancient Rome, 31, 34, 35
demand
  in Islamic economic thought, 50–53, 59
  Smith on, 120–21, 138
development strategies
  protective tariffs and, 143–53
  in Soviet Union, 182–3, 185, 197, 200–202
distributive justice, Quesnay on, 98–102
division of labour, 114, 128
double-entry bookkeeping, 179
duopoly, 73

Economist, The, 161
Edinburgh Review, 159–60
education: in Tamil society, 24
education movement in UK, 163–72
egalitarianism, Smith and, 112, 114, 118–19, 122
entrepreneurship
  Quesnay on, 105–6

223